ENGLISH 100

First Edition

English 100 Program
Department of English
University of Wisconsin-Madison

CONCEPTS, CONVERSATIONS, CRITIQUE

HAYDEN
HM
McNEIL

Table of Contents

Writing Practices

Sequence 1:
Concepts: Invention and Inquiry

Sequence 2:
Conversations: Engaging the Ideas of Others

Sequence 3:
Critique: Developing a Critical Approach through
Research and Argumentation

Program Awards

Introduction

Concepts, Conversations, Critique was compiled by writing instructors of the University of Wisconsin-Madison English 100 Program. This reader has two primary purposes. First, it includes readings that will provide opportunities for you to engage with a wide variety of ideas, while offering illustrations of the kind of intellectual work you will do in this course. Second, this reader is meant to serve as a type of handbook for the course, providing you with information about policies, student support services, and other resources that you may find useful as you join the university community.

An Introduction to Composition

You may already appreciate the importance and central place writing plays in your everyday life, academic career, and other contexts. If so, you are probably wondering why you are taking an introduction to composition when you have been writing throughout your educational experience. As this course will emphasize, writing is a situated practice that takes into account purpose, context, audience, and other factors that may inform why you write, what you write, and how you write. Although we all appreciate some general qualities about "good" writing—such as clarity of thought and language —there are many more qualities about effective writing that are connected to specific situations and require writers to be both aware of their writing purposes and intentional in their writing choices. So while the types of writing that you've done during high school or for other occasions have developed and focused your writing for that context and those educational experiences, you'll find that the writing you do at the university and beyond will require a variety of new and/or different writing strategies and practices. You will need to *resituate* both yourself and the work you will do.

As an introduction to composition, English 100 seeks to prepare you to identify your purposes for writing and to make informed decisions about the writing you do. Even in the defined context of the university, these purposes and decisions will still vary widely. What are some of the strategies for writing that may be applied across your courses regardless of discipline, within your cocurricular and extracurricular activities, or as you began to create materials to use in your career beyond the university? What are those strategies for writing that may require specialized knowledge about the way information is communicated or arguments are made within specific disciplines? What are the kinds of questions that you need to ask in order to approach and execute your writing effectively and successfully?

An Introduction to *Concepts, Conversations, Critique*

As you will see as you read through *Concepts, Conversations, Critique*, this text provides you with a variety of essays to help you approach writing in the university. The essays in the first section, "Writing Practices," introduce you to practices that are foundational to the way English 100 is designed and taught. Invention, drafting, revision, and editing are important in the writing process as you move from exploring and developing ideas, to sharpening and clarifying your arguments, to presenting your work in clear, organized, and effective ways. Another emphasis of English 100 is the development of rhetorical awareness, the understanding of how writing and language can be persuasive. An important element of this is understanding audience. In your classroom, you'll find opportunities to engage with a variety of "real" audiences, from the peer review groups used in responding to drafts, to your instructors who work closely with you on revisions, to your entire class or possibly others with whom you will share your research presentations.

The rest of this reader is arranged to correspond with the writing sequences used in your class. In Sequence 1, you'll read essays that describe abstractions by drawing evidence from a wide variety of particular phenomena. These essays illustrate how ideas or concepts can be developed through writing, from the inkling of an idea that arises from curiosity to the full realization of a line of inquiry. Sequence 2 will guide you through a process of learning to locate and use texts, as you identify and engage with written conversations that provide context for your own writing and work. The essays in this section illustrate how writers summarize, analyze, and synthesize the work of others in order to support their own arguments. And finally, in Sequence 3 you will find essays that bring together the kinds of work done in Sequences 1 and 2 to illustrate fully developed arguments, which situate a writer's ideas in relation to others' ideas, develop and utilize evidence, and reach new understandings. What is also important about the work you do in Sequence 3 is that you develop a critical method, that is, an approach to investigating your topic; a way to identify materials for developing, framing, and supporting your analysis; and a completed project that shows you understand how to best present your work to make your argument persuasive.

Writing at Wisconsin

As the cover of this reader illustrates, writing at the University of Wisconsin-Madison happens in a variety of locations and through a variety of practices, from sitting on the Terrace with your laptop, to having pens and notebook at hand, to being surrounded by your papers and books in the Memorial Union lounge. As you begin your career at Wisconsin, you will see writing is everywhere. As you experience writing in English 100, you should see this as an invitation to participate in the university community, contribute to scholarly conversations, and become engaged learners. Welcome!

Acknowledgements

This first edition of the reader has been a collaborative effort of the English 100 Program. English 100 instructors who taught during the 2007–2008 academic year suggested a wide variety of materials, and while we could not include everything we thank them for their work.

English 100 Program Policies and Resources

Attendance

Attendance is required. English 100 is a small seminar-like course and the presence of each student matters. You need to be in class, on time, prepared, every meeting. This matters for your own learning as well as for the contributions you can make to the learning of others. For those unavoidable times when you are sick or otherwise unable to come to class, the attendance policy allows 3 absences without penalty. It is always considerate to notify your instructor by email about an absence. If you miss class, it is *your* responsibility to find out what you missed and to make up any work as required. Excessive or habitual tardiness may be counted as an absence.

The final course grade will be lowered for each additional absence beyond the first 3 absences (An A will become an AB; an AB will become a B; a B will become a BC, and so on). An absence beyond 6 absences in a MWF class or beyond 4 absences in a TR class (the equivalent of 2 full weeks of class) will result in a student failing the course.

An instructor has the discretion to take into account *extraordinary* reasons for an absence such as a severe accident or illness, a family emergency or death, a recognized religious holiday, or jury duty. Documentation may be required. Too many absences for whatever reason will prevent you from completing the required coursework and in the case of excessive absences, your instructor may recommend that you drop the class.

Dropping or Withdrawing from the Course

Dropping and Withdrawing from a course are separate formal administrative procedures and it is the student's responsibility to initiate these procedures. If you simply stop attending class this is not the same as either formally dropping or withdrawing from the course. Before choosing either option, a student should meet with his/her instructor and advisor.

Academic Honesty and Plagiarism

The University of Wisconsin-Madison and the English 100 Program expect students to present their work honestly and to credit others responsibly and with care. University policy states: "Academic honesty and integrity are fundamental to the mission of higher education and of the University of Wisconsin system" (Wisconsin Administrative Code 14.01). Plagiarism is a serious offense, and it can occur in drafts as well as in final papers. Because this course relies heavily on sharing knowledge and information in the learning and writing processes, it is important that students learn how to work with sources without plagiarizing. Plagiarism includes all of the following:

- Cutting and pasting from another source without using quotation marks and citing the source;
- Using someone else's words or ideas without proper documentation when quoting and paraphrasing;
- Copying any portion of your text from another source without proper acknowledgement;
- Borrowing another person's specific ideas without documenting the source;
- Having someone rewrite or complete your work (This does not include getting and using feedback from a writing group or individual in the class.);
- Turning in a paper written by someone else, an essay "service," or from a World Wide Web site (including reproductions of such essays or papers); and
- Turning in a paper that you wrote for another course, or turning in the same paper for more than one course, without getting permission from your instructors first.

In all of the above cases, plagiarism has occurred when the use of someone else's words and/or ideas takes place without proper citation and documentation *no matter* what kind of text is the origin of the words and/or ideas. That is, material must still be documented even if it comes from a source such as an email, personal writing, oral or written interviews, classroom conversations, or formal presentations or lectures—not just from materials published as books, journal articles, or essays in popular magazines or websites.

The University of Wisconsin-Madison has established a range of penalties for students guilty of plagiarism or academic dishonesty. Appropriate penalties include a reduced grade, a failing grade for an assignment, a failing grade for the course, or even suspension or expulsion from the university. All instances of plagiarism are reported to the English 100 administration. For more information, see <**http://www.wisc.edu/students/conduct/uws14.htm**>

University General Education Requirements: Communication

English 100 fulfills Part A of the university's general education requirement in communication (commonly known as "Comm A"). The Comm A general education requirement seeks to prepare students in the communication skills (both written and oral) that they will need at the university. Below you will find a description of the Comm A requirement itself and more detailed descriptions of the objectives and learning outcomes expected of a Comm A course such as English 100.

(From 2007–2009 University Undergraduate Catalog and the College of Letters and Science General Education website: http://www.ls.wisc.edu/gened/)

Part A. Literacy Proficiency: 2-3 credits at first-year level dedicated to reading, listening, and discussion, with emphasis on writing. While most incoming freshmen are required to complete course work to fulfill this requirement, students may be exempted from Part A by approved college course work while in high school, AP test scores, or placement testing. Students are expected to satisfy this requirement by the end of their first year.

Purpose: The first course is to be a basic course in communication skills at the college level, developing student abilities in writing and public speaking, for both exposition and argumentation. As such, the course is to serve as a general foundation in the central skills and conventions required for student success in a variety of subsequent course work, as well as in careers after college.

Objectives: The course will advance basic skills in:
- The four modes of literacy: writing, speaking, reading & listening, with special emphasis on writing
- Critical thinking
- Information-seeking skills and strategies

These skills should be taught through continuous practice in the process of writing and speaking. Although the items listed below suggest a sequence, many or all of them are simultaneously learned in this process. Courses which satisfy the new University requirement must advance student skills in the following areas:

Planning:
- Selecting, narrowing, and focusing topics
- Identifying and analyzing audience information needs
- Generating and organizing ideas
- Comprehending and analyzing text

Drafting:
- Learning structures of exposition and argument and the use of evidence
- Organizing and developing paragraphs, papers, and speeches
- Adapting writing and speaking for intended audiences
- Learning conventions of academic writing
- Mastering elements of grammar, usage, and style
- Preparing speeches for oral delivery
- Citing sources, avoiding plagiarism, and compiling accurate bibliographies

Revising:
- Developing critical skills for reading and listening—in review of peer writing/speaking
- Revising and editing essays and speeches—for spelling, punctuation, grammar, style, organization, and logic
- Critiquing assigned readings and speeches delivered outside class

Information-Seeking Skills and Strategies:
- Identifying and retrieving source materials needed to evaluate, organize, and select information from print and electronic sources
- Acquiring basic critical, technical, and mechanical skills needed to find relevant information

Campus Resources

There are a number of English department and campus resources available to you that may assist your transition to college life and your success in English 100. Described below are some services that may be especially useful as you negotiate this large campus and the number of demands that you face as a student.

The English 100 Tutorial. The English 100 Tutorial Program offers individualized writing instruction specifically geared for English 100 students. The tutorial website at **www.wisc.edu/english/100tutorial/** offers information about the tutorial program, and you should also schedule appointments there. English 100 instructors have seen strong interest from many students, effective writers and novices alike, for extra help beyond what is offered in the classroom and during office hours. Since the Writing Center is not funded to provide tutoring for Communication A courses like English 100, the English 100 Tutorial provides an opportunity for you to receive one-on-one help from experienced English 100 instructors. These instructors are willing to work with you on any issue related to English 100, from brainstorming plans for a paper to the most effective strategies for a final revision. Please visit the website above to learn how you can make tutorial sessions an effective part of your writing process!

The Writing Center. While the Writing Center will *not* schedule appointments for English 100 assignments, it offers a wide array of classes on specific issues throughout the semester. You can access this semester's Writing Center class schedule at **http://www.wisc.edu/writing**. You may also make an appointment with the Writing Center if you are seeking assistance with assignments in other courses.

The McBurney Center. If you have a disability or particular circumstance that may have an impact on your academic work, you may want to meet with a counselor at the McBurney Center. The McBurney Disability Resource Center is located on the first floor of the Middleton Building at 1305 Linden Drive (1/2 block west of Van Hise Hall) (263-2741). Students need to provide documentation of a disability to this office in order to receive official university services and accommodations: **http://www.mcburney.wisc.edu/**

Other Resources. You'll find other helpful resources listed at http://www. wisc.edu/wiscinfo/student/ and through the Dean of Students office: **http://www.wisc.edu/students/**

The University Health Service offers a variety of counseling services. Their web page is **http://www.uhs.wisc.edu**. To make an appointment, call 262-1744. For emergency crisis intervention services, call 262-1744; for after hours and weekend emergencies, call 265-6565.

Course Directors

Morris Young
Director of English 100 and Associate Professor of English
6187C Helen C. White Hall
(608) 263-3367
msyoung4@wisc.edu.

Mary Fiorenza
Associate Director of English 100
Assistant Faculty Associate
6183 Helen C. White Hall
(608) 263- 4512
fiorenza@wisc.edu.

Katie Lynch
Senior Assistant Director of English 100
6189 Helen C. White Hall
(608) 265-9125
kelynch@wisc.edu.

Jacqueline Preston
Assistant Director of English 100
6189 Helen C. White Hall
(608) 265-9125
jspreston@wisc.edu

WRITING
PRACTICES

Introduction

The readings in "Writing Practices" provide ideas about how to approach any writing project, but especially writing in English 100. They give you strategies you can use for invention, drafting, revision, and editing. During the semester, you'll move through this process several times, as you explore and develop ideas; sharpen and clarify descriptions, narratives, and arguments; and, finally, present your work in clear, organized, and effective ways.

At the beginning of an assignment, you'll be facing a blank page or screen. How can you know what to write? What will work? Essayist and novelist Anne Lamott counsels you to think small, give yourself "short assignments" that "quiet the voices in your head," especially if they are overly critical and get in the way of your first draft. She describes writing mainly from her own experience, but her approach can work in other contexts as well, because what's important to Lamott's first draft is getting something down—not necessarily getting it down right. Her suggestion to allow yourself "shitty first drafts" can apply to just about any situation.

For instance, much academic writing involves reading, and then incorporating what you read into your own writing in some way. You might feel intimidated by the ideas of other, more experienced scholars. How can you present these ideas in relation to your own? Take a risk and don't worry about getting it right the first time, says Lamott. You might also try the strategies laid out in Joseph Harris's "Coming to Terms." His essay demystifies some key moves in academic writing, including how to integrate different types of quotations. (Think of quotations as "flashpoints," he says.)

Once you have a draft, you'll need readers. English 100 is designed to create opportunities for getting feedback from a variety of readers. Hephzibah Roskelly, in "The Cupped Hand and the Open Palm" and Lamott, in "Someone to Read Your Drafts," both help you think about making feedback a regular part of your writing process. What's more, these readings can help you understand why it's important in developing rhetorical awareness.

The point of feedback is to help you revise. Journalist and writing teacher Don Murray discusses the difference between real revision and editing in two readings from his book *Crafting a Life in Essay, Story, Poem.* A reader-centered approach to revision is provided by Kate Ronald in "Style: The Hidden Agenda in Composition Classes." She, too, provides practical strategies you can use to develop your style and make your writing hard to forget.

Coming to Terms

Joseph Harris

"Who's against shorthand? No one I know. Who wants to be short-changed? No one I know." So said the New Jersey poet and doctor William Carlos Williams to another doctor and writer, the psychiatrist Robert Coles. Williams's remark appears in an essay by Coles, "Stories and Theories,"[1] in which he warns against the damage that can be done when complex views and experiences are reduced to easy labels. And yet, to respond to another text you *have* to summarize it, put its key phrasings and ideas in some kind of shorthand. So how do you do that without short-changing it, too?

The usual advice is to restate the "main idea" or "thesis" of a text. Such advice imagines a piece of writing as something fixed or static, as an argument that a writer has "constructed" or a position that she has "defended"—and which can thus be condensed and reified into something like a "thesis statement." But there are many writers who don't so much argue for a single claim or position as *think through* a complex set of texts and problems. Their books and essays offer not sharply defined positions but ways of talking about a subject. The questions to ask of such work draw on metaphors of movement and growth: What issues drive this essay? What ideas does it explore? What lines of inquiry does it develop? To try to reduce this kind of open-ended text to a single main idea or claim would almost certainly be to shortchange it.

Instead the question to ask is: What is the writer trying *to do* in this text? What is his or her *project*? A *project* is usually something far more complex than a main idea, since it refers not to a single concept but to a plan of work, to a set of ideas and questions that a writer "throws forward" (Latin, *pro + jacare*). The idea of a project thus raises questions of intent. A project is something that a writer is working on—and that a text can only imperfectly realize. (Of course, any text you write will also hint at possibilities of meaning you had not considered, imply or suggest things you had not planned. A text always says both less and more than its writer intends.) To define the project of a writer is thus to push beyond his text, to hazard a view about not only what someone has said but also what he was trying to accomplish by saying it.

An example may help here. In her book *In a Different Voice*, Carol Gilligan shows how mainstream theories of psychology stumble in helping us understand why women respond to moral conflicts in ways that often differ from men. Gilligan doesn't suggest that previous generations of psychologists were wrong but rather that their views of the self were shaped and limited by their focus on the development of men. And so here, for instance, is how she approaches a seminal essay by Sigmund Freud:

> In 1914, with his essay "On Narcissism," Freud swallows his distaste at the thought of "abandoning observation for barren theoretical controversy" and extends his map of the psychological domain. Tracing the development of the capacity to love, which he equates with maturity and psychic health, he locates its origins in the contrast between love for the mother and love for the self. But in thus dividing the world between narcissism and "object" relationships, he finds that while men's development becomes clearer, women's becomes increasingly opaque. The problem arises because the contrast between mother and self yields two different images of relationships. Relying on the imagery of men's lives in charting the course of human growth, Freud is unable to trace in women the development of relationships, morality, or a clear sense of self. This difficulty of fitting the logic of his theory to women's experience leads him in the end to set women apart, marking their relationships, like their sexual life, as "a 'dark continent' for psychology."[2]

The first thing I'd note about this passage is its generosity. Gilligan is describing a view that she feels is deeply flawed, that indeed she is writing her book in an effort to correct, but her goal here seems to be to offer an account of Freud's thinking that he might have himself agreed with. Even the problem with his theory that she points out is one that Freud himself recognized, as Gilligan makes clear by quoting his comment about women remaining a "dark continent" for psychology. This isn't to say that her view of Freud is disinterested. Gilligan is trying to clear space in this passage for her own study of women's moral growth through showing how his theories are grounded in the experiences of men alone. In giving Freud his due, she lends a sense of weight to her own response to his work.

Gilligan does not so much summarize "On Narcissism"[3] as describe Freud's aims and strategies in writing it. The subject or actor of nearly every one of her sentences is Freud—whom Gilligan pictures as "swallowing his distaste" about theory, "extending his map" of psychology, "tracing the development" of love, "locating its origins," and so on. In doing so, she describes "On Narcissism" less as a structure supporting a single main idea than as a series of moves that Freud makes as a writer. One strength of this approach is stylistic: We tend to find it easier to follow prose that offers a narrative than prose that elaborates a set of abstract propositions—and Gilligan here offers us a brief story of ideas with Freud at its center. More important, to describe his plan of work, Gilligan needs to say something about Freud's *aims*, *methods*, and *materials*. This allows her, in her brief account of his essay, both to honor his project and to begin to point to some of its problems—through representing what he was trying to do (trace the origins of love), how he did it (examining the child's relationship with his mother), and where his data or insights came from (the early experiences of male children).

You can ask much the same questions in defining the projects of other writers:

- *Aims*: What is a writer trying to achieve? What position does he or she want to argue? What issues or problems does he or she explore?

- *Methods*: How does a writer relate examples to ideas? How does he or she connect one claim to the next, build a sense of continuity and flow?

- *Materials*: Where does the writer go for examples and evidence? What texts are cited and discussed? What experiences or events are described?

And, to follow Gilligan's lead once again, you need to ask and answer these questions in a generous mode. To make effective use of the work of other writers, you have to show the force of their thinking, to suggest in your rewriting of their work *why* they said what they said in the particular ways they said it. And the best way to do that is to pay close attention to how their texts are worded.

Noting Keywords and Passages

One mark of a strong academic writer is the ability to move from the global to the local, from projects to phrasings, from talking about a text as a whole to noticing moments of particular interest in it. To come to terms with a complex text you need to be able to shift levels in this way, to ground how you define the project of a writer by citing key passages from his or her text. Such quotations may often be short and pointed. If you return to Gilligan's paragraph on Freud, for instance, you'll note that she quotes the language of his essay at only three points, and each time quite briefly: once to show that Freud was concerned that in "On Narcissism" he was entering the realm of "theoretical controversy," another time to note the key concept of "object" relations, and a final time to show that he was aware that his views had turned the experiences of women into a "dark continent." (In each case, the words quoted are Freud's.) While these touches are light, they are also crucial: Delete them, and one might ask, "But is that really what Freud said?" Keep them, and even if you disagree with her account of Freud, you still need to admit that Gilligan has noticed something about his text and project.

There is a subtle but important distinction to make here: You don't quote from a text to explain what it means in some neutral or objective way. *You quote from a text to show what your perspective on it makes visible.* If we all read a text in the same way, there'd be little need for us to argue over the meaning of its specific lines or phrasings. But academic writing is based on the idea that we read texts differently. Intellectuals often discuss books and articles that their readers are familiar with, and sometimes may even know quite well. But the interest of an academic essay usually has less to with its subject than with the approach of its writer. You don't need to reexplain a text to somebody who has already read it. But you can offer a different way of reading that text, to point out how your perspective allows you to notice something new about it.

In deciding when to quote, then, the question to ask is not *What is the writer of this text trying to say?* but *What aspects of this text stand out for me as a reader?* Quote to illustrate your view of a text, to single out terms or passages that strike you in some way as interesting, troubling, ambiguous, or suggestive. Weak academic essays are often marked by an overreliance on quotation, as the words of the authors quoted begin to drown out those of the person writing about them. You don't want the writers you quote to do your work for you. You want the focus of your readers instead to be on your ideas, to draw their attention not to the texts you're quoting but to the work you're doing *with* those texts. And so, when what you need to do is to restate what a certain writer is trying to do, to represent her or his project, try to paraphrase the work as quickly and accurately as you can. Save quotation for moments that advance your project, your view of the text.

Or let me put it this way: Summarize when what you have to say about a text is routine and quote when it is more contentious. Here, for instance, is I. F. Stone, in *The Trial of Socrates*, pointing to what he sees as a key difference between the worldviews of the ancient Greek philosophers Aristotle and Plato:

> Plato was a theorist, Aristotle a scientific observer. Aristotle prized practical over theoretical knowledge in dealing with human affairs. Aristotle had a strong bias in favor of experience and common sense. In contrast, Plato in a famous passage of *The Republic* proposed to limit his study of "the dialectic"—and thus the future rulers of his utopia—to those who could "let go of the eyes and other senses and rise to the contemplation of *to on*"—"pure being" or "being itself." This would no doubt be a contemplative joy to the mystic, but it hardly offers guidance to the statesman, forced to deal with tangled affairs and obdurate human nature.
>
> Aristotle takes issue with Plato at the very beginning of his own masterwork on philosophy, the *Metaphysics*. It starts off by saying, "All men naturally desire knowledge. An indication of this is our esteem for the senses." Without them, and especially sight, Aristotle asks, how can we know and act?[4]

Plato and Aristotle both wrote many works, and their thought has been the focus of an uncountable number of commentaries over the past 2,500 years. (Alfred North Whitehead once remarked that European philosophy in large part "consists of a series of footnotes to Plato.") So there is no way that Stone (or anyone else) could possibly "prove" that Plato was a theorist and Aristotle an observer—at least not in terms quite so simple. But I don't understand that to be his aim in this passage. Rather, I think that what Stone wants to show is that there is a *way of looking* at Plato and Aristotle that is both reasonably fair to their work and useful to his own project. (He goes on later in his book to link Plato's bent for theory to the antidemocratic politics of his mentor, Socrates.) Stone makes the case for his approach through a pointed use of quotation, contrasting Plato's exhortation to "let go of the eyes and other senses" with Aristotle's "esteem for the senses." These sentences do not summarize the work of either philosopher. No sentence or two ever could. Rather, they illustrate Stone's particular view of the differences between Plato and Aristotle. They are salient moments from his perspective as a reader. They show him rewriting their work as part of his own project.

You'll have noticed that I say of Stone's approach that it seems "reasonably fair" to Plato and Aristotle. Those may seem waffle words, but I don't mean them as such. On the contrary, the question of what counts as a fair reading lies at the center of much academic argument. Several of Stone's critics felt that he failed to represent the work of Plato and Socrates very well, just as some of Gilligan's readers thought that she misunderstood Freud. Such disagreements are inevitable. The best you can do as a reader is to try to show *why* you view a text in a certain way, both in terms of the values you bring to the text and the moments you notice in it. Your readers can then point to different values and different moments, and your ways of reading the text can then be contrasted and argued for, if not resolved.

You can see quotations as *flashpoints* in a text, moments given a special intensity, made to stand for key concepts or issues. A useful rule of thumb, then, is to quote only those phrases or passages that you want to do further work with or bring pressure upon—whose particular implications and resonances you want to analyze, elaborate, counter, revise, echo, or transform. Such pressure does not have to be skeptical; you can quote from a text in order to highlight the power of a particular way of phrasing an issue. For instance, here is Cornel West, philosopher and cultural critic, near the start of his book *Race Matters*:

> The common denominator of these views of race is that each still sees black people as a "problem people," in the words of Dorothy I. Height, president of the National Council of Negro Women, rather than as fellow American citizens with problems. Her words echo the poignant "unasked question" of W. E. B. Du Bois, who, in *The Souls of Black Folk* (1903), wrote:
>
>> They approach me in a half-hesitant way, eye me curiously or compassionately, and then instead of saying directly, How does it feel to be a problem? they say, I know an excellent colored man in my town... Do not these Southern outrages make your blood boil? At these I smile, or

am interested, or reduce the boiling to a simmer, as the occasion may require. To the real question, How does it feel to be a problem? I answer seldom a word.

Nearly a century later, we confine discussions about race in America to the "problems" black people pose for whites rather than considering what this way of viewing black people reveals about us as a nation.

This paralyzing framework encourages liberals to relieve their guilty consciences by supporting public funds directed at "the problems"; but at the same time, reluctant to exercise principled criticism of black people, liberals deny them freedom to err. Similarly, conservatives blame the "problems" on black people themselves—and thereby render black social misery invisible or unworthy of public attention.[5]

Making use of the words of Height, Du Bois, and others, West constructs a jazzlike progression that moves from "problem people" to "citizens with problems" to "how does it feel to be a problem?" to "the 'problems' black people pose" to "the problems" to "blame the 'problems' on black people themselves." I especially admire the finesse with which he distinguishes between the "problems" that liberals see as besetting blacks and the "problems" that conservatives see blacks as causing. The net effect of these echoes-with-a-difference is to give the word *problem*, as it is used in discussions of race, a rich and disturbing complexity of meanings. West uses a series of quotations to pull the term out of general usage, as it were, and to grant it instead a particular history and meaning, to ask his readers to consider how race poses a specific and unusual sort of "problem" for us.

Quotation thus has two distinct uses in coming to terms with the work of another writer. On the one hand, it can serve as a *brake* on paraphrase. In quoting key passages from a text, you show respect for the specificity of its tone, ideas, and phrasings. You make it clear that you have not carelessly substituted its language with your own. On the other hand, quotation can *intensify* paraphrase. It allows you to scrutinize particular moments in a text—to suggest either the usefulness of a certain way of phrasing an issue (as West does with "problem") or its limitations (as Gilligan does with Freud's "dark continent"). I will return to this second use of quotation in the following chapters—since bringing pressure on a writer's phrasings is a crucial aspect of forwarding, countering, or transforming her project. For now, though, I need to say a little more about *coming to terms* as a form of reckoning or negotiation.

Assessing Uses and Limits

We live in a culture prone to naming winners and losers, rights and wrongs. You're in or out, hot or not, on the bus or off it. But academics seldom write in an all-or-nothing mode, trying to convince readers to take one side or the other of an argument. Instead their work assumes that any perspective on an issue (and there are often more than two) will have moments of both insight and blindness. A frame offers a view but also brackets something out. A point of view highlights certain aspects and obscures others. And so, in dealing with other writers, your aim should be less to prove them right or wrong, correct or mistaken, than to assess both the uses and limits of their work. That is to say, academic writing rarely involves a simple taking of sides, an attack on or defense of set positions, but rather centers on a weighing of options, a sorting through of possibilities.

In writing as an intellectual, then, you need to push beyond the sorts of bipolar oppositions (pro or con, good or evil, guilty or innocent) that frame most of the arguments found on editorial pages and TV talk shows. Intellectual writers usually work not with simple antitheses (either *x* or *not-x*) but with *positive opposing terms*—that is, with words and values that don't contradict each other yet still exist in some real and ongoing tension. For instance, I have suggested in this chapter that you need to deal with the work of others in ways that are both *generous* and *assertive*. These terms are not direct opposites, but neither are they congruent. Rather, they name different and competing values in writing that I believe you need to learn to negotiate. Or, for another example, you might look back at the piece on "Stories and Theories" by Robert Coles that I mentioned earlier. In that essay, Coles distinguishes between two kinds of discourse: *stories*, which we use in evoking the felt quality of events, and *theories*, which we use in analyzing their meanings. A story is not merely a bad version of a theory or vice versa. The two words describe distinct uses of language, each with its own strengths and weaknesses. They are positive opposing terms.

Academic writers often bring a cluster of texts and perspectives into this sort of positive opposition or tension. This is more complex and interesting work than simply taking sides in a debate, since it involves thinking through the potential uses of a number of positions rather than arguing for or against a fixed point of view. In coming to terms with a text, then, the key questions to ask have to do not with correctness but use. What does this text do or see well? What does it stumble over or occlude?

Here, for instance, is how John Seely Brown and Paul Duguid, in their book on *The Social Life of Information*, approach the work of one of their colleagues:

> Let us begin by taking a cue from MIT's Nicholas Negroponte. His handbook for the information age, *Being Digital*, encouraged everyone to think about the differences between atoms, a fundamental unit of matter, and bits, and the fundamental unit of information. Here was a provocative and useful thought experiment in contrasts. Moreover, it can be useful to consider possible similarities between the two as well.

Consider, for example, the industrial revolution, the information revolution's role model. It was a period in which society learned how to process, sort, rearrange, recombine, and transport atoms in unprecedented fashion. Yet people didn't complain that they were drowning in atoms. They didn't worry about atom overload. Because, of course, while the world may be composed of atoms, people don't perceive it that way. They perceive it as buses and books and tables and chairs, buildings and coffee mugs, laptops and cell phones, and so forth. Similarly, while information may come to us in quadrillions of bits, we don't consider it that way. The information reflected in bits comes to us, for example, as stories, documents, diagrams, pictures, or narratives, as knowledge and meaning, and in communities, organizations, and institutions.[6]

The strength of this passage hinges on that *moreover* near the end of the first paragraph. Brown and Duguid use this term to signal a complex stance toward Negroponte. They don't deny the suggestiveness of the contrast he draws between atoms and bits; in fact, they play with and elaborate upon it. But they also suggest that there is something that this contrast fails to make visible, or may even hide—something that has to do with the structures and contexts in which atoms and bits are always embedded. They thus neither simply endorse nor reject his perspective but point out its uses and limits.

They "take a cue" from Negroponte, that is, not by simply restating his view of how atoms and bits are different but by thinking more about their relationship and deciding that they can also be seen as similar. They come to terms with his work by showing both what he sees powerfully and what he fails to notice.

Indeed, you might use *moreover* as a catchword for much of the work of coming to terms with another text—in which you need not only to indicate what a writer does well but also to suggest what she or he has left undone. In arguing that academic writing needs to hold a number of competing views in tension, though, I don't mean to advocate tepid or bland prose. Rather, I am urging you to approach writing with an active mix of skepticism and generosity—both to look for gaps or difficulties in perspectives you admire and also to try to understand the strengths of those you don't. Form the habit of questioning your first responses: So, here's a text that seems to offer a compelling way of looking at an issue— what does it also bracket out of sight? Or, here's a text that seems curiously wrongheaded or obtuse—what might account for its seeming strangeness? what is its writer trying to accomplish? (If you really can't answer such questions, you're probably not dealing with a text that you can put to good use, since simply proving someone else wrong rarely advances your own thinking.) To forward the phrasings or ideas of other writers, you need to know what they can't do as well as what they can. And to counter the work of another, you need to recognize not just its limits but its strengths. I'll have more to say about those forms of rewriting in the next two chapters. My point here, though, is that to come to terms with a text, you need not only to restate its project but also to take its measure.

Quotation: Some Terms of Art

This is not a handbook but a text that tries to think through some ways of working as a writer with the words, images, and ideas of others. I will thus not review here the many and arcane rules for punctuating quotations and citing sources—which, to my point of view, have more to do with typing than writing and which, in any case, vary widely from one context to the other. The best advice I can offer you is to ask your teacher or editor what manual or style sheet you need to follow, buy a copy, and consult it carefully in preparing the final version of your work.[7] There are plenty of details but few intellectual issues involved in compiling a list of references or works cited; it's the kind of thing you want to get right the first time. The same goes for citing sources and page numbers. Most academic disciplines now use some version of parenthetical or in-text citation rather than footnotes, in which you place key information about a text you've quoted (name, author, page number, etc.) in parentheses following the quotation. If a reader then wants to look up the text you've quoted, he or she can consult its fuller entry in your list of works cited. Exactly what information should go in these parentheses, in what order, with what sorts of punctuation, as well as where the parentheses themselves should be placed in your own sentence—the answers to such questions can once again vary widely from one context or discipline to the next. The only way to make sure you get it right is to learn what style sheet to use. After that, pretty much the only thing you need to do is to follow the format it lays out.

But how you actually go about incorporating other texts into your own prose can also say a good deal about the stance or attitude you want to take toward them, and in ways that cannot be reduced to a simple matter of rules. There is, for instance, the question of how much you want to emphasize the *otherness* of the texts you quote, to what degree you want to make the difference between their language and yours visible on the page. The advice given by most writing manuals, it seems to me, urges you to downplay this sense of otherness, to quote in ways that work toward the illusion of a seamless text, incorporating the words of others as much as you can within your own sentences. On the other end of this spectrum is a text like the Vulgate Bible, which sets the words of Jesus in red type, separating them from the prose of the evangelists in a way that can be seen, literally, from across the room. My own sense, as I hope is suggested by the look and feel of this book, is that you want to develop a flexible repertoire of forms of quotation, including:

- *Block quotes*: Setting or "blocking" off the text of another writer from your own. Most of the key examples in this book take this

form. Block quotes are often indented from the main text and set in
a different font and spacing. They are seldom framed with quotation marks. Block quotes tend to make the work of others highly
visible in your writing. They are often used when you need to quote
several lines from a work, but also, and more important, as a form
of emphasis, as a way of saying that this is a text that you, as a writer,
plan to return to and work more with.

- *In-text quotes*: Incorporating the words of another writer as part of
  your own text, while marking and framing your use of their work
  with quotation marks. In-text quotes are most often used to note
  and emphasize particular terms and phrasings, to add to and qualify
  paraphrase. They are usually brief, although you may sometimes
  want to quote a full sentence or two without giving it the weight of
  a block quote. The rules for punctuating in-text quotes are byzan-
  tine and contested, although the basic principle is simple enough:
  Punctuation creates distance. A quotation introduced by a colon
  or a comma, or one that stands on its own as a sentence, feels more
  separate from your words and thinking than one that is dropped
  into the flow of your own prose with little or no punctuation.

- *Scare quotes*: Putting quotation marks around a word to signal that
  it is not one that you feel is apt. Scare quotes are the visual marker
  of sarcasm. They often refer not to a specific moment in a text but
  to a more general usage of a term. Cornel West makes effective use
  of them in the passage I quoted previously, when he says, "This
  paralyzing framework encourages liberals to relieve their guilty
  consciences by supporting public funds directed at 'the problems'…
  Similarly, conservatives blame the 'problems' on black people themselves." However, a little irony can go a long way. Often the best test
  is reading aloud. If you find yourself dropping your voice senten-
  tiously each time you reach a quoted term, consider limiting your
  use of scare quotes. Italics offer an alternative way of putting emphasis on a word without giving it a negative spin.

- *Epigraphs*: Setting a quotation at the head of a book, chapter, essay,
  or section of an essay. The term epigraph comes from the Greek,
  epi + *graphos*, "to write upon"; it thus refers literally to an inscrip-
  tion—as on a statue, gravestone, or building. Some of this meaning
  has carried over to its use in writing, as an epigraph is the one form
  of quotation that a writer is not expected to comment on. Rather,
  it is usually the epigraph that comments on the text that follows—
  that sets a tone or suggests a perspective, sometimes quite obliquely.
  When done well, an epigraph can serve as a kind of poetic précis of
  a text, summing up its aim or scope—even if its full meaning does
  not always become clear until the piece has been read through and

the epigraph considered a second time. Done less well, epigraphs can sometimes appear self-importantly literary, too erudite by half.

- *Allusions*: Leaving a brief quotation unmarked, in the expectation that readers will hear the echo of the other text in your own. The term derives from the Latin, *ad* + *ludere*, "to play with," and suggests something more on the lines of a hint and a wink than a direct statement. Academic writing often routinely proceeds from direct quotation to a more mundane kind of allusion—as, for instance, when the work of a writer is introduced by means of a block quote, which is then followed by an analysis of key terms and passages that are quoted in text, and finally when those terms are used without quotation marks but still carrying a particular set of inflections and meanings. In *Race Matters*, for example, Cornel West follows the paragraph I've quoted with one that starts, "To engage in a serious discussion of race in America, we must begin not with the problems of black people but with the flaws of American society." By this point in his text, West has dropped the quotation marks from around *problem*, but his use of the term still clearly echoes those of Height, Du Bois, and the "liberals" and "conservatives" that he has just cited. His prose alludes to a set of meanings that he no longer needs to quote.

Block quotes, in-text quotes, scare quotes, epigraphs, allusions—these are *terms of art*, words that the practitioners of a craft use to describe their work. In learning such terms, you acquire not simply a vocabulary but a sense of what distinctions matter in the practice of a craft. In this case, the range of terms used to describe forms of quotation speaks to the key role that dealing with the work of others plays in academic writing. The value placed on representing other texts accurately is further shown by the set of practices that academics have developed to show when a writer has needed to alter a quotation, however slightly—as with the use of ellipses (…) to mark a break in a quoted passage, of [brackets] to mark additions or changes made to a text, and of the notation (emphasis added) to indicate when terms in a passage have been italicized or otherwise highlighted. A strong use of the work of others is always grounded in a scrupulous care in citing their texts.

Coming to terms in some ways offers the clearest example of what I mean by *rewriting*. You come to terms with a text by translating its words and ideas into your own language, making them part of your own prose—not only re-presenting the work of another writer but also, at times, actually retyping it as you quote key terms and passages from a text. But I suspect that you will also find that in trying seriously to come to terms with another text, and especially in assessing its uses and limits, your focus as a writer soon shifts away from simply restating what that text has to say and toward the uses you can make of its concepts and phrases, or toward the gaps and problems you encounter in trying to do so. I will turn to such *forwarding* and *countering* moves in the next chapters.

Notes

1. Robert Coles, "Stories and Theories" in *The Call of Stories* (Boston Houghton Mifflin, 1989).

2. Carol Gulligan, *In a Different Voice: Psychological Theory and the Women's Development* (Cambridge; Harvard University Press, 1982), 24.

3. Freud's "On Narcissism" (1914) is reprinted in the *Standard Edition of the Complete Psychological Works*, vol. 14, ed. and trans. James Strachey (London: Hogarth, 1961).

4. I. F. Stone, *The Trial of Socrates* (Boston: Little, Brown, 1988), 13. Stone quotes from the Loeb Classical Library editions of both Plato and Aristotel. Whitehead's remark has itself been quoted (and often misquoted) in hundreds of other texts. It first appeared in his *Process and Reality*, rev. ed, (New York: Free Press, 1978), 39.

5. Cornel West, *Race Matters* (Boston: Beacon, 1993), 2-3. *The Souls of Black Folk* (1903) is reprinted in The Oxford W.E.B. DuBois Reader (New York; Oxford University Press, 1996). The passage quoted is found on p. 101. West does not provide a reference for the Heigh quotation.

6. John Seely Brown and Paul Duguid, *The Social Life of Information* (Boston: Harvard Business School Press, 2000), 15-16. Brown and Duguid are discussing Nicholas Negroponte's *Being Digital* (New York: Basic Books, 1995).

7. Several academic disciplines publish their own quides to documenting sources. Among those most often used are:

   Joseph Gibaldi, *The MLA Handbook for Writers of Research Papers*, 5th ed. (New York: Modern Language Association, 1999). (literature)

   The APA Publication Manual, 4th ed. (Washington, DC: American Psychological Association, 1994). (social sciences)

   Kate Turabian, *A manual for Writers of Term Papers, Theses, and Dissertations*, 6th ed. (Chicago: University of Chicago Press, 1996). Often simply called *Turabian* this manual a version of the format defined by the voluminous Chicago Manual of Style, 15th ed. (University of Chicago Press, 2003) (humanities)

   Most good handbooks provide brief guides to the MLA, APA and Chicago Styles.

Joseph Harris, "Coming to Terms," from *Rewriting: How to Do Things With Texts*. Logan, UT: Utah State University Press, 2006 pp. 16–32. Reprinted by permission.

Bird by Bird: Some Instructions on Writing and Life

Anne Lamott

Short Assignments

The first useful concept is the idea of short assignments. Often when you sit down to write, what you have in mind is an autobiographical novel about your childhood, or a play about the immigrant experience, or a history of—oh, say—say women. But this is like trying to scale a glacier. It's hard to get your footing, and your fingertips get all red and frozen and torn up. Then your mental illnesses arrive at the desk like your sickest, most secretive relatives. And they pull up chairs in a semicircle around the computer, and they try to be quiet but you know they are there with their weird coppery breath, leering at you behind your back.

What I do at this point, as the panic mounts and the jungle drums begin beating and I realize that the well has run dry and that my future is behind me and I'm going to have to get a job only I'm completely unemployable, is to stop. First I try to breathe, because I'm either sitting there panting like a lapdog or I'm unintentionally making slow asthmatic death rattles. So I just sit there for a minute, breathing slowly, quietly. I let my mind wander. After a moment I may notice that I'm trying to decide whether or not I am too old for orthodontia and whether right now would be a good time to make a few calls, and then I start to think about learning to use makeup and how maybe I could find some boyfriend who is not a total and complete fixer-upper and then my life would be totally great and I'd be happy all the time, and then I think about all the people I should have called back before I sat down to work, and how I should probably at least check in with my agent and tell him this great idea I have and see if he thinks it's a good idea, and see if *he* thinks I need orthodontia—if that is what he is actually thinking whenever we have lunch together. Then I think about someone I'm really annoyed with, or some financial problem that is driving me crazy, and decide that I must resolve this before I get down to today's work. So I become a dog with a chew toy, worrying it for a while, wrestling it to the ground, flinging it over my shoulder, chasing it, licking it, chewing it, flinging it back over my shoulder. I stop just short of actually barking. But all of this only takes somewhere between one and two minutes, so I haven't actually wasted that much time. Still, it leaves me winded. I go back to trying to breathe, slowly and calmly, and I finally notice the one-inch picture frame that I put on my desk to remind me of short assignments.

It reminds me that all I have to do is to write down as much as I can see through a one-inch picture frame. This is all I have to bite off for the time being. All I am going to do right now, for example, is write that one paragraph that sets the story in my hometown, in the late fifties, when the

17

trains were still running. I am going to paint a picture of it, in words, on my word processor. Or all I am going to do is to describe the main character the very first time we meet her, when she first walks out the front door and onto the porch. I am not even going to describe the expression on her face when she first notices the blind dog sitting behind the wheel of her car—just what I can see through the one-inch picture frame, just one paragraph describing this woman, in the town where I grew up, the first time we encounter her.

E. L. Doctorow once said that "writing a novel is like driving a car at night. You can see only as far as your headlights, but you can make the whole trip that way." You don't have to see where you're going, you don't have to see your destination or everything you will pass along the way. You just have to see two or three feet ahead of you. This is right up there with the best advice about writing, or life, I have ever heard.

So after I've completely exhausted myself thinking about the people I most resent in the world, and my more arresting financial problems, and, of course, the orthodontia, I remember to pick up the one-inch picture frame and to figure out a one-inch piece of my story to tell, one small scene, one memory, one exchange. I also remember a story that I know I've told elsewhere but that over and over helps me to get a grip: thirty years ago my older brother, who was ten years old at the time, was trying to get a report on birds written that he'd had three months to write, which was due the next day. We were out at our family cabin in Bolinas, and he was at the kitchen table close to tears, surrounded by binder paper and pencils and unopened books on birds, immobilized by the hugeness of the task ahead. Then my father sat down beside him, put his arm around my brother's shoulder, and said, "Bird by bird, buddy. Just take it bird by bird."

I tell this story again because it usually makes a dent in the tremendous sense of being overwhelmed that my students experience. Sometimes it actually gives them hope, and hope, as Chesterton said, is the power of being cheerful in circumstances that we know to be desperate. Writing can be a pretty desperate endeavor, because it is about some of our deepest needs: our need to be visible, to be heard, our need to make sense of our lives, to wake up and grow and belong. It is no wonder if we sometimes tend to take ourselves perhaps a bit too seriously. So here is another story I tell often.

In the Bill Murray movie *Stripes*, in which he joins the army, there is a scene that takes place the first night of boot camp, where Murray's platoon is assembled in the barracks. They are supposed to be getting to know their sergeant, played by Warren Oates, and one another. So each man takes a few moments to say a few things about who he is and where he is from. Finally it is the turn of this incredibly intense, angry guy named Francis. "My name is Francis," he says. "No one calls me Francis—

anyone here calls me Francis and I'll kill them. And another thing. I don't like to be touched. Anyone here ever tries to touch me, I'll kill them," at which point Warren Oates jumps in and says, "Hey—lighten up, Francis."

This is not a bad line to have taped to the wall of your office.

Say to yourself in the kindest possible way, Look, honey, all we're going to do for now is to write a description of the river at sunrise, or the young child swimming in the pool at the club, or the first time the man sees the woman he will marry. That is all we are going to do for now. We are just going to take this bird by bird. But we are going to finish this *one* short assignment.

Shitty First Drafts

Now, practically even better news than that of short assignments is the idea of shitty first drafts. All good writers write them. This is how they end up with good second drafts and terrific third drafts. People tend to look at successful writers, writers who are getting their books published and maybe even doing well financially, and think that they sit down at their desks every morning feeling like a million dollars, feeling great about who they are and how much talent they have and what a great story they have to tell; that they take in a few deep breaths, push back their sleeves, roll their necks a few times to get all the cricks out, and dive in, typing fully formed passages as fast as a court reporter. But this is just the fantasy of the uninitiated. I know some very great writers, writers you love who write beautifully and have made a great deal of money, and not *one* of them sits down routinely feeling wildly enthusiastic and confident. Not one of them writes elegant first drafts. All right, one of them does, but we do not like her very much. We do not think that she has a rich inner life or that God likes her or can even stand her. (Although when I mentioned this to my priest friend Tom, he said you can safely assume you've created God in your own image when it turns out that God hates all the same people you do.)

Very few writers really know what they are doing until they've done it. Nor do they go about their business feeling dewy and thrilled. They do not type a few stiff warm-up sentences and then find themselves bounding along like huskies across the snow. One writer I know tells me that he sits down every morning and says to himself nicely, "It's not like you don't have a choice, because you do—you can either type or kill yourself." We all often feel like we are pulling teeth, even those writers whose prose ends up being the most natural and fluid. The right words and sentences just do not come pouring out like ticker tape most of the time. Now, Muriel Spark is said to have felt that she was taking dictation from God every morning—sitting there, one supposes, plugged into a Dictaphone, typing away, humming. But this is a very hostile and aggressive position. One might hope for bad things to rain down on a person like this.

For me, and most of the other writers I know, writing is not rapturous. In fact, the only way I can get anything written at all is to write really, really shitty first drafts.

The first draft is the child's draft, where you let it all pour out and then let it romp all over the place, knowing that no one is going to see it and that you can shape it later. You just let this childlike part of you channel whatever voices and visions come through and onto the page. If one of the characters wants to say, "Well so what, Mr. Poopy Pants?," you let her. No one is going to see it. If the kid wants to get into really sentimental, weepy, emotional territory you let him. Just get it all down on paper, because there may be something great in those six crazy pages that you would never have gotten to by more rational, grown-up means. There may be something in the very last line of the very last paragraph on page six that you just love that is so beautiful or wild that you now know what you're supposed to be writing about, more or less, or in what direction you might go—but there was no way to get to this without first getting through the first five and a half pages.

I used to write food reviews for *California* magazine before it folded. (My writing food reviews had nothing to do with the magazine folding, although every single review did cause a couple of canceled subscriptions. Some readers took umbrage at my comparing mounds of vegetable puree with various ex-presidents' brains.) These reviews always took two days to write. First I'd go to a restaurant several times with a few opinionated, articulate friends in tow. I'd sit there writing down everything anyone said that was at all interesting or funny. Then on the following Monday I'd sit down at my desk with my notes, and try to write the review. Even after I'd been doing this for years, panic would set in. I'd try to write a lead, but instead I'd write a couple of dreadful sentences, xx them out, try again, xx everything out, and then feel despair and worry settle on my chest like an x-ray apron. It's over, I'd think, calmly. I'm not going to be able to get the magic to work this time. I'm ruined. I'm through. I'm toast. Maybe, I'd think, I can get my old job back as a clerk-typist. But probably not. I'd get up and study my teeth in the mirror for a while. Then I'd stop, remember to breathe, make a few phone calls, hit the kitchen and chow down. Eventually I'd go back and sit down at my desk, and sigh for the next ten minutes. Finally I would pick up my one-inch picture frame, stare into it as if for the answer, and every time the answer would come: all I had to do was to write a really shitty first draft of, say, the opening paragraph. And no one was going to see it.

So I'd start writing without reining myself in. It was almost just typing, just making my fingers move. And the writing would be *terrible*. I'd write a lead paragraph that was a whole page, even though the entire review could only be three pages long, and then I'd start writing up descriptions of the food, one dish at a time, bird by bird, and the critics would be sitting on my shoulders, commenting like cartoon characters. They'd be pretending to snore, or rolling their eyes at my overwrought descriptions, no matter how hard I tried to tone those descriptions down, no matter how conscious I was of what a friend said to me gently in my early days of restaurant reviewing. "Annie," she said, "it is just a piece of *chicken*. It is just a bit of *cake*."

But because by then I had been writing for so long, I would eventually let myself trust the process—sort of, more or less. I'd write a first draft that was maybe twice as long as it should be, with a self-indulgent and boring beginning, stupefying descriptions of the meal, lots of quotes from my black-humored friends that made them sound more like the Manson girls than food lovers, and no ending to speak of. The whole thing would be so long and incoherent and hideous that for the rest of the day I'd obsess about getting creamed by a car before I could write a decent second draft. I'd worry that people would read what I'd written and believe that the accident had really been a suicide, that I had panicked because my talent was waning and my mind was shot.

The next day, though, I'd sit down, go through it all with a colored pen, take out everything I possibly could, find a new lead somewhere on the second page, figure out a kicky place to end it, and then write a second draft. It always turned out fine, sometimes even funny and weird and helpful. I'd go over it one more time and mail it in.

Then, a month later, when it was time for another review, the whole process would start again, complete with the fears that people would find my first draft before I could rewrite it.

Almost all good writing begins with terrible first efforts. You need to start somewhere. Start by getting something—anything—down on paper. A friend of mine says that the first draft is the down draft—you just get it down. The second draft is the up draft—you fix it up. You try to say what you have to say more accurately. And the third draft is the dental draft, where you check every tooth to see if it's loose or cramped or decayed, or even, God help us, healthy.

What I've learned to do when I sit down to work on a shitty first draft is to quiet the voices in my head. First there's the vinegar-lipped Reader Lady, who says primly, "Well, *that's* not very interesting, is it?" And there's the emaciated German male who writes these Orwellian memos detailing your thought crimes. And there are your parents, agonizing over your lack of loyalty and discretion; and there's William Burroughs, dozing off or shooting up because he finds you as bold and articulate as a houseplant; and so on. And there are also the dogs: let's not forget the dogs, the dogs in their pen who will surely hurtle and snarl their way out if you ever *stop* writing, because writing is, for some of us, the latch that keeps the door of the pen closed, keeps those crazy ravenous dogs contained.

Quieting these voices is at least half the battle I fight daily. But this is better than it used to be. It used to be 87 percent. Left to its own devices, my mind spends much of its time having conversations with people who aren't there. I walk along defending myself to people, or exchanging repartee with them, or rationalizing my behavior, or seducing them with gossip, or pretending I'm on their TV talk show or whatever. I speed or run an aging yellow light or don't come to a full stop, and one nanosecond later am explaining to imaginary cops exactly why I had to do what I did, or insisting that I did not in fact do it.

I happened to mention this to a hypnotist I saw many years ago, and he looked at me very nicely. At first I thought he was feeling around on the floor for the silent alarm button, but then he gave me the following exercise, which I still use to this day.

Close your eyes and get quiet for a minute, until the chatter starts up. Then isolate one of the voices and imagine the person speaking as a mouse. Pick it up by the tail and drop it into a mason jar. Then isolate another voice, pick it up by the tail, drop it in the jar. And so on. Drop in any high-maintenance parental units, drop in any contractors, lawyers, colleagues, children, anyone who is whining in your head. Then put the lid on, and watch all these mouse people clawing at the glass, jabbering away, trying to make you feel like shit because you won't do what they want—won't give them more money, won't be more successful, won't see them more often. Then imagine that there is a volume-control button on the bottle. Turn it all the way up for a minute, and listen to the stream of angry, neglected, guilt-mongering voices. Then turn it all the way down and watch the frantic mice lunge at the glass, trying to get to you. Leave it down, and get back to your shitty first draft.

A writer friend of mine suggests opening the jar and shooting them all in the head. But I think he's a little angry, and I'm sure nothing like this would ever occur to you.

Someone to Read Your Drafts

There's an old *New Yorker* cartoon of two men sitting on a couch at a busy cocktail party, having a quiet talk. One man has a beard and looks like a writer. The other seems like a normal person. The writer type is saying to the other, "We're still pretty far apart. I'm looking for a six-figure advance, and they're refusing to read the manuscript."

Now, I've been wrong before, but I'd bet you anything that this guy never shows his work to other writers before trying to get someone to buy it. I bet he thinks he's above that.

Whenever I'm giving a lecture at a writing conference and happen to mention the benefits of finding someone to read your drafts, at least one older established writer comes up to me and says that he or she would never in a million years show his or her work to another person before it was done. It is not a good idea, and I must stop telling my students that it will help them. I just smile, geishalike, and make little fluttery sounds of understanding. Then I go on telling people to consider finding someone who would not mind reading their drafts and marking them up with useful suggestions. The person may not have an answer to what is missing or annoying about the piece, but writing is so often about making mistakes and feeling lost. There are probably a number of ways to tell your story right, and someone else may be able to tell you whether or not you've found one of these ways.

I'm not suggesting that you and another writer sit in a cubby somewhere and write together, as though you were doing potato prints side by side at the institution, and that then you beam at each other's work the way you gape when your kid first writes his name. But I am suggesting that there may be someone out there in the world—maybe a spouse, maybe a close friend—who will read your finished drafts and give you an honest critique, let you know what does and doesn't work, give you some suggestions on things you might take out or things on which you need to elaborate, ways in which to make your piece stronger.

In the first story of Donald Barthelme's I ever read, twenty years ago, he said that truth is a hard apple to catch and it is a hard apple to throw. I know what a painful feeling it is when you've been working on something forever, and it feels done, and you give your story to someone you hope will validate this and that person tells you it still needs more work. You have to, at this point, question your assessment of this person's character and, if he or she is not a spouse or a lifelong friend, decide whether or not you want them in your life at all. Mostly I think an appropriate first reaction is to think that you don't. But in a little while it may strike you as a small miracle that you have someone in your life, whose taste you admire (after all, this person loves you and your work), who will tell you the truth and help you stay on the straight and narrow, or find your way back to it if you are lost.

I always show my work to one of two people before sending a copy to my editor or agent. I feel more secure and connected this way, and these two people get a lot of good work out of me. They are like midwives; there are these stories and ideas and visions and memories and plots inside me, and only I can give birth to them. Theoretically I could do it alone, but it sure makes it easier to have people helping. I have girlfriends who had their babies through natural childbirth—no drugs, no spinal, no nothing—and they secretly think they had a more honest birth experience, but I think the epidural is right up there with the most important breakthroughs in the West, like the Salk polio vaccine and salad bars in supermarkets. It's an individual thing. What works for me may not work for you. But feedback from someone I'm close to gives me confidence, or at least it gives me time to improve. Imagine that you are getting ready for a party and there is a person at your house who can check you out and assure you that you look wonderful or, conversely, that you actually do look a little tiny tiny tiny bit heavier than usual in this one particular dress or suit or that red makes you look just a bit like you have sarcoptic mange. Of course you are disappointed for a moment, but then you are grateful that you are still in the privacy of your own home and there is time to change.

One of the best writers I know has a wife who reads everything he writes and tells him when she loves it and when she doesn't, why it does or doesn't work for her. She is almost like an equal partner in the process. Two other writers I know use each other. As I said, I have two people who read my stuff. One is another writer, who is one of my best friends and probably the most neurotic, mentally ill person in my galaxy. Another is a librarian who reads two or three books a week but has never written a word. What I do is to work over a piece until it feels just about right, and then I send it to one of these two friends, who have agreed in advance to read it.

I always send my work Federal Express, because I am too impatient to wait for the mail to deliver it. I spend the entire next day waiting to hear, pacing, overeating, feeling paranoid and badly treated if I haven't heard from my friends by noon. Naturally I assume that they think it is tripe but that they don't have the courage to tell me. Then I'll think about all the things I don't like about either of them, how much in fact I hate them both, how it is no wonder that neither of them has many friends. And then the phone will ring and they usually say something along the lines of "I think it's going to be great, I think it's really good work. But I also think there are a few problems."

At this point, I am usually open to suggestion, because I'm so relieved that they think it's going to be great. And I ask gaily where they think there's room for improvement. This is where things can get ever so slightly dicey. They might say that the whole first half is slow, and they couldn't get into it, but that on page six or thirty-eight or whatever, things finally got going, and then they couldn't put it down. They absolutely raced through the rest of it—except that maybe they had a bit of trouble with the ending, and they wonder if I really understand one character's motivation and whether I might just want to spend—oh—five minutes, no more, rethinking this person.

My first response if they have a lot of suggestions is never profound relief that I have someone in my life who will be honest with me and help me do the very best work of which I am capable. No, my first thought is, "Well. I'm sorry, but I can't be friends with you anymore, because you have too many problems. And you have a bad personality. And a bad character."

Sometimes I can't get words to come out of my mouth because I am so disappointed, as if they had said that Sam is ugly and boring and spoiled and I should let him go. Criticism is very hard to take. But then whichever friend is savaging my work will suggest that we go through it together page by page, line by line, and in a clipped, high-pitched voice I'll often suggest that this won't be necessary, that everything's just fine. But these friends usually talk me into going through the manuscript with them over the phone, and if I'll hang in there, they'll have found a number of places where things could be so much stronger, or funnier, or more real, or more interesting, or less tedious. They may even have ideas on how to fix those places, and so, by the end, I am breathing a great sigh of relief and even gratitude.

When someone reliable gives you this kind of feedback, you now have some true sense of your work's effect on people, and you may now know how to approach your final draft. If you are getting ready to send your work to a potential agent for the first time, you don't want to risk burning that bridge by sending something that's just not ready.

You really must get your piece or book just right, as right as you can. Sometimes it is just a matter of fine-tuning, or maybe one whole character needs to be rethought. Sometimes the friend will love the feel of the writing, the raw material, and yet feel that it is a million miles from being done. This can be deeply disappointing, but again, better that your spouse or friend tell you this than an agent or an editor.

I heard Marianne Williamson say once that when you ask God into your life, you think he or she is going to come into your psychic house, look around, and see that you just need a new floor or better furniture and that everything needs just a little cleaning—and so you go along for the first six months thinking how nice life is now that God is there. Then you look out the window one day and see that there's a wrecking ball outside. It turns out that God actually thinks your whole foundation is shot and you're going to have to start over from scratch. This is exactly what it can be like to give, say, a novel to someone else to read. This person can love it and still find it a total mess, in need of a great deal of work, of even a new foundation.

So how do I find one of these partners? my students ask. The same way you find a number of people for a writing group. The only difference is that in this case, you're looking for one partner instead of several. So if you are in a class, look around, see if there's someone whose work you've admired, who seems to be at about the same level as you. Then you can ask him or her if he or she wants to meet for a cup of coffee and see if you can work with each other. It's like asking for a date, so while you are doing this, you will probably be rolfed by all your most heinous memories of seventh and eighth grade. If the person says no, it's good to wait until you get inside your car before you fall apart completely. Then you can rend your clothes and keen and do a primal scream. Of course, you probably want to be sure that the person hasn't followed you out to your car. But it actually doesn't matter if he or she sees you break down, because you don't have to be friendly with that person anymore. That person is a jerk. You double up therapy sessions for a few weeks until you're back in the saddle, and then you ask someone else, someone you like much better.

If you know for sure that some smart and civilized person loves your work, you can ask that person if she would be willing to look at a part of your novel or your latest short story. If this person writes, too, ask if she would like you to take a look at her draft. If she says no to both offers, pretend to be friendly, so she won't think less of you than she already does. Then you can move into a trailer park near your therapist's house until you're well enough again to ask someone else.

The second question my students ask about a writing partner is this: what if someone agrees to read and work on your stuff for you, and you have agreed to do the same for him, say, and it turns out that he says things about your work, even in the nicest possible tone of voice, that are totally negative and destructive? You find yourself devastated, betrayed. Here you've done this incredibly gutsy thing, shown someone your very heart and soul, and he doesn't think it's any good. He says how sorry he is that this is how he feels. Well, let me tell you this—I don't think he is. I think destroying your work gave him real pleasure, pleasure he would never cop to, pleasure that is almost sexual in nature. I think you should get rid of this person immediately, even if you are married to him. No one should talk to you like this. If you write a long piece, and it is your first, and you are wondering if it's publishable, and it isn't, even by a long shot, someone should be able to tell you this in a way that is gentle yet not patronizing, so that you are encouraged—maybe not to pursue publication, but to pursue writing. Certainly this person might suggest you get a second opinion. But if he is too strident or adamant, ditch the sucker. Would you stand for someone talking this way to your children—for instance, telling them that they are not very talented at painting and shouldn't even bother? Or that their poetry is not very interesting? Of course not. You'd want to go pay this person a little visit with your flamethrower. So why, if someone says something like this to you, would you want anything further to do with him? Why waste what little time you may have left with such scum?

I worry that Jesus drinks himself to sleep when he hears me talk like this. But about a month before my friend Pammy died, she said something that may have permanently changed me.

We had gone shopping for a dress for me to wear that night to a nightclub with the man I was seeing at the time. Pammy was in a wheelchair, wearing her Queen Mum wig, the *Easy Rider* look in her eyes. I tried on a lavender minidress, which is not my usual style. I tend to wear big, baggy clothes. People used to tell me I dressed like John Goodman. Anyway, the dress fit perfectly, and I came out to model it for her. I stood there feeling very shy and self-conscious and pleased. Then I said, "Do you think it makes my hips look too big?" and she said to me slowly, "Annie? I really don't think you have that kind of time."

And I don't think you have that kind of time either. I don't think you have time to waste not writing because you are afraid you won't be good enough at it, and I don't think you have time to waste on someone who does not respond to you with kindness and respect. You don't want to spend your time around people who make you hold your breath. You can't fill up when you're holding your breath. And writing is about filling up, filling up when you are empty, letting images and ideas and smells run down like water—just as writing is also about dealing with the emptiness. The emptiness destroys enough writers without the help of some friend or spouse.

There are always a couple of rank beginners in my classes, and they need people to read their drafts who will rise to the occasion with respect and encouragement. Beginners always try to fit their whole lives into ten pages, and they always write blatantly about themselves, even if they make the heroine of their piece a championship racehorse with an alcoholic mother who cries a lot. But beginners are learning to play, and they need encouragement to keep their hands moving across the page.

If you look around, I think you will find the person you need. Almost every writer I've ever known has been able to find someone who could be both a friend and a critic. You'll know when the person is right for you and when you are right for that person. It's not unlike finding a mate, where little by little you begin to feel that you've stepped into a shape that was waiting there all along.

Crafting a Life in Essay, Story, Poem

Donald M. Murray

The Art of Revision

Rewriting begins before you put the first word on paper and continues until you edit the final draft—which may, in turn, inspire revision.

At first, this may seem discouraging. In school and on the job, revision has been analogous to punishment. Rewriting is seen only as the solution to failure. But revision lies at the center of the writing process, the activity that provides joy, inspiration, surprise, concentration, closure. Revision for yourself, the first reader, and editing for other readers is necessary for effective writing. Listen to what the following writers say about revision.

> I love revision. Where else can spilled milk be turned into ice cream?
>
> Katherine Patterson

> Rewriting is when playwriting really gets to be fun. In baseball you only get three swings and you're out. In rewriting, you get almost as many swings as you want and you know, sooner or later, you'll hit the ball.
>
> Neil Simon

> In my own case there are days when the result is so bad that no fewer than five revisions are required. However, when I'm greatly inspired, only four revisions are needed before, as I've often said, I put in that note of spontaneity which even my meanest critics concede.
>
> John Kenneth Galbraith

> I love the flowers of afterthought.
>
> Bernard Malamud

Revision is too often confused with editing. In rewriting, the focus is on the writer's own reseeing, in exploring and developing the topic so the writer can discover what to say and how to say it. Revision is a private act with an eye cocked toward the reader. In editing, the focus is on the reader, making sure that what the writer has decided to say is clear to the reader. Editing is a public act with attention on the reader, only a glance given to the writer's needs. The revision process takes all the writer knows about the subject and narrows it down to a final draft; the editing process clarifies that draft so that it can be read and understood by many readers.

During revision the writer looks forward from the point of view of the creator who is discovering the evolving meaning; during editing, the writer looks backward from the point of view of the reader.

There are genre differences in revision but they are only matters of emphasis. In poetry and fiction the attention may linger longer with the writer; but if the most "creative" writing is to be read, attention must be paid to the reader, and there must be editing as well as revision. In the corporate memo and the research grant proposal, the writer had better take the time to explore and understand the subject through revision if editing is to make that message clear. Revision is the craft of seeing what you have written, not what you planned, hoped or thought you wrote. Revision is the ability to read your own drafts with the writer's eye, distancing yourself from yourself.

The Revision Attitude

Writing is an experimental act. In the search for meaning, the writer—and the artist, the actor, and the scientist—proceeds by trial and error. I hook one word to another, reach up above the workbench and grab a different word; plug a clause into a sentence, turn it around and try it again; shape a paragraph, taking a little off the end, building up the middle, sharpening the leading edge.

There are many potential right ways and wrong ways to say something, ways that are right or wrong in the evolving context of the draft. The question is what works and what needs work.

Effective writing develops from error—the wrong word allows the writer to hear the right word, the collapse of syntax exposes the possibility of an unexpected meaning, the harsh sound of a poor sentence allows the writer to hear the melody that supports the meaning, the paragraph that runs off the road shows where the road should go.

Attitude controls revision, and the writer should know that failure is necessary, failure is instructive. Only when we fail to say what we imagined we would say do we discover what we should say and how we should say it. We should train ourselves to welcome and make use of instructive failure.

Revision Before Drafting

Meditation tells us to empty our minds and we find that almost impossible. Awake and asleep, talking to others, doing our work, reading, watching TV driving the car, attending meetings—we carry on continuous inter weaving conversations with ourselves. Writers tune in to those conversations: What are we saying to our other selves, what are we saying to others? We surprise ourselves by what we hear.

This morning a breakfast crony asked me why I had made the decision to come to the university when I was thirty-nine. As we drove home I told him the story, but I also heard another story telling itself underneath the oral draft. It would keep surfacing in a word, a phrase, a line.

After I left him off, I found a word that would capture and trigger this story that I needed to tell myself: *discontent*. When I went to my computer I found myself typing in a note that would lead to a future column. It is my habit to put these notes into the format I use to send my columns in to the *Globe*, as the notes may turn into a lead or when typing in the notes I may find myself drafting the first half of the column. Here is today's note:

Sitting on the porch looking back...   } Realize a
                                                } powerful vein
                                                } of discontent
                                                } runs through
Computer down, anxious to get to work   } my life

[1st marriage—strain—not to be here but there.]

Discontent has its unhappy aspects for the person feeling it AND the people around them. What are they...

BUT
better than content.
{et

I have been revising in my head and on the page, and I will continue to do this naturally, considering and reconsidering the role of discontent in my life arid in the lives of others. I brought the topic of discontent up in a conversation with Minnie Mae in the car and in a conversation with Chip Scanlan on the phone. In those conversations I pay as much attention to what I am saying as to what the other person is saying. I may write nothing down or I may capture an idea or a voice on the 3" × 5" cards I carry in my pocket all the time, in my daybook, on the laptop beside my chair in the living room.

Revision During Drafting

As I write, I revise. What I intend to say changes as I say it. Each word predicts the next word, each clause the next clause, each sentence the next sentence, and so on. Writing is revising: the hint, the guess, the suspicion, the intent changed by its language, its audience, its context, its evolving meaning, its amplifying voice.

In drafting I often write in spurts of one to three paragraphs to get started, then in chunks of six to eight paragraphs, going back and reading the chunk of writing to discover what I said rather than what I thought I was saying. Once I know what I have said, I can put it back on track or, more often, follow the track, developing and clarifying what I have found myself saying. As John Fowles says, "Follow the accident, fear the fixed plan—that is the rule." I start to write the column on discontent:

Driving down the highway, a young friend asks why I made the decision, at the age of 39, to come to the university and, as old men will, I told him more than he probably wanted to know.

Of course I wasn't so much telling him as telling myself in the hope of discovering a meaning or order I had not seen before. ~~Writers~~, I confess what Minnie Mae knows only too well, that writers talk to listen to themselves. I "write" as I speak, telling a story I do not expect.

At one level it was familiar, the lines worn with use, personal cliches I have told before: "When I was in college I wrote nothing but poetry, never worked on the college newspaper. I wanted to be a great poet but those jobs were taken."

I added a another familiar line, "I also wanted to be a great novelist but those jobs were also taken" and then I added a flourish, "I looked in the want ads. Nothing."

My friend seemed to nod in an encouraging manner. No matter, I would have gone on anyway. "I went to work on a newspaper because I wanted to write poetry, went to *Time* because the newspaper publisher wanted me to be an editor and I wanted to write a novel, freelanced after I was fired by *Time*—they wanted to make me a TV producer—and freelanced magazine articles because I didn't want to write magazine articles."

As my friend got out of my car at his house, I finished the story of my life. "I came to the university to teach journalism because I wanted to write fiction and poetry."

He laughed and I went on telling my story to myself, how I wrote—and continue to write—books on writing and teaching because I want to write fiction and poetry.

As I went down to my office, I felt the familiar old man's guilt that I hadn't done what I should have with my life and I even heard my first wife's voice during a divorce more than forty-five years ago saying that I was never content. I wanted to be out of college when I was in college, whatever I was doing I always wanted to be doing something else.

I sat before my computer and waited for the guilt. But it didn't come. I heard the new story that lay under the story I had told my friend. I had lived a life of discontent.

As I wrote this, I kept waiting for the spot where I stopped and revised during the drafting but it didn't come. I have to remind myself that one revision decision is not to revise, to accept the flowing text. I rush on towards the end I don't yet know but can sense just ahead of me, in the last three hundred or four hundred words.

This is typical. My columns are about eight hundred words long. About half-way through I stop, read what I have written, accept or change it, and get a feel for how much space I have left. Trained to write at this length, I feel I have all the room in the world left to discover what I have to say.

And in saying that I realize that it may have been in the genes. I have a great-grandfather who emigrated from the Hebrides to begin a new life when he was 88. One grandfather had a "fiddle foot," he was always going off dancing to a new tune, a new enterprise, a new dream. So did my other grandfather, and my father kept changing jobs until he was in his seventies, always discontent.

Their story was the story that lay under the new story I told myself when telling my friend the familiar story of my life. At my age, I have within me, layer upon layer of story, a mind that is like an archeological dig.

I retold myself the story of my ancestors and the discontent that brought them from Scotland to New England. I would not, I had pledged when I was young, follow their path of discontent, chasing after rainbows that had no pot of gold.

But of course I had, finding a wife who understood, or at least accepted, a husband who often scorned the publications he had accomplished, the awards he was given, because they were for the writing he did not intend to do but only the writing he had done.

I look at my blank computer screen and relive, for a moment the private—and not so private—aching dissatisfaction that has rubbed raw almost all my adult life.

I say aloud, "I have lived a life of discontent" and hear not guilt but pride for the first time. I want no Eastern, zen-like state of bliss, but the familiar Western itch to better myself, to get on, to do what probably can't be done.

I realize, with a shock, that I have accomplished what I have done because I didn't want to do it but was driven toward another goal, a rainbow bending over the horizon.

And telling myself—and you—this story I recognize the final irony: I am content with my discontent.

Three hundred and thirty-five words, seven hundred and fifty-four in all. I am home free. I will read it again and revise if it is necessary, but I realize that all through this draft the story was telling me about my life. In writing this short essay, I came to understand my heritage in a way I never had before, and I had come to accept and understand the way I had lived my own life as I never had before. The draft had revised me.

Revision After Drafting

When I was writing magazine articles I used to do three major drafts, reading and revising each ten times, thirty readings in all. That was in the days before computers and I would cross out and revise by hand, attaching inserts by tape or staple, producing long kite tails of drafts that Minnie Mae would type. Each of the three major revisions had its own focus.

Revision for content. I read the first draft to discover what I had to say, decide if it was worth saying and if I wanted to say it. There was no point in going on unless I knew what I was saying and was willing to say it. My meaning would be the North Star that would guide all other revisions. Often I would steal an idea from John Steinbeck and put what the article said in a single sentence. If I could not do that, I needed to revise. I also made sure I had the specific details that would satisfy the reader's hunger for information, the documentation that would support each point, and the examples that would clarify the message I had to deliver.

Revision for order. After I knew what I had said, I could order the information so that each word, each sentence, each paragraph drove the meaning forward. For years I cut the draft into individual paragraphs, rearranging them until I found a simple, clear line through the article, a sequence that answered the reader's questions at the moment they were asked.

Revision for language. This stage I would now call editing. I read aloud, line-by-line, tuning the voice to my meaning and my audience. The heard text that comes aloud in the reader's ear must be heard first by the writer. In this draft, I paid close attention to everything in the text, checking each fact or citation for accuracy, making sure the spelling was correct, the attributions in place, the mechanics and rhetorical conventions broken only when they were essential to communicate or clarify meaning.

In recent decades, I find that I am doing all three readings or drafts simultaneously. But if I have difficulty with a piece I may break down my readings into that former sequence. I also find on the computer that I do all of them in chunks of writing or in my head as I write. My columns really are a first draft, as is this book—a first draft that is revised as it is written. The column that I have written is ready for editing although, as I have said above, the line between revising and editing overlaps.

Tricks of the Revision Trade

Each craft—baking or quilt making, pot throwing or gardening, cabinet making or antique restoration—has its own tricks. Here are some of the tricks I use in revising.

- I scan the draft, flying over the territory, to see if there are any large omissions.

- I read aloud to hear the music of the draft, making sure it communicates the meaning.

- I look for what works and develop that.

- I cut what can be cut. Less has always been more in my drafts.

- I ask the reader's questions and make sure they are answered.

- I consider the pace, slowing down the text so that the reader can absorb each point and speeding it up so the reader will not put it down.

I revel in the art of revision. I am rarely as happy as I am when I am crafting my text and therefore my life.

The Art of Editing

When you revise, you are your own reader. You revise, primarily, to discover, develop and clarify the subject for yourself. Now you become your own editor and clarify what you have written for your reader. You are your reader's advocate.

The Editing Attitude

To edit your own copy—or anyone else's—effectively, you have to have three levels of respect.

First of all, you have to respect the draft. Each piece of writing has its own integrity. The writer is not the creator but the midwife who assists the draft as it comes into the world. Each text has its own identity, and the editor has to cultivate it, making it clear to readers without turning it into something it is not.

As you edit your own copy, listen to the draft and follow it. It may have to be changed, but the draft is a rational product. It was produced by a process of thinking, of making intelligent choices. You may disagree with those choices, but first try to understand why they were made. The most unexpected turns in the draft, the ones that first look like errors or failures, even typos, may end up being the strongest points in the piece. Respect doesn't mean agreement. It doesn't mean leaving everything as it is. It means listening respectfully to the draft, considering the case the draft has made and then doing what has to be done.

Next you have to respect the writer. It is easy (normal, for me) to read my own draft and despair. It doesn't read as I expected; of course not. Writing changes in its writing. What is most strange, however, may be what is most important. Doris Lessing reminds us, "You have to remember that nobody ever wants a new writer. You have to create your own demand." Milan Kundera said, "To write a novel, you must be true to your obsessions, your ideas, and your imagination, and these are things with roots in your childhood. It is the images from your childhood and youth which form the imaginary country of your novels, and this imaginary country, in my case, is called Prague."

Be demanding of your own copy but on your own terms. Realize that every time you write you are developing your own voice, your own vision of the world, your own understanding of what that vision means. Respect yourself.

And also respect the reader. When I edit, I am the reader's advocate. I have been hired to represent the reader. I am no longer the author and have the responsibility to make sure my text speaks to someone other than myself.

There is great joy in editing. Now I have a draft that deserves close attention. I have a meaning, a form, abundant material, a focus and an order, a voice and I can, word-by-word, reveal the text.

There's nothing quite like the eagerness I feel when I sit down to edit. I will find out what I have said and, in making it clear to others, I will make it clear to myself. I will mark with a strikeout what I cut, insert new words in caps and add a commentary explaining what I have done and why. Join me as I edit the column, second- and third-guess me. I might edit it differently tomorrow: There is no single right way or wrong way.

> Driving down the highway, a young friend asks why I made the decision, at the age of 39, to come to the university and, as old men will, I told him more than he probably wanted to know.

I have a few strict rules. One of them is never, never ever begin a paragraph with a dependent clause and I can't remember having done it in years, but here it seems to catch a moment on the fly and establish the conversational tone of the essay. I'll keep it. I cut the comma after 39 and questioned "as old men will" but it seems to establish an appropriate discursive tone.

> Of course I wasn't so much telling him as telling myself in the hope of discovering a meaning or order I had not seen before. I confess what Minnie Mae knows only too well, that writers talk to listen to themselves. I "write" as I speak, telling a story I do not expect.

I feel guilty that I am not cutting but I read it over three times and feel each sentence pulls its weight. If I had to cut, I would take out the middle sentence but I think it sets up the last sentence in the paragraph and I think that sentence carries an idea that may be interesting to the reader.

> At one level it MY STORY THE STORY I TOLD was familiar, the lines worn with use, personal clichés I have told before: "When I was in college I wrote nothing but poetry, never worked on the college newspaper. I wanted to be a great poet but those jobs were taken WHEN I GRADUATED IN 1948."

I edited to make the paragraph simpler, to make it set up the quote but get to it faster.

I added a another familiar line, "I also wanted to be a great novelist but those jobs were also taken" and then I added a flourish, "I looked in the want advs. Nothing."

I was particularly proud of this paragraph yesterday for reasons I do not understand today. Cut.

My friend seemed to nod in an encouraging manner. No matter, I would have gone on anyway. "I went to work on a newspaper because I wanted to write poetry, went to *Time* because they wanted me to be an editor and I wanted to write a novel, freelanced after I was fired by *Time*—they wanted to make me a TV producer—and freelanced magazine articles because I didn't want to write magazine articles."

I realize that my experience in writing fiction makes me break the story and bring in the listener. Having the listener there sets up what happens when I become my own listener a few paragraphs on. Of course, I didn't know I would continue the story when I drafted this paragraph, and I didn't know I would document what I had said in the beginning. The text knew but I didn't. Pay attention to the text. It will tell you what to write and how to write it.

As my friend got out of the car at his house, I finished the story of my life. "I came to the university to teach journalism because I wanted to write fiction and poetry."

He laughed and I went on telling my story to myself, how I wrote—and continue to write—books on writing and teaching because I want to write fiction and poetry.

I am simply filling out the story I know for the reader and the copy seems clean enough. I will not touch it.

As I went down to my office, I feel the familiar old man's guilt that I hadn't done what I should have with my life, and I even heard my first wife's voice during a divorce more than 45 years ago saying that I was never content. I wanted to be out of college when I was in college, whatever I was doing I always wanted to be doing something else.

In writing this I confronted the monster I did not want to face and I heard a complaint from my first wife that I had not heard for decades. I needed to do this as the writer but do I need to share this with the reader? I decide I do, because readers will have their own monsters, their own old complaints from others in the past. It is essential to say this to set up what will come next.

I sat before my computer and waited for the guilt. But it didn't come. I heard the new story that lay under the story I had told my friend. I had lived a life of discontent.

This is the turning point of the column. Unless I arrive at such a discovery I will not submit the column. I take the reader along on a voyage of discovery. We share the journey, and if we have no destination, I have no column. I questioned the story under the story, but it seems essential to what I am saying.

And in saying that I realize that it may have been in the genes. ~~I have~~ A ~~a~~ great grandfather ~~who~~ emigrated from the Hebrides to begin a new life when he was 88.~~O~~ ; one grandfather had a "fiddle foot," he was always ~~going off~~ dancing to a new ~~tune, a new enterprise, a new~~ dream; ~~So did my other grandfather and my~~ father kept changing jobs until he was in his seventies. ~~, always discontent.~~

I am surprised by the genetic discovery. It should have been obvious but it was not obvious to me before I wrote it. It was reason enough to write the piece. Now it has to be lined up more clearly for the reader. It was hard not to go on telling all the other stories of discontent but this was enough for the reader to establish the point.

~~Their story was the story that lay under the new story I told myself when telling my friend the familiar story of my life. At my age, I have within me, layer upon layer of story, a mind that is like an archeological dig.~~

This is difficult. It is a hard read but I think it is important. I have to read ahead to see if it can be cut or if I need to clarify it. *I can cut it and I can cut the first sentence of the following paragraph.*

~~I retold myself the story of my ancestors and the discontent that brought them from Scotland to New England.~~ I would not, I had pledged when I was young, follow their path of discontent, chasing after rainbows that had no pot of gold.

But of course I had, finding a wife who understood, or at least accepted, a husband who often scorned ~~the~~ HIS publications, ~~he had accomplished, the~~ EVEN awards ~~he was~~ THEY WERE given, because they were NOT for the writing he ~~did not~~ intendED to do. ~~but only the writing he had done.~~

I return to the monster and to the wife mentioned above but I have to make the sentence run clear.

I look at my blank computer screen and relive, for a moment the private—and no so private—aching dissatisfaction that has rubbed me raw almost all my adult life.

I might be able to cut this but I think it establishes the seriousness of my—and perhaps the reader's—neuroses.

I say aloud, "I have lived a life of discontent" and hear not guilt but pride for the first time. I want no Eastern, zen-like state of bliss, but the familiar Western itch to better myself, to get on, to do what probably can't be done.

This had surprised me and I wondered in writing it if I were pushing it a bit much but it seems to run counter to a great deal of popular culture and therefore may add an interesting tension in the piece. It also seems to make me a member of another time, another generation, appropriate to a column called "Over 60."

I realize, with a shock, that I have accomplished what I have because I didn't want to do it but was driven toward ~~another goal,~~ a rainbow bending over the horizon.

I always worry that I am telling the reader what to think in the end of a column. The essayist should make the reader think in the reader's own way, not instruct and therefore attempt to control the reader's thinking. I decide to keep the paragraph, partially to set up the last one.

And telling myself—and you—this story I recognize the final irony: I am content with my discontent.

The seven hundred and fifty-four words before editing have shrunk to six hundred and twenty-seven, one hundred and twenty-seven words fewer than before but I think the content will expand in the reader's mind. Now I will submit it to Minnie Mae for her inspection and, if it passes, to Louise Kennedy at the *Globe*.

And since I started this section on editing with the concept of respect, I should end by saying I respect my editors. I am fortunate in having editors I can respect. It allows me freedom. When I have good editors I can try things I wouldn't dare if I knew my copy was going in as I had written it. I have had that situation and I have to be both the creator and the final censor. With good editors I can take a chance and they will tell me if it works—or does not work.

 Do I accept what they suggest? More often than not. If they have a problem understanding the text, so will readers. My ego is greater than protecting the text. I believe that I can say what needs to be said in a hundred different ways so I listen to the editor and, more often than not, revise when there is a problem.

Tricks of the Editing Trade

Each writer develops techniques that work for the writer. My editing techniques include:

- I *hear* the draft, editing for the music of the text that will reveal and support its meaning.

- I play the devil's advocate, questioning the text, checking every fact, especially those that are so familiar I know without question they are accurate.

- I cut what can be cut, remembering the advice of Will Strunk as quoted by E. B. White. These words were over my writing desk for decades:

    > Vigorous writing is concise. A sentence should contain no unnecessary words, a paragraph no unnecessary sentences, for the same reason that a drawing should have no unnecessary lines and a machine no unnecessary parts. This requires not that the writer make all his sentences short, or that he avoid all detail and treat his subjects only in outline, but that every word tell.

- I edit with verbs and nouns, and with admiration for the subject-verb-object sentence.

- I imagine the flight of the sea gull and try to use the simplest word that will carry my meaning.

- The more complex the idea, the more important the information, the more likely I will write with short words, short sentences, short paragraphs.

- I am aware of the points of emphasis: most important at the end of a sentence, paragraph, section, piece, next-most important at the beginning and least important in the middle and make sure what should be emphasized is.

- I ask the reader's questions, and answer them immediately.

- I am aware of pace, the speed at which the reader is being carried through the text, and proportion, the size of each part of the text in relation to the other parts.

- Like the murderer, I try to erase my tracks. I remember George Orwell's statement, "Good writing is like a window pane." I want to call attention to my subject, not myself.

- While I am editing, George Orwell's list from "Politics and the English Language" always lurks in my memory.

- I am a poor speller so I have a word book by my computer and use Spellcheck and Minnie Mae to make sure each word is spelled correctly.

- I'll put a piece of paper over the last sentence or paragraph. If I can read the piece and understand without that last piece of writing, then I move the paper up another paragraph. I keep doing that until I can't understand the poem, story, article, chapter without the covered paragraph. I did this on a novel and never published the last chapter in the final draft. The novel was finished before that chapter and, although I thought it was the best-written chapter in the novel, it was zapped.

Can you ruin a piece by revising and editing it too much? I haven't yet. It may happen, but not yet. I have kept revising so much I never finished a draft. I have a perfect beginning but no middle and no end, but I have found that even severe cuts—75 percent of the copy—strengthen the draft. Each revision and each editing goes to the center of what I have to say, and each time I make it better. Sometimes I stop when I discover nothing or no new way to say what I have written, but most of the time I stop revising and editing because I have a deadline.

Most writers become obsessed with getting it right and revise and edit too much. The danger is not that the writer will edit too little but edit too much. The writer has to let the draft go into the world, and that can be as hard (and essential) as letting a child go into the world.

Donald M. Murray, "The Art of Revision," pp. 135-141; and "The Art of Editing," pp. 141-149, from *Crafting a Life in Essay, Story, Poem*. Portsmouth, NH: Boynton/Cook, 1996. Reprinted by permission.

The Cupped Hand and the Open Palm

Hephzibah Roskelly

When I was in first grade, I was a bluebird. Funny that I remember that after so many years. Or maybe not so funny. I suspect you remember your label too. I remember being proud of being in the group I was in. Somehow everybody in Mrs. Cox's class knew it was pretty awful to be a yellowbird, common to be a redbird, and therefore best to be a bluebird. One student of mine remembers her experience in first grade this way: "My first-grade teacher waited for us to make a mistake in our group and then she'd pounce. She always stood behind our desks. That's because I wasn't in the fast reading group. I was in the bears." She laughs. "To this day I think bears are stupid." For Susan, like for many of us, the first-grade reading group is our first real experience with group work, and for many of us, like for Susan, it's not remembered fondly. Especially if you happened to be a yellowbird or a bear.

By third or fourth grade, though, your early memory may have dimmed a little as group work began to get less attention. You and your fellow students were "tracked" by this point, grouped into classes according to the results of standardized achievement tests, so the need for "ability level" groups like the blue/red/yellowbirds within the classroom became less pressing. And by the time you entered middle school or seventh grade, probably there wasn't much group work at all. In its place was "seat work," which meant some sort of writing. If you were like most students, you wrote alone. Nobody ever saw your writing except your teacher and, very rarely, other students, if they happened to look at the bulletin board where the teacher occasionally posted the "A" papers. If you were writing answers to questions or coming up with ideas in class, you were often reminded to "cover your work" so that your friend in the desk across from you wouldn't be tempted to copy. So you used a sheet of paper to cover your writing, or you hid your marks behind a wall you made with your hand, cupping it to keep what you wrote private. Covering your work became so natural that you might have even cupped your hand anytime you wrote *anything* in school—the beginning of a short story, a letter to the editor of your school paper or to your girlfriend—the kind of writing where "copying" would never occur. But you continued to cup your hand because by this time you had gotten the message. Writing is solitary, individual, something others can take away from you if you don't keep it from them, and something others don't see except when it's "clean."

These elementary school lessons about groups and about writing are deeply imbedded, so much so that you may react with suspicion or even hostility now when your writing class—a freshman composition course or some other—encourages group work. Your past experience with group work in reading hasn't led you to feel that it will do much more than put you in some category you'd rather not be in, and past experience with writing suggests that sharing your work with someone else is foolish or illegal. Your college, after all, probably has an honor code that says something about giving and receiving help. Why should a composition teacher force the connection between writing and the small group, asking you to come up with ideas together, make plans together, read and revise together, and, strangest of all, write together?

I try to answer that question here. One of the reasons that group work fails in the classroom is that neither our past experiences in the reading group nor those with the writing lesson have given us much of a rationale for working in groups. When a person doesn't know why she's doing something, doing it seems relatively useless. Working in small groups, even though it's an idea touted by theorists and teachers in composition, is limited in actual practice for just this reason: Students and sometimes their teachers don't know why they're doing what they're doing when they meet in the small group. Just as important, students and their teachers aren't aware of why they're often so disposed against working in groups. I describe what underlies these attitudes so that you can begin to understand why group work fails sometimes and why it's so potentially useful for your development as a writer.

Why Group Work Fails

I asked a group of students who will be student teaching in high school English classrooms this semester to use their own past experiences and their developing ideas about teaching to speculate about what makes groups fail in the classroom. Their list may mesh with your own feelings about the small group in the classroom.

Too Many Chefs; No Chefs; Untrustworthy Chefs

Students mentioned the possibility of the "one member who dominates," who "thinks he knows it all," who "can't let the group decide." Or the possibility of having several members who all wanted to lead. What some described as a domineering personality in the group, others saw as responsible. "Somebody always ends up doing the most work. And that's usually me," says Beth, one of my first-year students at the beginning of the semester. "When I was in high school there were always a few who didn't want to do the work and goofed off, and they left the rest of us poor slobs to do it." The fear that the work won't be shared but shuffled off to one wimpy or guilty person is echoed in comments about who's prepared, who volunteers, who shows up. A student teacher reports on her experience with being given too much responsibility for her group's operation: "My classmates saw me as one of the smart kids and so in groups I was always expected to emerge as a leader and to get things done. There were many times when I felt I was carrying the load."

An even bigger fear about responsibility and personality centers on trust. "I don't know the other people in my group. Why would I want to talk to them about how I feel about anything?" asks a student teacher. And one freshman writer writing in her journal before her group met for the first time writes about her fears that the group won't be responsible to her: "What if they think my ideas are terrible? What if they think I'm stupid?"

Chaos Rules

At first, the fear of spinning out of control in the group may seem primarily to be a teacher complaint rather than a student one. And it's true that the fear that there will be too much talk or that the talk will quickly get "off task" does prevent teachers from using group work at all, or they use it only sparingly and with rigid guidelines to control it. But students fear loss of control as well. When students are conditioned to the quiet classroom where only one person has the right to talk (the teacher) and the rest have the right to remain silent (the students)—and this is the typical classroom—students aren't comfortable with a lot of noise and movement either. "It gets too disorganized," one student lamented. "I'm an organized person. And I don't like hearing what the other groups are saying."

If You Want Something Done Well—

One student teacher remembers her 101 class doing revision of essays in small groups:

> We had writing groups to comment on each other's papers. This was fine except that no one would make any comments about my papers. I guess because my grammar is sound they couldn't find anything to say because they didn't know what else to look for.

> A typical group dialogue went something like this:

> *First person:* I don't see anything wrong with your paper.
> *Second person:* Me neither.
> *Third person:* Yeah, it's a good paper. You'll get an A.
> *Me:* Well, what did you think about it?
> *First person:* Everything. The whole paper is fine.
> *Second person:* I liked your topic. How did you think of such a good topic?
> *Third person:* Yeah. You'll get an A.

> Not only did this fail to give me any useful feedback, but it also put me in an awkward position when the time came for me to comment on others' papers. They were so full of admiration and praise for mine, how could I say anything negative about theirs? So a vicious cycle where no one benefited was created.

Related to this feeling of the group not helping because no one knov what to do within the group is the feeling that the work they do is no very important. "It's a waste of time. I think teachers have us get in gro when they don't have anything left to say and don't want to let the clas go. We just read the paper in my last class. Or maybe talked for five mii utes and then read the paper." Another writer says, "1 kept changing wh my group said or changing what I said to match them. It would have taken a lot less time and been better just to do it myself."

Why—and How—a Group Works

These students tell the story of why group work fails in the classroom. The stories reveal deep and often unconscious beliefs about how the writing class is supposed to proceed, about how writers are supposed to work. The beliefs come from those old experiences with reading groups and with writing. But they also come from what we've' all imagined about how peo- ple learn in school. School, we've determined, is competitive, not coopera- tive, and therefore it's the individual not the group effort that counts. And counting is what school is all about. Who has the most points, the most stars, the most A's? Who's the bluebird? The fact is we assume that effort can only be measured by a grade and that a grade can't fairly be given to a group. So attempts to work as a group seem futile and unnecessary given what we've assumed school is all about—keeping not sharing, winning not collaborating, cupping the hand, not opening the palm.

If it were true that people learn to think and write primarily alone in solitary confinement so to speak—it might also be true that group work is wasted effort, or unhelpful or too chaotic or too hard. But the truth is that people don't learn—in fact, can't learn much at all—in isola- tion. They learn *by engaging in the world*. They come to terms with what's around them, understand it, through sound and movement, through talk. A child who never hears talk, as tragic cases show, never talks or talks only very little. Talking presumes at least one listener or commenter. Group work, then, because it encourages engagement—talk and reflection and response—mirrors the way people learn things inside and outside the classroom, the ways in which they make sense out of the world.

So conversation, communication with others, is vital to our under- standing of others and ourselves. And people can't communicate unless they listen—work toward a shared notion about how to proceed. Do you know the movie *Airplane*? It's actually one long joke about how commu- nications gets muddled when that shared notion doesn't exist.

"These people need to be taken to a hospital," the doctor says.

Walking up, stewardess Julie looks at them. "What is it?" she asks.

The doctor is impatient. "It's a big white building with sick people in it. But that's not important right now." Or:

"Surely you can't mean it," Julie says.

"I mean it," the doctor says. "And stop calling me Shirley."

Julie and the doctor don't communicate because they haven't decided on a shared basis for their talk. They mistake words and ideas and don't care enough (because then it wouldn't be funny) to get it right before they go on. In the classroom group, when shared work and talk do take place, real communication can occur. People learn to listen to one another and use one another's talk to test and explore their own talk more fully. This notion of learning and understanding as essentially shared rather than possessed by one individual can be tested using a little game I came up with called Trivial Literacy (after E. D. Hirsch's best-selling book *Cultural Literacy: What Every American Needs to Know*, 1987):

1. Choose part of Hirsch's list (or any list of words). A part of one list might read something like *hambone, harridan, Holden Caulfield, Huguenot.*

2. Mark every word you don't know or can't guess about.

3. In your group, see how many marks you can eliminate by getting information from others.

4. In class, see how many marks remain when the group pools all information.

5. Are there any words left? Guess about them. Ask somebody outside class.

You know what will happen before you do the test. You find out more and more by talking. You bear the contexts people have for knowing things like *Harlem Globetrotters*, and you bring up the context you have for knowing *Huguenot*. In other words, you'll illustrate how your knowledge gets stronger, better developed, more insightful, and more complete the more you combine your knowledge with others'. This combining always works better if it's informal, conversational, unpressured, in some way equal. That's why Trivial Literacy usually teaches so much. Because it's a game—it's fun, and the stakes aren't high. Group works need to be nurtured because it works, often playfully, to encourage the development of individual thought.

All writers need to hear their own voices, but I think they can only hear them clearly when they find them in the chorus of lots of other voices. Otherwise, for many writers the writing is hollow, without a sense of commitment or investment that characterizes the voices of confident, effective writers. Kenneth Bruffee (1984), who's a composition teacher and writer, makes this connection between the social and the individual explicit. "Thought is an artifact created by social interaction," he says. "We can think because we can talk, and we think in ways we have learned to talk" (640). We're stronger and better developed individual thinkers and writers because we interact with people in groups.

Partially because so much of writing is done in silence and solitude, college writers often fear the investment required in writing. They don't trust their voices; the only thing they do trust is the certain knowledge that they will be graded on what that voice is able to produce. They want control, and so they ask "How long does this have to be?" or "Can we use first person?" And they want to minimize risk, so they count words and number of footnotes, use simple sentence and forms they've read, and write with passive verbs that take them out of the writing. "It can be seen that Jane Austen was expressing feminist concerns," they might say, as a way of avoiding a declaration that *they've* been the ones to see it. They avoid the personal commitment that writing requires because it seems too dangerous to risk. It's as though you walked into a dark auditorium to speak to a group, knowing they were out there waiting but not knowing how many there were, how big the room was, or if you had a microphone. You'd probably clear your throat a few times, and test the sound, but if you could see nothing but your speech, and you knew you were being judged each time you opened your mouth, you might likely be stunned into silence.

Your small group functions as a visible audience, a literal sounding board for your voice, and, as Bruffee (1984) and others suggest, a source of your growing knowledge of the world. As such, the group alleviates the sense of powerlessness in writing (and thinking) that so many student writers feel and thus reduces the fear of commitment and investment by helping you to hear your voice clearly.

The Group at Work: First-Year Writers Writing Together

The group lessens writers' deep and real fear of taking responsibility for what's on the page in lots of ways—by supporting and strengthening individual writer's attempts, providing other perspectives on ideas, and sharing responsibility. All of these benefits for the writer occur when groups do all kinds of activities together—read, comment, discuss, plan, interpret—but they're most visible and dramatic when groups write together. That's why I'm using this example of the work of the group from my freshman writing course.

Students had been in their 101 class and in groups for five or six weeks when I gave the assignment. They were already comfortable talking about writing and ideas. But this task asked them to go a step farther, to write together a short (two- or three-page) collective response to Dorothy

Parker's funny and bitter short story "You Were Perfectly Fine." The story is primarily a dialogue between a male and female character discussing the events at a party the night before. The man's guilt about getting drunk leads him to pretend he remembers a "promise" he's made to the woman, who pretends too in order to hold him to it. After reading the story and doing some quick in-class writing, groups met to begin to decide how they felt about the hungover, guilty man, the seemingly sympathetic woman, and the reasons for the dishonesty in the dialogue. As groups talked, they jotted down notes, often asking one another to repeat or clarify, often interrupting one another with revisions. Some groups talked mostly about the distinctions between social life in the twenties, when the story was written, and the present. Others concentrated on whether it was the man or the woman who was more to blame for the hypocrisy. In the next week and a half, groups argued about men and women and Dorothy Parker, and they worked out ways to allow for varying perspectives and to combine them. Everybody had to negotiate what to say and how to say it, who would write the final copy, where they would revise. All the talk and writing helped them find new ways to make points and gave them finally the new voices they needed to write together.

Here's the first paragraph of one of the papers:

> Dorothy Parker's negative view of relationships between men and women is obvious in "You Were Perfectly Fine." We analyzed the story as readers and listeners. Reading it, we felt that the woman was basically honest and the man without credibility. Then listening to it our ideas changed. We got more of a sense of the female being manipulative, romantic and lovesick, but dishonest and deceitful. Peter, the man, seems sensitive and witty, although he ends up being weak and panic-stricken. They seem like real people. Between reading and listening, we've learned that both these characters are dishonest and the relationship probably doesn't stand a chance.

This group ends their piece with a modern tale of deceit that connects romance in Parker's time and in their own, using one of the group member's own experience with deceit in relationships: "It's hard for men and women to be honest with each other whether they live in the Roaring Twenties or right now. Nobody wants to hurt somebody or get hurt themselves."

Notice that the voice in this excerpt is strong. It's controlled; that is, students talk both about the story and the relationships within it, but they feel free enough to be personal too, using the personal pronoun "we" and including a real-life example. There's a clear sense of commitment, interest, and investment in the task.

Collaboration in the group removed or alleviated some of the most debilitating fears about writing for the freshman writers in my class, and this ability of the group to nurture confidence proves how useful the group can be in strengthening the writing process in individual writers. I bet that these fears about writing hit close to your own.

Fear of Starting

Many writers find a blank page of paper so intimidating that they delay beginning as long as possible, searching for the perfect sentence opening, the right title, the best word. But because in the group there were four or five sets of ideas about a particular sentence or a way to open or a character, no writer stared at her paper waiting for inspiration. Inspiration, in fact, came from the talk that went on in the group. "Wait a minute," a group writer would say. "Is this what you said?" And she'd read it back. Another member would say, "It sounds better like this." "And why don't we add something about his past?" another would add. Writing happened so fast that nobody had time to dread not being able to find the idea or the word they wanted to begin.

Fear of Stopping

One first-year writer told me once that her writing was like a faucet with no water pressure—"it won't turn on hard—it just dribbles till it stops." Lots of writers fear that once they get the one good thought said, or the two points down, they'll be left with nothing but dead air time, and that they'll have to fill it with what one of my students calls "marshmallow fluff." But none of the groups had difficulty maintaining writing after they began. The group kept ideas flowing, and changing, and if one person was losing momentum, another would be gathering it. Ken Kesey, the author of *One Flew over the Cuckoo's Nest* (1962) and a teacher, comments on this effect as he describes a collaborative project—an entire novel— that his creative writing class worked on in one group: "Some days you just don't have any new sparkling stuff. But when you got thirteen people, somebody always has something neat and it's as though somebody on your team is on and you're off" (Knox-Quinn 1990, 315).

Fear of Flying

When you have a personal stake in your writing, a belief in your voice and in what you're saying, and a trust in your reader to hear you out, your writing soars. "Everyone can, under certain conditions, speak with clarity and power," composition teacher Peter Elbow says. "These conditions usually involve a topic of personal importance and an urgent occasion." The group helped make the topic personally important since each writer had to justify decisions and ideas to the others, and the occasion was urgent since talk, writing, and real communication were necessary to make decisions in a limited time.

The Group and Changing the World

So what does this long example from my first-year class prove? First, the group validates rather than hurts or lessens the individual voice. The group reinforces the effort involved in writing, talking, by the energy and specificity with which they both support and challenge the writer's thinking. Ken Kesey watched larger perspectives get developed on character and plot in the novel his class wrote: "When we would sit down around the table… and start writing our little section, boy you could hear the brain cells popping. They knew they had to write and had to fit in with the other stuff. You couldn't be too much yourself" (Knox-Quinn 1990, 310). But knowing that gives writers a clearer sense of self when they write individually. Not being "too much yourself" is a way of finding what your writing self really is.

"People think it's about competing with each other," Kesey says, speaking of writers and writing. "But the real things that you compete with are gravity and inertia—stagnation" (Knox-Quinn 1990, 315). Writing is not some sort of contest between you and everybody in the class, with the one who has the best grade—the fewest red marks—winning at the end of it, and that's why the cupped hand is a poor metaphor for what happens when you produce writing in a classroom. The struggle, the contest, is internal, between your desire to talk on paper and your fear or distrust of it. The group helps us compete with the real opponent of creative, critical thought—inertia, the fear of making a move.

As Kesey's work with his creative writers and my work with my first-year writers suggest, the group gives writers the strategies for winning that contest. I remember a few years ago, a freshman writer was writing an essay whose topic turned out to be something about the advantages of watching TV. She was bored with it, but chose it quickly as she was casting about for anything to do. The essay began, "There are many disadvantages to sitting in front of a TV. But there are some positive things about TV." Well, you get the idea. It was uncommitted, with no sense of the personal investment I've been describing, and a feeling in the writing of inertia. The writer wasn't just writing about couch potatoes; she was writing couch potato prose. When she read aloud her opening to her group the next day, she became aware that the group was growing glassy-eyed. She finally gave up. "It's bad, huh?" They laughed. Then she started talking. All of a sudden the couch potato had stood up. She was exploring an idea she was creating for and with her group.

Look back at the idealistic subheading that began this last section. Changing the world seems a pretty grandiose goal for group work, doesn't it? "Freshman Arrive But Not to Change the World" read the headline in an article this fall in the *Greensboro News and Record* that described how first-year students in colleges across the country didn't believe they would make real changes in the world outside themselves. I think the article was wrong. I think people want to change the worlds they live in, but they feel increasingly powerless to do it. And here's the last and best reason for the group. Because they force writers and thinkers to consciousness, groups foster action and change.

Deciding on what's significant about what you're reading, what you're writing, what you're listening to, what you're writing in a group, is the beginning of an understanding that you make knowledge in the classroom. You don't just find it in a book, and you don't just apply it from a lecture. You *create* it. That's a potentially powerful piece of information. Once you realize that you make knowledge, you see that you can act to change the knowledge that's there. As students of writing, your work in the group can help you become aware that the knowledge of the subject matter you work with of voice, of forms and styles can be determined by you and those around you. The more your group meets and talks about reading, writing, and ideas, the more your group collaborates, the more *authoring* you do. What seat work and the bluebirds taught you to see as private and unique the group can help you recognize as also shared and social. And that realization really can help you make a difference in the world around you and within you.

Works Cited

Bruffee, Kenneth (1984). "Collaborative Learning and the Conversation of Mankind." *College English, 46,* 635–652.

Hirsch, E. D. (1987). *Cultural Literacy: What Every American Needs to Know.* Boston: Houghton Mifflin, 1987.

Kesey, Ken (1962). *One Flew over the Cuckoo's Nest.* New York: New American Library.

Knox-Quinn, Carolyn (1990). "Collaboration in the Writing Classroom: An Interview with Ken Kesey." *College Composition and Communication, 41,* 309–317.

Parker, Dorothy (1942). "You Were Perfectly Fine." *Collected Stories of Dorothy Parker.* New York: Modern Library.

Hephzibah Roskelly, "The Cupped Hand and the Open Palm," from *The Subject is Writing*, 4th ed., Wendy Bishop & James Strickland, eds., Portsmouth, NH: Boynton/Cook, 2006, pp. 141-151. Reprinted by permission.

Style: The Hidden Agenda in Composition Classes or One Reader's Confession

Kate Ronald

In some ways I see this essay as a confession. I have been teaching writing and theorizing about how it should be taught for almost fifteen years now. During those fifteen years, you, the students reading this essay, have been in school, taking English classes and writing compositions. I have been teaching those classes and reading those compositions; plus I've been teaching some of your teachers for the past ten years, and so I feel responsible to you even though I've never had you in one of my classes. Now I'm going to tell you something you might already know. Since you started school in the first grade, there's been a revolution in the way you've been "taught" to write. It used to be that teachers focused on and evaluated your writing according to two main things: its structure and its correctness. Those were the days of diagramming sentences and imitating types of organization. In the 1960s and '70s, however, many people who studied writing began to talk about teaching the "process" of writing rather than the "products" of writing. In other words, the focus has shifted in the 1980s from organization and correctness to generating ideas, appealing to audiences, and developing a "voice" in writing.

Composition or "rhetoric" as it used to be called, is an ancient discipline going all the way back at least to Plato and Aristotle in the third century B.C.E. You are the most recent in a long, long line of students sitting in classes where teachers assign writing tasks and evaluate your ability. In ancient times, the art of writing was divided into five steps: invention (coming up with ideas), arrangement (organizing them), style (making them sound right), memory (remembering speeches), and delivery (oratorical ability). One way to think about the history of writing instruction is to look at the different emphases that different eras have put on these five steps. Today, with computers and photocopy machines, we don't worry much anymore about memory, for example, but it was terribly important in the time before the printing press. And we don't "deliver" what we write orally very much anymore, although the kind of font you choose from your word-processing program might be considered a matter of delivery. Of course all writers have to think about invention, arrangement, and style, no matter what age they work in. However, different eras have emphasized different parts of composition. Plato and Aristotle were upset by what they saw as an enchantment with style; they worried that writers could dazzle audiences without caring much about telling them the truth. And so they focused on invention, on figuring out issues by thinking and writing. By the sixteenth and seventeenth centuries, the focus had shifted back to style, going so far as giving students manuals that provided hundreds of ways to say "I enjoyed your letter very much." How a person sounded was more important than what a person had to say.

I see the shift from "product" to "process" while you've been in school as a reaction to that overemphasis on style. Once again, the focus has changed back to make *invention* the most important step in composition. Writing teachers who are up-to-date these days (including me) tell you (our students) not to worry, for example, about grammar or spelling or organization as you write your early drafts. We invite you to choose your own topics for writing and to get feedback from responsive small groups in your classes. We don't grade individual papers, but instead ask you to write multiple drafts and submit for final evaluation the ones you think best represent you as a writer. We don't lecture on punctuation or topic sentences. It's what you say, not how you say it, that counts. No doubt you all are familiar with this kind of teaching—I doubt you'd be reading this essay right now if you weren't in a class with a thoroughly "new rhetoric" teacher. Obviously this whole collection is focused on the *processes* of writing, the main theme of writing instruction in the 1980s.

But here comes my confession. Your teacher, and I, and all the others who were part of this latest revolution in rhetoric, haven't been exactly honest with you about the matter of style. We say we aren't overly interested in style, that your ideas and your growth as writers is uppermost in our minds, but we are still influenced by your writing style more than we admit, or perhaps know. In other words, despite all the research and writing I've done in the past ten years about composing, revising, responding, contexts for writing, personal voice, and all I know about the new rhetoric, I'm still rewarding and punishing my students for their writing styles. And here's the worst part of my confession: I'm not sure that I'm teaching them style. Of course any teacher quickly realizes that she can't teach everything in one semester, but I worry that I'm responding to something in my students' writing that I'm not telling them about—their style, the sound of their voices on paper. This essay is my attempt to atone for that omission in my own teaching. Despite that selfish motive, I also want to suggest to you ways in which you might become aware of your own writing styles and your teachers' agendas about style, as well as show you some strategies for studying and improving your own style in writing.

Let me stop to define what I mean and what I don't mean by "style." I don't mean spelling, grammar, punctuation, or usage, although if I'm going to be completely honest, I'd have to tell you that mistakes along those lines do get in my way when I'm reading. But those can be fixed, easily, by editing and copyreading. By style, I mean what my student, Margaret, said last semester after another student, Paul, had read a paper out loud for the whole class. She got this longing look on her face and cried, "I want to write the way Paul does!" You know students like Paul.

He's clever, he surprises with his different perspectives on his topics, and he has a distinctive voice. I call this "writing where somebody's home," as opposed to writing that's technically correct but where there's "nobody home," no life, no voice. Let me give you some examples of these two kinds of voices.

Much Too Young to Be So Old

The neighborhood itself was old. Larger than most side streets, 31st Street had huge cracks that ran continuously from one end to the other of this gray track that led nowhere special. Of the large, lonely looking houses, there were only six left whose original structures hadn't been tampered with in order to make way for inexpensive apartments. Why would a real family continue to live in this place was a question we often asked and none of us could answer. Each stretch of the run-down rickety houses had an alley behind them. These alleys became homes, playgrounds, and learning areas for us children. We treasured these places. They were overgrown with weeds and filled with years of garbage, but we didn't seem to care. Then again, we didn't seem to care about much. (Amy)

The Dog

In 1980 I lived in a green split-level house. It was a really ugly green but that is beside the point. The neighborhood was really rather pretty, with trees all over the place and not just little trees: They were huge. My friends and I played football in my backyard right after school every day. The neighbors had a white toy poodle that barked forever. You would walk by the fence and it would bark at you. I had no idea whatsoever that the dog was mean. (Corey)

Even though both these writers begin these essays by describing the settings of their stories, and both end with a suggestion of what's coming next, Amy's opening paragraph appeals to me much more than Corey's. I could point out "flaws" in both openings: I think Corey's suffers from lack of concrete detail, and he takes a pretty long time telling us only that the trees were "huge." Amy uses too much passive voice ("hadn't been tampered with"). However, I'm much more drawn into the world of 31st Street than I am to the neighborhood with huge trees. And I think that's because I know more about Amy from this opening—her words and her rhythm evoke a bittersweet expectation in me—whereas I'm not sure what Corey's up to. In other words, I get the distinct feeling that Amy really wants to tell her readers about her childhood. I don't see that kind of commitment in Corey. I know Corey's going to write a dog story, and usually those are my favorites, but somehow I don't very much want to read on.

But teachers have to read on, and on and on, through hundreds and hundreds of drafts a semester. So I can't just say to Corey, "This is boring." And, being a believer in the "new rhetoric," I'm interested in the process that leads to these two different styles. How does Amy come up with this voice? Was she born clever? And why does Corey make the decision to take himself out of his writing? I can think of many reasons why he would choose to be safe; in fact, he admitted to me later in that course that he had "copped out," choosing to write in what he called his "safe, public style" rather than take chances with what he thought was a more risky, personal style. That makes sense, if you consider the history of writing instruction up until the past fifteen to twenty years. Certainly it's been better to get it right, to avoid mistakes, than to get it good, to try for a voice. And it makes sense that Corey wouldn't want to expose his personal style—writing classrooms traditionally have not been places where students have felt safe. Writing and then showing that writing to someone else for evaluation and response is risky, a lot like asking "Am I OK? Am I a person you want to listen to?"

And so, to play it safe in a risky environment, it's tempting to take on a voice that isn't yours, to try to sound like you know what you're talking about, to sound "collegiate," to be acceptable and accepted. There's also a sort of mystique about "college writing," both in composition courses and in other disciplines. To write in college, this thinking goes, means to be "objective," to make your own opinions, your own stake in the subject, completely out of your writing. That's why people write, "It is to be hoped that" rather than, "I hope" or, "There are many aspects involved" rather than, "This is complicated." And then there's also a real fear of writing badly, of being thought stupid, and so it's tempting simply to be bland and safe and not call too much attention to yourself.

And teachers have encouraged you, I think, to remain hidden behind your own prose. Remember when you got a "split grade" like this: "C+/B"? One grade for content and another for style. That sends a clear message, I think, that what you say and how you say it can be separated and analyzed differently. That's crazy—we can't split form and content. But teachers tend to encourage you to do that when they ask you to read an essay by Virginia Woolf or E. B. White from an anthology and then tell you to "write like that." Or, we teachers have been so concerned with form that we've discouraged you from real communication with another person. One of my students just yesterday described her English classes this way: "I wanted to learn how to write and they were trying to teach me what my writing should look like." Preoccupation with correctness, with organization, and with format (margins, typing, neatness, etc.), all get in the way of style and voice. So, too, do prearranged assignments, where each student in the class writes the same essay on the same subject ("Compare high school to college," "Discuss the narrator's attitude in this short story," "My most embarrassing moment"). Such assignments become exercises in competition, in one sense, because you've got somehow to set yourself apart from the rest of the essays your teacher will be reading. But they are also exercises in becoming invisible, for while you want to be noticed, you don't want to be too terribly different, to stick out like a sore thumb. And so you write safely, not revealing too much or taking many chances.

I used to teach that way, giving assignments, comparing one student with another and everyone with the "ideal" paper I imagined in my head (although I never tried writing with my students in those days) correcting mistakes and arriving at a grade for each paper. The new rhetoric classes I teach now have eliminated many of these traps for students, but I've also opened up new ones, I'm afraid. Now my students choose their own topics, writing whatever they want to write. And sometimes I'm simply not interested in their choices. In the old days, when I gave the assignment, naturally I was interested in the topic—it was, after all, *my* idea. Now I read about all sorts of things every week—my students' families, their cars, the joys and sorrows in their love lives, their athletic victories and defeats, their opinions on the latest upcoming election, their thoughts about the future, etc. Frankly, I don't approach each of these topics in the same way. For example, a dog story almost always interests me, while a car story might not. Or, a liberal reading of the latest campus debate on women's issues will grab my attention much more quickly than a fundamentalist interpretation. That's simply the truth. But, as a teacher of "process," I try my best to get interested in whatever my students are writing. And, I'm usually delighted by how much my students can move me with their ideas. So what makes me interested? I'm convinced it has to do with their style. And here I'm defining style not simply as word choice or sentence structure, but as a kind of "presence" on the page, the feeling I get as a reader that, indeed, somebody's home in this paper, somebody wants to say something—to me, to herself, to the class, to the community.

Mine is not the only response students receive in this kind of classroom. Each day, students bring copies of their work-in-progress to their small groups. They read their papers out loud to each other, and we practice ways of responding to each writer that will keep him or her writing, for starts, and that will help the writer see what needs to be added, changed, or cut from the draft. This can get pretty tricky. It's been my experience that showing your writing to another student, to a peer, can be much more risky than showing it to a teacher. We've all had the experience of handing in something we knew was terrible to a teacher, and it's not so painful. People will give writing to teachers that they'd never show to someone whose opinion they valued. But sitting down in a small group with three or four classmates and saying, "I wrote this. What do you think?" is, again, like asking "Do you like me? Am I an interesting person?" And so my classes practice ways of responding to one another's writing without being overly critical, without taking control of the writing out of the writer's hands, and without damaging egos. And they become quite sophisticated as the semester goes along. Still, one of the worst moments in a small group comes when someone reads a draft and the rest of the group responds like this: "It's OK. I don't see anything wrong with it. It seems pretty good." And then silence. In other words, the writer hasn't grabbed their attention, hasn't engaged the readers, hasn't communicated in any meaningful way. What's the difference between this scenario and one where the group comes back with responses like "Where did you get that idea? I really like the way you describe the old man. This reminds me of my grandfather. I think you're right to notice his hands"? I think the difference is in *style*, in the presence of a writer in a group who is honestly trying to communicate to his or her readers.

But I know I still haven't been exactly clear about what I mean by style. That's part of my dilemma, my reason for wanting to write this essay. All of us, teachers and students, recognize good style when we hear it, but I don't know what we do to foster it. And so for the rest of this essay I want to talk to you about how to work on your own writing styles, to recognize and develop your own individual voice in writing, and how to listen for your teachers' agendas in style. Because, despite our very natural desires to remain invisible in academic settings, you *want* to be noticed; you want to be the voice that your teacher becomes interested in. I think I'm telling you that your style ultimately makes the difference. And here I'm talking about not only your writing styles, but the reading styles of your audiences, the agendas operating in the contexts in which you write.

I'll start backward with agendas first. There are several main issues that I think influence English teachers when they are reading students' writing. First, we have a real bent for the literary element, the metaphor, the clever turn of phrase, the rhythm of prose that comes close to the rhythm of poetry. That's why I like sentences like these: "As the big night approached I could feel my stomach gradually easing its way up to my throat. I was as nervous as a young foal experiencing its first thunderstorm" (from an essay about barrel racing) and "Suddenly the University of Nebraska Cornhusker Marching Band takes the field for another exciting half-time performance, and the Sea of Red stands up *en masse* and goes to the concession stand" (from an essay about being in the band). I like the surprise in this last sentence, the unexpectedness of everyone leaving the performance, and I like the comparison to a young foal in the first one, especially since the essay is about horses. I tell my students to "take chances" in their writing. I think these two writers were trying to do just that. And I liked them for taking that chance.

But you don't want to take chances everywhere. Of course this kind of writing won't work in a biology lab report or a history exam, which brings me to another troublesome issue when we talk about style in college writing. You move among what composition researchers call "discourse communities" every day—from English to Biology to Sociology to Music to the dorm to family dinners to friends at bars—you don't talk or write the same way, or in the same voice to each of these groups. You adjust. And yet many professors still believe that you should be learning to write one certain kind of style in college, one that's objective, impersonal, formal, explicit, and organized around assertions, claims, and reasons that illustrate or defend those claims. You know this kind of writing. You produce it in response to questions like "Discuss the causes of the Civil War," or "Do you think that 'nature' or 'nurture' plays the most important role in a child's development?" Here's a student trying out this kind of "academic discourse" in an essay where he discusses what worries him:

> Another outlet for violence in our society is video games. They have renewed the popularity that they had earlier in the 1980s and have taken our country by storm. There is not one child in the country who doesn't know what a Nintendo is. So, instead of running around outside getting fresh air and exercise, most children are sitting in front of the television playing video games. This is affecting their minds and their bodies.

Why wouldn't Jeff just say "Video games are popular again" instead of saying that "they have renewed their popularity" or "Kids are getting fat and lazy" rather than "This is affecting their minds and bodies"? Besides using big words here, Jeff is also trying to sound absolutely knowledgeable: He states that every child in this country knows Nintendo, they are all playing it, when if he thought about that for a minute, he'd know it wasn't true. I don't like this kind of writing very much myself. Jeff is trying so hard to sound academic that "there's nobody home," no authentic voice left, no sense of a real human being trying to say something to somebody. I prefer discourse that "renders experience," as Peter Elbow (1991) puts it, rather than discourse that tries to explain it. He describes this kind of language (or style) as writing where a writer "conveys to others a sense of experience—or indeed, that mirrors back to themselves a sense of their own experience, from a little distance, once it's out there on paper" (137). Here's an example of that kind of "rendering" from Paul's essay about a first date:

> Her mother answers the door. My brain says all kinds of witty and charming things which my larynx translates in a sort of amphibious croak. (Ribbitt, Ribbitt. I can't remember what it was I actually attempted to say.) She materializes at the top of the stairs, cast in a celestial glow. A choir of chubby cherubim, voices lifted into a heavenly chorus, drape her devine body with a thin film of gossamer. (No, not really. She did look pretty lovely, though. I tried to tell her as much. Ribbitt. Ribbitt.)

Now, perhaps Paul goes too far here, trying a little too hard to be clever, but I like this better than the discussion of video games. (And not just because I like the topic of dating better—since I've gotten married, I don't date anymore and I confess I'm addicted to Mario Brothers 3.) Paul here is conveying the *feeling* of the moment, the sense of the experience, and he's complicating the memory by moving back and forth between the moment and his interpretation of it. In other words, he's letting me into the story, not explaining something to me. Paul is involved in what he's writing while Jeff is detached. And Paul's funny. Besides dog stories, I like humor in my students' writing.

Now, this brings me to another issue in the matter of style. I prefer the rendering style over the explanatory style, perhaps because I'm an English major and an English teacher, and therefore I like the allusion over the direct reference, description over analysis, narrative over exposition. But perhaps there's another reason I like the more personal style: I'm a woman. There's a whole body of recent research that suggests that men and women have different writing styles, among all sorts of other differences. Theorists such as Pamela Annas and Elizabeth Flynn suggest that women writers in academic situations often are forced to translate their experiences into the foreign language of objectivity, detachment, and authority that the male-dominated school system values. Women strive for connection, this thinking argues, while men value individual power. Feminist theory values writing that "brings together the personal and the political, the private and the public, into writing which is committed and powerful because it takes risks, because it speaks up clearly in their own voices and from their own experiences" (Annas 1985, 370; see also Flynn 1988). Here's an example of that kind of writing, an excerpt from an essay titled, "Grandma, You're Not So Young Anymore":

> My grandma was always so particular about everything. Everything had to be just so. The walls and curtains had to be spotless, the garden couldn't have a weed, the kolaches had to be baked, and the car had to be washed.... Each spring she was always the first to have her flowers and garden planted. She could remember the littlest details about our family history and ancestors.... There were always kolaches in the oven and cookies in the refrigerator....
>
> I really didn't notice the aging so much at first... When I would come home from college Mom would always say, "Grandma's really lonely now. Grandpa was her company, and now he's gone. You should really go and visit her more often. She won't be around forever."
>
> I had to admit I didn't visit her all that often... I didn't notice how much slower she'd gotten until Thanksgiving Day. Grandma took us to Bonanza because she didn't want to cook that much. I noticed the slower, more crippled steps she took, the larger amount of wrinkles on her face, and most of all, her slowed mental abilities. She sometimes had trouble getting words out as if she couldn't remember what she wanted to say. She couldn't decide what foods she wanted to eat, and when she did eat, she hardly

touched a thing. I didn't think my grandma would ever get old. Now I don't think she will last forever anymore.

Here, Deanna uses her own experience and observations to go on and talk about how the elderly are treated in our culture. She could have written a statistical report on nursing homes or a more formal argument about how Americans don't value their old people. But she chose instead to draw from her own life and therefore she draws me into her argument about the "frustration" of getting old. I like old people, and I can identify this woman's deterioration with my own mother's several years ago. But I still think it's more than my personal history that draws me to this essay. I suspect it's Deanna's willingness to explore her own experience on paper. Deanna definitely needs to work on editing this draft to improve her style (something more specific, for example, than "larger amounts of wrinkles" and "slowed mental abilities"). But she doesn't need to work to improve her style in the sense of her commitment to this topic, her presence on the page, or her desire to figure out and to explain her reaction to her grandmother's aging.

Each of these three issues might lead me to advise you that you should write metaphors for English teachers, formal explanations for male teachers in other disciplines, and personal narratives for your women professors. But you know that would be silly, simplistic advice about style. You have to maneuver every day through a complex set of expectations, some of which aren't made explicit, and the whole idea of teacher-as-audience is much more complex that simply psyching out a teacher's background or political agenda. "Style" in writing means different things to different people. I have to be honest and admit that my definition of style as presence on paper is simply my own definition. I hope this essay will lead you to your own thinking about what style means, in all contexts. But I am going to end by giving you some advice about your own style in writing anyway—the teacher in me can't resist. That advice is: Work on your style without thinking about school too much. Here are five suggestions to help you do this.

In School or Out, Write as if You're Actually Saying Something to Somebody. Even if you're not exactly sure who your audience is, try to imagine a real person who's interested in what you have to say. Probably the most important thing I can tell you about working on your style is: Think of your writing as actually saying something to somebody real. Too often in academics we can imagine no audience at all, or at the most an audience with evaluation on its mind, not real interest or response. When I'm able to get interested in my students' writing, no matter what the topic, it's because I hear someone talking to me. My colleague Rick Evans calls this kind of writing "talking on paper," and if you keep that metaphor in mind, I think you'll more often avoid the kind of "academese" or formal language that signals you're hiding or you've disappeared.

I can illustrate the difference in style I'm talking about through two journals that Angie gave me at the beginning and the end of a composition and literature course last year. All through the course, I asked students to write about how the novels we were reading connected to their own lives:

> January 24: Well, I'm confused. I haven't written a paper for an English class that wasn't a formal literary analysis since 8th grade. Now, all of a sudden, the kind of writing my teachers always said would be of no use in college *is*, and what they said *would* be, *isn't*. Go figure. Now, if Kate had asked me to churn out a paper on some passage or symbol in *Beloved*—even one of my own choosing—I could get out 5-8 (handwritten) pages easy. But this life stuff? Who wants to know about that anyway?

> May 1: This portfolio represents the work closest to my guts. It's *my* story, not *Beloved's* or Carlos Rueda's. I hasten to point out that this may not be my best work or even my favorite work, but it's the work that sings my song. My goal was to communicate a set of ideas, to spark a dialogue with *you*, as my reader, to inspire you to think about *what* I have written, not *how* I have written it. So here it is, bound in plastic, unified, in a manner, ready for reading. I hope you like what I have woven.

Notice how Angie's attitude toward me as her reader changed from January to May. At first she referred to "Kate" as if I wouldn't be reading what she had written, even though this was a journal handed in to me; later I become some one she wants to engage in a dialogue. (She had expected the kind of writing class I described at the beginning of this essay, but she found herself writing for a new rhetoric teacher.) Notice, too, how at first she talks about how she could write five to eight pages *even if she had to choose her own topic*. The implication is clear—that it's easier to write when someone else tells her what to do, what to write about. In other words, it's easier to perform rather than to communicate. Notice, finally, Angie's relationship to the literature we were reading in these two journals. At first she wants only to write about the symbols in Toni Morrison's novel *Beloved* (1987), focusing all her attention on the literary work and not on herself. At the end of the course, she subordinates the novels almost completely to her own stories. This is an engaged writer, one with a clear sense of her own style, her own presence.

Write Outside of School. Play with writing outside of school. You'll need to write much more than just what's assigned in your classes to develop a beautiful writing style. (Sorry, but it's true.) One of the truisms about good writers is that they are good readers; in other words, they read a lot. (And they were probably read to as kids, but we can't go into that right now.) So, here's an exercise in style that I recommend to my students.

Find an author whose writing you admire. Copy out a particular, favorite passage. Then imitate that style, word for word, part-of-speech for part-of-speech. Here's an example from one of my students last semester. We were reading *Beloved*, and Sarah used its opening passage to talk about the first day of class. I'll show you Morrison's passage and then Sarah's:

> 124 was spiteful. Full of a baby's venom. The women in the house knew it and so did the children. For years each put up with the spite in his own way, but by 1873, Sethe and her daughter Denver were its only victims. The grandmother, Baby Suggs, was dead, and the sons, Howard and Buglar, had run away by the time they were thirteen years old—as soon as merely looking in a mirror shattered it (that was the signal for Buglar); as soon as two tiny hand prints appeared in the cake (that was it for Howard). Neither boy waited to see more. (3)

> Andrews 33 was quiet. Full of a new semester's uneasiness. The students in the room knew it and so did the teacher. For a few minutes, everyone took in the tension in their own way, but by 12:45 the roll call and Kate's lame jokes broke the ice a little bit. The course, a new program, was explained, and the syllabus, papers and papers, looked simple enough by the time Kate explained her marvelous approach—as soon as really deciding on a topic excited us (that was the reason for the authority list); as soon as four friendly voices read to each other (that was the reason for small groups). No students lingered too write more. (Sarah)

Sarah told me later that doing this imitation surprised her—she had never written with parentheses before, nor had she stopped sentences in the middle this way ("the syllabus, papers and papers"). She wasn't sure she liked this imitation, but it showed her she could write in different ways. And playing with different voices on paper will help you make choices about your own style in different situations.

Read Your Work-in-progress out Loud, Preferably to a Real Person. Looking back over this essay, I realize that so much of what I've said about style revolves around the sense of sound. Teachers have good ears, and so do you. Listen to your own voice as you read out loud. Do you sound like a person talking to someone? Or a student performing for a grade?

Practice Cutting All the Words You Can out of Your Drafts and Starting from There. This is one of the hardest things for any writer to do, and yet I think it's one of the most effective ways to make your writing more interesting. Most of the time there are simply too many words getting in the way of your meaning, making too much noise for you to be heard. Look closely at your drafts and be hard on yourself. Let me give you a few quick examples:

> The first thing that really upsets me is the destruction of our environment due to ignorance, capitalism, and blindness in the world. The attitude that most people take is that by ignoring the problem it will go away. An example of this attitude is the turnout for elections in America.

> Revision: Ignorance, capitalism, and blindness destroy our environment. Most people look the other way. Many don't even vote.

Once Jim revised this opening sentence from an essay on what worries him, he realized that he hadn't said much yet and that he was moving way too quickly. He learned that he had several ideas he felt strongly about, ideas worth slowing down to develop. Here are two more examples:

> I also think that we need to provide more opportunities for the homeless to receive an education so they can compete in today's job market. Another reason for educating these people is because the increasing numbers of unemployed persons is a factor that is contributing to homelessness in our country. There are declining employment opportunities for unskilled labor in todays job market, and since many homeless are unskilled laborers, they are not able to acquire a decent job. Therefore they cannot afford to buy a home. I think it is critical that these people be educated if the homeless problem in our country is going to be resolved.

> Revision: We need to educate the homeless so they can compete in a market where jobs are becoming more scarce.

> There are so many things that a person can fill their mind with. I find that when talking with friends the majority of their thoughts are filled with worries. I don't really believe that it is all negative to worry unless it becomes an obsession. So many people are worried about so many different things. Some of which are personal while others are more societal. When I try to figure out what worries me most I find it to be on a more personal level.

> Revision: I'm sort of worried that I worry so much about myself.

Each of these last two writers realized that they hadn't said much of anything yet in their initial drafts. Going back to cut words, asking themselves questions about what they meant to say to a reader, allowed them to start over with a different, clearer perspective. I know this isn't easy, especially in school, where you've been trained to "write 1000 words" and, by God, you'll write 1000 words whether you have one or 1000 words to say on the subject. Try to stop padding and counting words in the margins. Cut words. This is probably the most practical piece of advice I have.

Finally, Write About Your Own Writing Style. Keep a record of your reactions to what you write, a list of your favorite sentences, and a reaction to the reactions you get from readers. Most of all, forgive yourself for writing badly from time to time. One of my professors in graduate school told me that I was capable of writing "awkward word piles," and here I am with the nerve to be writing an essay to you about style. I've tried to practice what I preach, and now I'm suggesting that you throw out more than you keep and to notice and remember what works for you. Writing about your own writing is another piece of practical advice.

This is really my last word: Don't let *me* fool you here. Even though I understand what Angie meant in her last journal to me about my being more interested in what she has to say than *how* she said it, I'm still very in tune with the how, with her style, I'm happy that her focus has moved away from me as evaluator toward herself as a creator. But I'm still influenced by her style. Don't forget that. And I'm happy that the emphasis in composition has shifted from style back to invention. But I still reward and punish style in my reactions to students' writings. Yes, I try to be an interested reader, but my agendas also include listening for the sound of prose I like.

I suppose what I'm really confessing to you all in this essay is that I am not only a teacher, but I'm also a reader, with her own tastes, preferences, and phobias about what I like to read. And, as a reader, I look for style. There's a play that I love that I think can show you what I mean by style, by presence in writing. *The Real Thing*, by Tom Stoppard (1983) is about real love and real life, but it's also about real writing. At about the end of Act One, Henry, the playwright/hero, talks about good writing. He's picked up a cricket bat (could be a Louisville slugger, but this play is set in London) to make his point. (Read this out loud and listen to the sound):

> This thing here, which looks like a wooden club, is actually several pieces of particular wood cunningly put together in a certain way so that the whole thing is sprung, like a dance floor. It's for hitting cricket balls with. If you get it right, the cricket ball will travel two hundred yards in four seconds, and all you've done is give it a knock like knocking the top off a bottle of stout, and it makes a noise like a trout taking a fly. What we're trying to do is write cricket bats, so then when we throw up an idea and give it a little knock, it might... *travel*. (22)

This image has stayed with me for seven years, ever since I first saw and read Stoppard's play, and it's an idea that I think all writers and readers understand. "Ideas traveling"—surely that's what I want for myself as a writer and for my students. I love the image of the dance floor too—the idea of a piece of writing as an invitation to movement, a place to join with others, a site of communal passion and joy. But I don't think people in school always think of writing as something that travels, or as a dance floor, and I would like somehow to help you a little toward Henry's vision. Later in the same speech he picks up a badly written play that he's been asked to "fix" and describes it:

> Now, what we've got here is a lump of wood of roughly the same shape trying to be a cricket bat, and if you hit a ball with it, the ball will travel about ten feet and you will drop the bat and dance about shouting "Ouch!" with your hands stuck in your armpits (23).

I've read writing, my own and my students' and professionals', that makes me want to do this different kind of dancing. Many of your textbooks read like "lumps of wood," yes? Henry tells us that no amount of simple editing will fix something that has no life or passion to begin with. But how to transform lumps of wood into cricket bats? It seems to me the key lies in this play's other theme—the "real thing," meaning real love and real passion. When I encourage you to develop your style in writing, I'm inviting you into the game, onto the dance floor, encouraging you to commit yourself to your ideas and to your readers. That's the essence of *style*, which, without knowledge and passion, amounts only to a performance that dazzles without touching its readers, and which, without practice, amounts to very little. In that sense, Plato and 'Aristotle were right to say that we shouldn't emphasize style over invention, ideas, and voice. And in another sense, my last piece of advice would apply to students in ancient Greece as well as modern America: write about something you care about to someone you care about. Even if you are writing in school, try to have a presence—show them that somebody's home, working. Writers must know and love not only their subjects but their audiences as well, so that ideas will dance, so that ideas will travel.

Works Cited

Annas, Pamela. (1985). "Style as Politics." *College English*, 4, 370.

Elbow, Peter (1991). "Reflections on Academic Discourse." *College English*, 2, 137.

Flynn, Elizabeth (1988). "Composing as Woman." *College Composition and Communication*, 39, 423–435.

Morrison, Toni (1987). *Beloved*. New York: Knopf.

Stoppard, Tom (1983). *The Real Thing*. London: Faber & Faber.

Kate Ronald, "Style: The Hidden Agenda in Composition Classes or One Reader's Confession," from *The Subject is Writing*, 4th ed., Wendy Bishop & James Strickland, eds., Portsmouth, NH: Boynton/Cook, 2006, pp. 195-209. Reprinted by permission.

SEQUENCE
1

CONCEPTS: INVENTION AND
INQUIRY

Introduction

Concepts: Invention and Inquiry

Writing, by its very nature, is a communicative act. Even when you write notes to yourself or enter secret thoughts into a private journal, you are engaging in acts of *communication* even if those acts are just with yourself. Effective communication with those around us depends upon the ability to take personal, private experience and connect it to the experiences of others in meaningful ways. One way of doing this is to take your concrete, and perhaps unique experience and use it as *evidence* for a more general or common experience. This is the process of abstraction—generating and describing ideas and concepts using evidence developed from particular experience.

In Sequence 1, you'll read essays that describe abstract ideas or concepts and draw evidence from a wide variety of particular phenomena. As you read through the essays in this section, pay special attention to the ways in which the authors move from the particular to the general, that is, the way that the authors generate abstractions or conceptualize ideas. How do they support their generalizations? How do they limit or contextualize them in ways that are convincing?

For example, in Carl Becker's short deliberation on the concept of "Democracy," we see a careful unpacking of an idea that can be understood and applied in many ways that might seem incongruous with commonly held beliefs. Aaron Copland's description of "How We Listen to Music" offers a method for experiencing and describing the effect that music can have on people. In describing this method, Copland uses both narrative and descriptive writing to provide detail to the idea of music that he is exploring. And in the essays by Richard Ford, Margaret Mead and Rhoda Metraux, and Jo Goodwin Parker, we see how these writers use specific metaphors to convey ideas and meanings about broad social experiences.

Democracy

Carl Becker

Democracy, like liberty or science or progress, is a word with which we are all so familiar that we rarely take the trouble to ask what we mean by it. It is a term, as the devotees of semantics say, which has no "referent"—there is no precise or palpable thing or object which we all think of when the word is pronounced. On the contrary, it is a word which connotes different things to different people, a kind of conceptual Gladstone bag[1] which, with a little manipulation, can be made to accommodate almost any collection of social facts we may wish to carry about in it. In it we can as easily pack a dictatorship as any other form of government. We have only to stretch the concept to include any form of government supported by a majority of the people, for whatever reasons and by whatever means of expressing assent, and before we know it the empire of Napoleon, the Soviet regime of Stalin, and the Fascist systems of Mussolini and Hitler are all safely in the bag. But if this is what we mean by democracy, then virtually all forms of government are democratic, since virtually all governments, except in times of revolution, rest upon the explicit or implicit consent of the people. In order to discuss democracy intelligently it will be necessary, therefore, to define it, to attach to the word a sufficiently precise meaning to avoid the confusion which is not infrequently the chief result of such discussions.

All human institutions, we are told, have their ideal forms laid away in heaven, and we do not need to be told that the actual institutions conform but indifferently to these ideal counterparts. It would be possible then to define democracy either in terms of the ideal or in terms of the real form—to define it as government of the people, by the people, for the people; or to define it as government of the people, by the politicians, for whatever pressure groups can get their interests taken care of. But as a historian I am naturally disposed to be satisfied with the meaning which, in the history of politics, men have commonly attributed to the word—a meaning, needless to say, which derives partly from the experience and partly from the aspirations of mankind. So regarded, the term democracy refers primarily to a form of government, and it has always meant government by the many as opposed to government by the one—government by the people as opposed to government by a tyrant, a dictator, or an absolute monarch. This is the most general meaning of the word as men have commonly understood it.

In this antithesis there are, however, certain implications, always tacitly understood, which give a more precise meaning to the term.

---

[1] A piece of hand luggage with two compartments.

Peisistratus,[2] for example, was supported by a majority of the people, but his government was never regarded as a democracy for all that. Caesar's power derived from a popular mandate, conveyed through established republican forms, but that did not make his government any the less a dictatorship. Napoleon called his government a democratic empire, but no one, least of all Napoleon himself, doubted that he had destroyed the last vestiges of the democratic republic. Since the Greeks first used the term, the essential test of democratic government has always been this: the source of political authority must be and remain in the people and not in the ruler. A democratic government has always meant one in which the citizens, or a sufficient number of them to represent more or less effectively the common will, freely act from time to time, and according to established forms, to appoint or recall the magistrates and to enact or revoke the laws by which the community is governed. This I take to be the meaning which history has impressed upon the term democracy as a form of government.

[2] Tyrant of Athens, 561–527 B.C.E.

Carl Becker, "Democracy," from *Modern Democracy*, by Carl Becker. New Haven: Yale University Press, 1941, excerpt from pp. 4-7. Reprinted by permission.

How We Listen to Music

Aaron Copland

We all listen to music according to our separate capacities. But, for the sake of analysis, the whole listening process may become clearer if we break it up into its component parts, so to speak. In a certain sense we all listen to music on three separate planes. For lack of a better terminology, one might name these: (1) the sensuous plane, (2) the expressive plane, (3) the sheerly musical plane. The only advantage to be gained from mechanically splitting up the listening process into these hypothetical planes is the clearer view to be had of the way in which we listen.

The simplest way of listening to music is to listen for the sheer pleasure of the musical sound itself. That is the sensuous plane. It is the plane on which we hear music without thinking, without considering it in any way. One turns on the radio while doing something else and absentmindedly bathes in the sound. A kind of brainless but attractive state of mind is engendered by the mere sound appeal of the music.

You may be sitting in a room reading this book. Imagine one note struck on the piano. Immediately that one note is enough to change the atmosphere of the room—proving that the sound element in music is a powerful and mysterious agent, which it would be foolish to deride or belittle.

The surprising thing is that many people who consider themselves qualified music lovers abuse that plane in listening. They go to concerts in order to lose themselves. They use music as a consolation or an escape. They enter an ideal world where one doesn't have to think of the realities of everyday life. Of course they aren't thinking about the music either. Music allows them to leave it, and they go off to a place to dream, dreaming because of and apropos of the music yet never quite listening to it.

Yes, the sound appeal of music is a potent and primitive force, but you must not allow it to usurp a disproportionate share of your interest. The sensuous plane is an important one in music, a very important one, but it does not constitute the whole story.

There is no need to digress further on the sensuous plane. Its appeal to every normal human being is self-evident. There is, however, such a thing as becoming more sensitive to the different kinds of sound stuff as used by various composers. For all composers do not use that sound stuff in the same way. Don't get the idea that the value of music is commensurate with its sensuous appeal or that the loveliest sounding music is made by the greatest composer. If that were so, Ravel would be a greater creator than Beethoven. The point is that the sound element varies with each composer, that his usage of sound forms an integral part of his style and must be taken into account when listening. The reader can see, therefore, that a more conscious approach is valuable even on this primary plane of music listening.

The second plane on which music exists is what I have called the expressive one. Here, immediately, we tread on controversial ground. Composers have a way of shying away from any discussion of music's expressive side. Did not Stravinsky himself proclaim that his music was an "object," a "thing," with a life of its own, and with no other meaning than its own purely musical existence? This intransigent attitude of Stravinsky's may be due to the fact that so many people have tried to read different meanings into so many pieces. Heaven knows it is difficult enough to say precisely what it is that a piece of music means, to say it definitely, to say it finally so that everyone is satisfied with your explanation. But that should not lead one to the other extreme of denying to music the right to be "expressive."

My own belief is that music has an expressive power, some more and some less, but that all music has a certain meaning behind the notes and that that meaning behind the note constitutes, after all, what the piece is saying, what the piece is about. This whole problem can be stated quite simply by asking, "Is there a meaning to music?" My answer to that would be, "Yes." And "Can you state in so many words what the meaning is?" My answer to that would be, "No." Therein lies the difficulty.

Simple-minded souls will never be satisfied with the answer to the second of these questions. They always want music to have a meaning, and the more concrete it is the better they like it. The more the music reminds them of a train, a storm, a funeral, or any other familiar conception the more expressive it appears to be to them. This popular idea of music's meaning—stimulated and abetted by the usual run of musical commentator—should be discouraged wherever and whenever it is met. One timid lady once confessed to me that she suspected something seriously lacking in her appreciation of music because of her inability to connect it with anything definite. That is getting the whole thing backward, of course.

Still, the question remains, How close should the intelligent music lover wish to come to pinning a definite meaning to any particular work? No closer than a general concept, I should say. Music expresses, at different moments, serenity or exuberance, regret or triumph, fury or delight. It expresses each of these moods, and many others, in a numberless variety of subtle shadings and differences. It may even express a state of meaning for which there exists no adequate word in any language. In that case, musicians often like to say that it has only a purely musical meaning. They sometimes go farther and say that *all* music has only a purely musical meaning. What they really mean is that no appropriate word can be found to express the music's meaning and that, even if it could, they do not feel the need of finding it.

But whatever the professional musician may hold, most musical novices still search for specific words with which to pin down their musical reactions. That is why they always find Tchaikovsky easier to "understand" than Beethoven. In the first place, it is easier to pin a meaning-word on a Tchaikovsky piece than on a Beethoven one. Much easier. Moreover, with the Russian composer, every time you come back to a piece of his it almost always says the same thing to you, whereas with Beethoven it is often quite difficult to put your finger right on what he is saying. And any musician will tell you that that is why Beethoven is the greater composer. Because music which always says the same thing to you will necessarily soon become dull music, but music whose meaning is slightly different with each hearing has a greater chance of remaining alive.

Listen, if you can, to the forty-eight fugue themes of Bach's *Well-Tempered Clavichord*. Listen to each theme, one after another. You will soon realize that each theme mirrors a different world of feeling. You will also soon realize that the more beautiful a theme seems to you the harder it is to find any word that will describe it to your complete satisfaction. Yes, you will certainly know whether it is a gay theme or a sad one. You will be able, in other words, in your own mind, to draw a frame of emotional feeling around your theme. Now study the sad one a little closer. Try to pin down the exact quality of its sadness. Is it pessimistically sad or resignedly sad; is it fatefully sad or smilingly sad?

Let us suppose that you are fortunate and can describe to your own satisfaction in so many words the exact meaning of your chosen theme. There is still no guarantee that anyone else will be satisfied. Nor need they be. The important thing is that each one feel for himself the specific expressive quality of a theme or, similarly, an entire piece of music. And if it is a great work of art, don't expect it to mean exactly the same thing to you each time you return to it.

Themes or pieces need not express only one emotion, of course. Take such a theme as the first main one of the *Ninth Symphony*, for example. It is clearly made up of different elements. It does not say only one thing. Yet anyone hearing it immediately gets a feeling of strength, a feeling of power. It isn't a power that comes simply because the theme is played loudly. It is a power inherent in the theme itself. The extraordinary strength and vigor of the theme results in the listener's receiving an impression that a forceful statement has been made. But one should never try to boil it down to "the fateful hammer of life," etc. That is where the trouble begins. The musician, in his exasperation, says it means nothing but the notes themselves, whereas the nonprofessional is only too anxious to hang on to any explanation that gives him the illusion of getting closer to the music's meaning.

Now, perhaps, the reader will know better what I mean when I say that music does have an expressive meaning but that we cannot say in so many words what that meaning is.

The third plane on which music exists is the sheerly musical plane. Besides the pleasurable sound of music and the expressive feeling that it gives off, music does exist in terms of the notes themselves and of their manipulation. Most listeners are not sufficiently conscious of this third plane. . . .

Professional musicians, on the other hand, are, if anything, too conscious of the mere notes themselves. They often fall into the error of becoming so engrossed with their arpeggios and staccatos that they forget the deeper aspects of the music they are performing. But from the layman's standpoint, it is not so much a matter of getting over bad habits on the sheerly musical plane as of increasing one's awareness of what is going on, in so far as the notes are concerned.

When the man in the street listens to the "notes themselves" with any degree of concentration, he is most likely to make some mention of the melody. Either he hears a pretty melody or he does not, and he generally lets it go at that. Rhythm is likely to gain his attention next, particularly if it seems exciting. But harmony and tone color are generally taken for granted, if they are thought of consciously at all. As for music's having a definite form of some kind, that idea seems never to have occurred to him.

It is very important for all of us to become more alive to music on its sheerly musical plane. After all, an actual musical material is being used. The intelligent listener must be prepared to increase his awareness of the musical material and what happens to it. He must hear the melodies, the rhythms, the harmonies, the tone colors in a more conscious fashion. But above all he must, in order to follow the line of the composer's thought, know something of the principles of musical form. Listening to all of these elements is listening on the sheerly musical plane.

Let me repeat that I have split up mechanically the three separate planes on which we listen merely for the sake of greater clarity. Actually, we never listen on one or the other of these planes. What we do is to correlate them—listening in all three ways at the same time. It takes no mental effort, for we do it instinctively.

Perhaps an analogy with what happens to us when we visit the theater will make this instinctive correlation clearer. In the theater, you are aware of the actors and actresses, costumes and sets, sounds and movements. All these give one the sense that the theater is a pleasant place to be in. They constitute the sensuous plane in our theatrical reactions.

The expressive plane in the theater would be derived from the feeling that you get from what is happening on the stage. You are moved to pity, excitement, or gayety. It is this general feeling, generated aside from the particular words being spoken, a certain emotional something which exists on the stage, that is analogous to the expressive quality in music.

The plot and plot development is equivalent to our sheerly musical plane. The playwright creates and develops a character in just the same way that a composer creates and develops a theme. According to the degree of your awareness of the way in which the artist in either field handles his material will you become a more intelligent listener.

It is easy enough to see that the theatergoer never is conscious of any of these elements separately. He is aware of them all at the same time. The same is true of music listening. We simultaneously and without thinking listen on all three planes.

In a sense, the ideal listener is both inside and outside the music at the same moment, judging it and enjoying it, wishing it would go one way and watching it go another—almost like the composer at the moment he composes it; because in order to write his music, the composer must also be inside and outside his music, carried away by it and yet coldly critical of it. A subjective and objective attitude is implied in both creating and listening to music.

What the reader should strive for, then, is a more active kind of listening. Whether you listen to Mozart or Duke Ellington, you can deepen your understanding of music only by being a more conscious and aware listener—not someone who is just listening, but someone who is listening *for* something.

Aaron Copland, "How We Listen to Music," Aaron Copland Fund for Music, Inc. Reprinted by permission of the Aaron Copland Fund for Music, Inc., copyright owner.

A City Beyond the Reach of Empathy

Richard Ford

East Boothbay, Me.
Who can write about New Orleans now? Tell us what it's like there. Bring us near to what people are experiencing, to their loss, to what will survive. People who are close should write that. Only they're in the city, or they're on a bus, or they're seeking shelter. We don't know where they are.

It's just a keyhole, and a small one, onto this great civic tragedy. The people who should be writing of it can't be found. An attempt to set out a vocabulary for empathy and for reckoning is frustrated in a moment of sorest need by the plain terms of the tragedy that wants telling. There are many such keyholes.

In America, even with our incommensurable memories of 9/11, we still do not have an exact human vocabulary for the loss of a city—our great iconic city, so graceful, livable, insular, self-delighted, eccentric, the one New Orleanians always said, with a wink, that care forgot and that sometimes, it might seem, forgot to care. Other peoples have experienced their cities' losses. Some bombed away (sometimes by us). Others gone in the flood. Here now is one more tragedy that we thought, by some divinity's grace that didn't arrive, we'd miss. But not. And our inept attempts at words run only to lists, costs, to assessing blame. It's like Hiroshima, a public official said. But no. It's not like anything. It's what it is. That's the hard part. He, with all of us, lacked the words.

For those away from New Orleans—most all of us—in this week of tears and wrenching, words fail. Somehow our hearts' reach comes short and we've been left with an aching, pointless inwardness. "All memory resolves itself in gaze," the poet Richard Hugo wrote once about another town that died.

Empathy is what we long for—not sadness for a house we own, or owned once—now swept away. Not even for the felt miracle of two wide-eyed children whirled upward into a helicopter as if into clouds. And we want more than that, even at this painful long distance: we want to project our sympathies straight into the life of a woman standing waist-deep in a glistening toxic current with a whole city's possessions all floating about, her own belongings in a white plastic bag, and who has no particular reason for hope, and so is just staring up. We would all give her hope. Comfort. A part of ourselves. Perform an act of renewal. It's hard to make sense of this, we say. But it makes sense. Making sense just doesn't help.

Tell me what you feel, a woman in Los Angeles said to me today by telephone. (I have a telephone, of course.) Tell me what you think of when you think of New Orleans. There must be special things you feel the loss of. Memories. And I realized, by her voice, that she had made a firm decision already about this loss.

Oh, yes, I said, though not always the memories you'd think. I have a picture of my parents on V-J Day, in City Park, holding a baby, staring at the camera and the sun. They are all dressed up and happy. The baby is me. So, I wonder, how is that park faring tonight.

I have a memory of my father and mother drunk as loons on New Year's Eve, in front of Antoine's. It was nearly midnight, 1951. There was no place to leave me, so they had their fight (only an argument, really) in front of me. My father held my mother against a wall on St. Louis Street and shouted at her. About what I don't know. Later, when we were in bed in the Hotel Monteleone, with me between them and the ceiling fan turning, they both cried. So. What of Antoine's now? What of the waiters who a week ago stood out on the street in tuxedos aprons and smoked? What of St. Louis Street?

I have a memory of a hot and breathless summer. It is many summers joined into one. My mother took me onto the Algiers Ferry, an open boat with cars driven onto the deck. Out on the great sliding brown river there was the only hint of breeze you could find anywhere. Back and across to the foot of Canal Street. Back and across, we went. She bought me pralines. I held her hand during it all, until the sun finally fell and the hot night rose. So, now, what of that river? And the Algiers Ferry? And Algiers? All memory resolves itself in gaze.

And a last one, more up to date. My wife and I are walking home from a friend's house down tree-shrouded Coliseum Street. It is 2003, and 11 o'clock on a warm January night. We are only steps from our door, just in a cone of street light, when a boy hops out of a car and says he will definitely kill us if we don't hand it over right away. He has a little silver pistol to persuade us. Let's say he's 16. And he is serious. But he laughs when we tell him we don't have a penny. And it's true. I pull my pockets out like a bum. "You people," he says, almost happily, his gun become an afterthought. "You shouldn't be out here this way." He shakes his head, looks at the pavement, then gets in his car and drives away. He, that boy—he'd be 19—I hope he's safe somewhere.

It is—New Orleans is—a city foremost for special projections, for the things you can't do, see, think, consume, feel, forget up in Jackson or Little Rock or home in Topeka. "We're at the jumping-off place," Eudora Welty wrote. This was about Plaquemines, just across the river. It is—New Orleans—the place where the firm ground ceases and the unsound footing begins. A certain kind of person likes such a place. A certain kind of person wants to go there and never leave.

And there are the streetcars (or there were). And there are the oak trees and the lovely French boulevards and the stately rich men's houses. And Buddy Bolden was born there and Satchmo grew up in Storyville.

Huey Long lived in the Roosevelt Hotel, where he really had a "de-duct box." His brother, Uncle Earl, was crazy as a betsy-bug. If you knew a waiter you could get a table anywhere. You couldn't get divorced or married or sell your house on Fat Tuesday. And while they didn't let Jews and blacks in the Boston Club, the races still mingled and often people danced in the streets. They subscribed to the Napoleonic Code.

But so much for memory now. It charms, but it confuses and possibly holds us back. It's hard enough to take things in. When I think of my friends in the city this morning, I think of them as high and dry, as being where they belong, being themselves in their normal life that was. I turn off the TV, as I did four years ago next week, just to think my own sorrowing and prospective thoughts of them.

From the ruins it's not easy to know what's best to think. Even the president may have felt this way in his low pass over that wide sheet of onyx water, the bobbing roofs peeking above the surfaces, the vast collapse, the wind-riddled buildings, that little figure (could he see who she was?) staring skyward. Something will be there when the flood recedes. We know that. It will be those people now standing in the water, and on those rooftops—many black, many poor. Homeless. Overlooked. And it will be New Orleans—though its memory may be shortened, its self-gaze and eccentricity scoured out so that what's left is a city more like other cities, less insular, less self-regarding, but possibly more self-knowing after today. A city on firmer ground.

I write in the place of others, today, for the ones who can't be found. And there is a blunt ending now, one we always feared, never wished for, and do not deserve. Don't get me wrong. We would all turn the days back if we could, have those old problems, those old eccentricities again. But today is a beginning. There's no better way to think of it now. Those others surely will be writing soon.

Richard Ford, "A City Beyond the Reach of Empathy," *The New York Times*, September 4, 2005. Reprinted by permission of The New York Times via PARS International.

On Friendship

Margaret Mead
Rhoda Metraux

Few Americans stay put for a lifetime. We move from town to city to suburb, from high school to college in a different state, from a job in one region to a better job elsewhere, from the home where we raise our children to the home where we plan to live in retirement. With each move we are forever making new friends, who become part of our new life at that time.

For many of us the summer is a special time for forming new friendships. Today millions of Americans vacation abroad, and they go not only to see new sights but also—in those places where they do not feel too strange—with the hope of meeting new people. No one really expects a vacation trip to produce a close friend. But surely the beginning of a friendship is possible? Surely in every country people value friendship?

They do. The difficulty when strangers from two countries meet is not a lack of appreciation of friendship, but different expectations about what constitutes friendship and how it comes into being. In those European countries that Americans are most likely to visit, friendship is quite sharply distinguished from other, more casual relations, and is differently related to family life. For a Frenchman, a German or an Englishman friendship is usually more particularized and carries a heavier burden of commitment.

But as we use the word, "friend" can be applied to a wide range of relationships—to someone one has known for a few weeks in a new place, to a close business associate, to a childhood playmate, to a man or woman, to a trusted confidant. There are real differences among these relations for Americans—a friendship may be superficial, casual, situational or deep and enduring. But to a European, who sees only our surface behavior, the differences are not clear.

As they see it, people known and accepted temporarily, casually, flow in and out of Americans' homes with little ceremony and often with little personal commitment. They may be parents of the children's friends, house guests of neighbors, members of a committee, business associates from another town or even another country. Coming as a guest into an American home, the European visitor finds no visible landmarks. The atmosphere is relaxed. Most people, old and young, are called by first names.

Who, then, is a friend?

Even simple translation from one language to another is difficult. "You see," a Frenchman explains, "if I were to say to you in French, 'This is my good friend,' that person would not be as close to me as someone about whom I say only, 'This is my friend.' Anyone about whom I have to say more is really less."

In France, as in many European countries, friends generally are of the same sex, and friendship is seen as basically a relationship between men. Frenchwomen laugh at the idea that "women can't be friends," but they also admit sometimes that for women "it's a different thing." And many French people doubt the possibility of a friendship between a man and a woman. There is also a kind of relationship within a group—men and women who have worked together for a long time, who may be very close, sharing great loyalty and warmth of feeling. They may call one another *copains*—a word that in English becomes "friends" but has more the feeling of "pals" or "buddies." In French eyes this is not friendship, although two members of such a group may well be friends.

For the French, friendship is a one-to-one relationship that demands a keen awareness of the other person's intellect, temperament and particular interests. A friend is someone who draws out your own best qualities, with whom you sparkle and become more of whatever the friendship draws upon. Your political philosophy assumes more depth, appreciation of a play becomes sharper, taste in food or wine is accentuated, enjoyment of a sport is intensified.

And French friendships are compartmentalized. A man may play chess with a friend for thirty years without knowing his political opinions, or he may talk politics with him for as long a time without knowing about his personal life. Different friends fill different niches in each person's life. These friendships are not made part of family life. A friend is not expected to spend evenings being nice to children or courteous to a deaf grandmother. These duties, also serious and enjoined, are primarily for relatives. Men who are friends may meet in a café. Intellectual friends may meet in larger groups for evenings of conversation. Working people may meet at the little *bistro* where they drink and talk, far from the family. Marriage does not affect such friendships; wives do not have to be taken into account.

In the past in France, friendships of this kind seldom were open to any but intellectual women. Since some women's lives centered on their homes, their warmest relations with other women often went back to their girlhood. The special relationship of friendship is based on what the French value most—on the mind, on compatibility of outlook, on vivid awareness of some chosen area of life.

Friendship heightens the sense of each person's individuality. Other relationships commanding as great loyalty and devotion have a different meaning. In World War II the first resistance groups formed in Paris were built on the foundation of *les copains*. But significantly, as time went on these little groups, whose lives rested in one another's hands, called themselves "families." Where each had a total responsibility for all, it was kinship ties that provided the model. And even today such ties, crossing every line of class and personal interest, remain binding on the survivors of these small, secret bands.

In Germany, in contrast with France, friendship is much more articulately a matter of feeling. Adolescents, boys and girls, form deeply sentimental attachments, walk and talk together—not so much to polish their wits as to share their hopes and fears and dreams, to form a common front against the world of school and family and to join in a kind of mutual discovery of each other's and their own inner life. Within the family, the closest relationship over a lifetime is between brothers and sisters. Outside the family, men and women find in their closest friends of the same sex the devotion of a sister, the loyalty of a brother. Appropriately, in Germany friends usually are brought into the family. Children call their father's and their mother's friends "uncle" and "aunt." Between French friends, who have chosen each other for the congeniality of their point of view, lively disagreement and sharpness of argument are the breath of *life*. But for Germans, whose friendships are based on mutuality of feeling, deep disagreement on any subject that matters to both is regarded as a tragedy. Like ties of kinship, ties of friendship are meant to be irrevocably binding. Young Germans who come to the United States have great difficulty in establishing such friendships with Americans. We view friendship more tentatively, subject to changes in intensity as people move, change their jobs, marry, or discover new interests.

English friendships follow still a different pattern. Their basis is shared activity. Activities at different stages of life may be of very different kinds—discovering a common interest in school, serving together in the armed forces, taking part in a foreign mission, staying in the same country house during a crisis. In the midst of the activity, whatever it may be, people fall into step—sometimes two men or two women, sometimes two couples, sometimes three people—and find that they walk or play a game or tell stories or serve on a tiresome and exacting committee with the same easy anticipation of what each will do day by day or in some critical situation. Americans who have made English friends comment that, even years later, "you can take up just where you left off." Meeting after a long interval, friends are like a couple who begin to dance again when the orchestra strikes up after a pause. English friendships are formed outside the family circle, but they are not, as in Germany, contrapuntal to the family nor are they, as in France, separated from the family. And a break in an English friendship comes not necessarily as a result of some irreconcilable difference of viewpoint or feeling but instead as a result of misjudgment, where one friend seriously misjudges how the other will think or feel or act, so that suddenly they are out of step.

What, then, is friendship? Looking at these different styles, including our own, each of which is related to a whole way of life, are there common elements? There is the recognition that friendship, in contrast with kinship, invokes freedom of choice. A friend is someone who chooses and is chosen. Related to this is the sense each friend gives the other of being a special individual, on whatever grounds this recognition is based. And between friends there is inevitably a kind of equality of give-and-take. The similarities make the bridge between societies possible, and the American's characteristic openness to different styles of relationship makes it possible for him to find new friends abroad with whom he feels at home.

Margaret Mead & Rhoda Metraux, "On Friendship," from *A Way of Seeing*. William Morrow, 1974, pp. 45-48. Copyright © 1961, 1970 by Margaret Mead and Rhoda Metraux. Reprinted by permission of HarperColllins Publishers.

What Is Poverty?

Jo Goodwin Parker

You ask me what is poverty? Listen to me. Here I am, dirty, smelly, and with no "proper" underwear on and with the stench of my rotting teeth near you. I will tell you. Listen to me. Listen without pity. I cannot use your pity. Listen with understanding. Put yourself in my dirty, worn out, ill-fitting shoes, and hear me.

Poverty is getting up every morning from a dirt- and illness-stained mattress. The sheets have long since been used for diapers. Poverty is living in a smell that never leaves. This is a smell of urine, sour milk, and spoiling food sometimes joined with the strong smell of long-cooked onions. Onions are cheap. If you have smelled this smell, you did not know how it came. It is the smell of the outdoor privy. It is the smell of young children who cannot walk the long dark way in the night. It is the smell of the mattresses where years of "accidents" have happened. It is the smell of the milk which has gone sour because the refrigerator long has not worked, and it costs money to get it fixed. It is the smell of rotting garbage. I could bury it, but where is the shovel? Shovels cost money.

Poverty is being tired. I have always been tired. They told me at the hospital when the last baby came that I had chronic anemia caused from poor diet, a bad case of worms, and that I needed a corrective operation. I listened politely—the poor are always polite. The poor always listen. They don't say that there is no money for iron pills, or better food, or worm medicine. The idea of an operation is frightening and costs so much that, if I had dared, I would have laughed. Who takes care of my children? Recovery from an operation takes a long time. I have three children. When I left them with "Granny" the last time I had a job, I came home to find the baby covered with fly specks, and a diaper that had not been changed since I left. When the dried diaper came off, bits of my baby's flesh came with it. My other child was playing with a sharp bit of broken glass, and my oldest was playing alone at the edge of a lake. I made twenty-two dollars a week, and a good nursery school costs twenty dollars a week for three children. I quit my job.

Poverty is dirt. You say in your clean clothes coming from your clean house, "Anybody can be clean." Let me explain about housekeeping with no money. For breakfast I give my children grits with no oleo or cornbread without eggs and oleo. This does not use up many dishes. What dishes there are, I wash in cold water and with no soap. Even the cheapest soap has to be saved for the baby's diapers. Look at my hands, so cracked and red. Once I saved for two months to buy a jar of Vaseline for my hands and the baby's diaper rash. When I had saved enough, I went to

87

buy it and the price had gone up two cents. The baby and I suffered on. I have to decide every day if I can bear to put my cracked, sore hands into the cold water and strong soap. But you ask, why not hot water? Fuel costs money. If you have a wood fire it costs money. If you burn electricity, it costs money. Hot water is a luxury. I do not have luxuries. I know you will be surprised when I tell you how young I am. I look so much older. My back has been bent over the wash tubs for so long, I cannot remember when I ever did anything else. Every night I wash every stitch my school age child has on and just hope her clothes will be dry by morning.

Poverty is staying up all night on cold nights to watch the fire, knowing one spark on the newspaper covering the walls means your sleeping children die in flames. In summer poverty is watching gnats and flies devour your baby's tears when he cries. The screens are torn and you pay so little rent you know they will never be fixed. Poverty means insects in your food, in your nose, in your eyes, and crawling over you when you sleep. Poverty is hoping it never rains because diapers won't dry when it rains and soon you are using newspapers. Poverty is seeing your children forever with runny noses. Paper handkerchiefs cost money and all your rags you need for other things. Even more costly are antihistamines. Poverty is cooking without food and cleaning without soap.

Poverty is asking for help. Have you ever had to ask for help, knowing your children will suffer unless you get it? Think about asking for a loan from a relative, if this is the only way you can imagine asking for help. I will tell you how it feels. You find out where the office is that you are supposed to visit. You circle that block four or five times. Thinking of your children, you go in. Everyone is very busy. Finally, someone comes out and you tell her that you need help. That never is the person you need to see. You go see another person, and after spilling the whole shame of your poverty all over the desk between you, you find that this isn't the right office after all—you must repeat the whole process, and it never is any easier at the next place.

You have asked for help, and after all it has a cost. You are again told to wait. You are told why, but you don't really hear because of the red cloud of shame and the rising black cloud of despair.

Poverty is remembering. It is remembering quitting school in junior high because "nice" children had been so cruel about my clothes and my smell. The attendance officer came. My mother told him I was pregnant. I wasn't but she thought that I could get a job and help out. I had jobs off and on, but never long enough to learn anything. Mostly I remember being married. I was so young then. I am still young. For a time, we had all the things you have. There was a little house in another town, with hot water and everything. Then my husband lost his job. There was un-employment insurance for a while and what few jobs I could get. Soon, all our nice things were repossessed and we moved back here. I was pregnant then. This house didn't look so bad when we first moved in. Every week it gets worse. Nothing is ever fixed. We now had no money. There were a few odd jobs for my husband, but everything went for food then, as it does now. I don't know how we lived through three years and three babies, but we did. I'll tell you something, after the last baby I destroyed my marriage. It had been a good one, but could you keep on bringing children in this dirt? Did you ever think how much it costs for any kind of birth control? I knew my husband was leaving the day he left, but there were no good-byes between us. I hope he has been able to climb out of this mess somewhere. He never could hope with us to drag him down.

That's when I asked for help. When I got it, you know how much it was? It was, and is, seventy-eight dollars a month for the four of us; that is all I ever can get. Now you know why there is no soap, no needles and thread, no hot water, no aspirin, no worm medicine, no hand cream, no shampoo. None of these things forever and ever and ever. So that you can see clearly, I pay twenty dollars a month rent, and most of the rest goes for food. For grits and cornmeal, and rice and milk and beans. I try my best to use only the minimum electricity. If I use more, there is that much less for food.

Poverty is looking into a black future. Your children won't play with my boys. They will turn to other boys who steal to get what they want. I can already see them behind the bars of their prison instead of behind the bars of my poverty. Or they will turn to the freedom of alcohol or drugs, and find themselves enslaved. And my daughter? At best, there is for her a life like mine.

But you say to me, there are schools. Yes, there are schools. My children have no extra books, no magazines, no extra pencils, or crayons, or paper and the most important of all, they do not have health. They have worms, they have infections, they have pinkeye all summer. They do not sleep well on the floor, or with me in my one bed. They do not suffer from hunger, my seventy-eight dollars keeps us alive, but they do suffer from malnutrition. Oh yes, I do remember what I was taught about health in school. It doesn't do much good. In some places there is a surplus commodities program. Not here. The county said it cost too much. There is a school lunch program. But I have two children who will already be damaged by the time they get to school.

But, you say to me, there are health clinics. Yes, there are health clinics and they are in the towns. I live out here eight miles from town. I can walk that far (even if it is sixteen miles both ways), but can my little children? My neighbor will take me when he goes; but he expects to get paid, *one way or another*. I bet you know my neighbor. He is that large man who spends his time at the gas station, the barbershop, and the corner store complaining about the government spending money on the immoral mothers of illegitimate children.

Poverty is an acid that drips on pride until all pride is worn away. Poverty is a chisel that chips on honor until honor is worn away. Some of you say that you would do *something* in my situation, and maybe you would, for the first week or the first month, but for year after year after year?

Even the poor can dream. A dream of a time when there is money. Money for the right kinds of food, for worm medicine, for iron pills, for toothbrushes, for hand cream, for a hammer and nails and a bit of screening, for a shovel, for a bit of paint, for some sheeting, for needles and thread. Money to pay *in money* for a trip to town. And, oh, money for hot water and money for soap. A dream of when asking for help does not eat away the last bit of pride. When the office you visit is as nice as the offices of other governmental agencies, when there are enough workers to help you quickly, when workers do not quit in defeat and despair. When you have to tell your story to only one person, and that person can send you for other help and you don't have to prove your poverty over and over and over again.

I have come out of my despair to tell you this. Remember I did not come from another place or another time. Others like me are all around you. Look at us with an angry heart, anger that will help you help me. Anger that will let you tell of me. The poor are always silent. Can you be silent too?

SEQUENCE
2

CONVERSATIONS: ENGAGING THE IDEAS OF OTHERS

Introduction

Conversations: Engaging the Ideas of Others.

Much of the writing that you'll do in college is connected to texts produced by people who have ideas about the same topic on which you're working. Academic writing is often thought of as part of a conversation, because of the way writers and researchers build from, disagree with, and respond to each others' work. The readings in Sequence 2 provide examples of how to effectively engage in these conversations through summary, analysis, synthesis, and interpretation of other people's research and ideas in relation to a writer's own project.

The sequence of writing assignments will guide you through a process of learning to locate and use texts that are related to a particular concept or theme. Working with course readings, you will practice thinking about the rhetorical elements of writing, and you'll investigate how rhetoric works to shape your audience's understanding of your topic. For example, Andrew Delbanco's essay "Scandals of Higher Education," is a review essay that summarizes, synthesizes and discusses the ideas of several authors whose books he evaluates. Gerald Graff's essay on "Deborah Meier's Progressive Traditionalism" focuses specifically on the ideas of this well-known educator and unpacks the impact that Meier's work may have on educational policy. And Beverly Daniel Tatum's essay on 'The Complexity of Identity," surveys research about identity construction in order to provide a foundation for her own research about identity.

Getting CLUED in: Library Assignment #1!

WELCOME TO THE UW-MADISON CAMPUS LIBRARIES! AS PART OF THE LIBRARY MODULE OF YOUR COMMUNICATION REQUIREMENT COURSE, YOUR FIRST ASSIGNMENT IS TO COMPLETE CLUE, OUR CAMPUS LIBRARY USER EDUCATION TUTORIAL.

What is CLUE?

- CLUE is a **Web-based, multimedia tutorial** that contains five instructional modules.

- CLUE will orient you to our campus library system and the **resources and services** available to you. It also will help you learn the **skills** you will need to find books and journal articles online and in our libraries.

- After you complete CLUE, your class will be coming over to the library for a library class session during which you will be doing a series of exercises that build on what you've learned in CLUE.

- CLUE also includes three quizzes which are embedded within the modules. You will need to print out your scores from these three quizzes and turn them in to your instructor in order to get credit for completing CLUE.

How long does it take to do CLUE?

CLUE usually takes between 40 minutes to an hour to complete. But you do NOT need to do the whole thing in one sitting. CLUE covers a lot of important information that you will need to know in order to complete most of your major college assignments, so give yourself enough time to work through the whole tutorial.

Where do I go to use CLUE?

- CLUE is available at **http://clue.library.wisc.edu/**

- In order to print your quiz scores, you will need to do CLUE on a PC. In order to run CLUE you also will need the following:

  ✓ A PC running Internet Explorer 5+ or Mozilla Firefox

  ✓ Macromedia Flash player version 6+

  ✓ Campus network or other **high speed bandwidth** such as DSL, cable modem, etc.

  ✓ Sound turned on (speakers or headphones)

  ✓ Printer

If you are having trouble running CLUE on your computer, go to any of the DoIT computer labs: www.doit.wisc.edu/computerlabs/labs.asp

- You can access CLUE in any of the DoIT computer labs (InfoLabs), including the ARCH InfoLabs in the residence halls.

If I do CLUE in an InfoLab, what should I bring?

✓ A set of **headphones**. If you don't own headphones, you can check out a set at: College Library's Computer and Media Center, Steenbock Library's Microcomputer Lab, or the Circulation Desk on the 2nd floor of Wendt Library.

✓ A **debit card** (a.k.a. copy card or print card) to print off your scores from the quizzes.

If you run into any problems, ask an InfoLab consultant for help.

What if I have questions about CLUE?

- If you have questions about any of the resources or skills described in CLUE, there is an option in CLUE that enables you to contact us by email with your questions. Librarians in the reference areas of any of our campus libraries also will be glad to help you. You also can get your questions answered by talking with librarians via IM or chat. Just go to http://www.library.wisc.edu/ask/ .

- If you have questions about getting into CLUE or run into technical difficulties using it, you can email us at cluehelp@library.wisc.edu or, if you're in a campus InfoLab, ask the lab consultant for help.

Tips for using CLUE:

- Don't forget to print off your scores for the three quizzes and to turn those in to your instructor for credit.

- When you come to the library for the class session that is a follow-up to CLUE, the assumption will be that you've spent enough time doing CLUE to have a basic understanding of the resources and skills it covers. The class exercises will build on what you've learned. So give yourself time to actually learn the skills CLUE covers.

UW-Madison Libraries, Rev 6/14/08

Characteristics of Popular and Scholarly Articles

Popular Articles

- Report current events, entertain, or summarize research of general interest

- Their intended audience is the general public

- The authors are often journalists or general writers

- The authors are often unnamed

- Usually include the following characteristics:

  - short (under 5 pages)

  - photographs and advertisements

  - no citations (sources)

  - everyday language

  - not peer reviewed* or refereed

Scholarly Articles

- Report the results of research or analytical studies

- Their intended audience includes scholars, researchers, and students in a particular field of study

- The authors are researchers and experts in their field

- The authors are <u>always</u> named

- Usually include the following characteristics:

  - Long (5+ pages; frequently shorter in the sciences)

  - describe their research methodology

  - citations

  - technical or specialized language

  - often peer reviewed* or refereed

---

* peer reviewed articles are those that have been accepted for publication in a journal by a panel of recognized experts in a specific field of study.

How Can I Tell If an Article is Popular or Scholarly?

Use This Checklist!

	Popular Articles	Scholarly Articles
Title of Article:	Often uses everyday or catchy language	Often uses technical and/or scholarly language
Title of Publication:	Title is one you can buy in the magazine rack of a drugstore or newsstand	Title suggests the journal is not written for the general public but for professionals in a particular field of study
Name of the Author(s):	Often not included	Included
Length of the Article:	Relatively short (often less than 5 pages)	Substantial length (5+ pages); frequently shorter in the sciences
Research Results:	Not included	Can include charts, graphs, diagrams, etc.
Bibliography:	Not included usually	Included usually

University of Wisconsin-Madison
Library & Information Literacy Instruction Office
443D Memorial Library

(wp\comcore\script\popvsscholhandoutfin-08b)06-08

How to Find Information on Your Research Topic in Journal Databases

Rev. 3-26-08

STEP 1 Identify the Information You Want to Find

- Write a persuasive argument that your research will defend

OR

- Write a question that your research will answer

STEP 2 Choose One or More Databases to Use for Your Topic
(e.g., Academic Search)

STEP 3 Create a Search

- Think of words that best describe the subject of your search
- Use **AND** between different concepts (e.g., prevention **AND** disease)
- Use **OR** between words that describe one concept (e.g., Severe Acute Respiratory Syndrome **OR** SARS)

STEP 4   Select Relevant Articles

- Select articles that are closely related to your topic

- Keep track of the citations (use RefWorks or email)

STEP 5   Locate the Journal Articles

- Click on the Full Text-HTML or Full Text-PDF link in an article record

- Click on the Find It button, to try to find the full text of an article in another database

- Click on the MadCat Catalog link (in the Find It menu box)

    1. Write down the name of the library and the call number of an item (from MadCat)

    2. Write down the citation (article) information from the Find It menu

        - Use what you have written to find the item on the shelf (use that library's stack guide to help you find the correct shelf)

        - Use what you have written to locate the article within a volume

Scandals of Higher Education

Andrew Delbanco

On the Tuesday before last Thanksgiving, *The Harvard Crimson* ran a protest article by a sophomore majoring in economics. His cause was the abolition of classes for the whole of Thanksgiving week. Since few students like to stick around past the weekend before the holiday, he wrote, Harvard ought to follow Yale in ending its "anti-family-friendly policy" of remaining officially in session through Wednesday. It did not occur to him that making a round-trip home shortly before leaving campus again for Christmas break might pose a financial hardship for some of his classmates.[1]

The facts bear him out. Ninety percent of Harvard students come from families earning more than the median national income of $55,000, and Harvard's dean of admissions was quoted in the *Crimson* a few months earlier defining "middle-income" Harvard families as those earning between $110,000 and $200,000. For these students, and certainly for their many wealthier classmates, it should be no problem to fly home, or, better yet, to hop over to Cancun or Barbados.

It is hardly surprising that lots of rich kids go to America's richest colleges. It has always been so. But today's students are richer on average than their predecessors. Between the mid-1970s and mid-1990s, in a sample of eleven prestigious colleges, the percentage of students from families in the bottom quartile of national family income remained roughly steady—around 10 percent. During the same period the percentage of students from the top quartile rose sharply, from a little more than one third to fully half. If the upscale shops and restaurants near campus are any indication, the trend has continued if not accelerated. And if the sample is broadened to include the top 150 colleges, the percentage of students from the bottom quartile drops to 3 percent.[2] In short, there are very few poor students at America's top colleges, and a large and growing number of rich ones.

All this may seem at odds with the stated commitment of Ivy League and other elite colleges to the high-sounding principle of "need-blind" admissions. To be "need-blind" means to take no account of a candidate's ability to pay in deciding the case for admission. And since this policy is usually accompanied by a pledge to provide sufficient scholarship funds to admitted applicants who cannot afford the full cost (around $45,000 in the Ivy League today), it is an expensive policy. It depends on a system of discount pricing by which students paying the published tuition and fees subsidize those who cannot pay, and it requires large institutional investments to sustain the scholarship fund.

These are worthy commitments—a residual form of redistributive liberalism in a society broadly hostile to liberalism. Yet as a matter of practice, "need-blind" is a slogan that does not mean much except in relation to the needs of the applicant pool. If most applicants come from places like Greenwich or Grosse Point, a college can be "need-blind" without having to dispense much aid.

What explains the scarcity of low-income students at America's selective colleges? The short answer is that very few apply. As William Bowen, Martin Kurzweil, and Eugene Tobin write in their book *Equity and Excellence in American Higher Education*, students from low-income families tend early in life to fall behind in "cognitive skills, motivation, expectations...and practical knowledge about the college admissions process."[3] Most lose hope of attending a top college long before the competition formally begins.

The causes and consequences of these dispiriting facts are complex, and the cost to society—moral and material—is high. There is moral cost in the shortfall between the professed ideal of equal opportunity and the reality of rising inequality. As for the material cost, "there has never been reason to believe that all outstanding candidates will be able to pay whatever fees are charged without help," as Bowen and his colleagues put it, and "society at large needs all the trained talent it can marshal."

Our richest colleges could and should do a better job of recruiting needy students, which would require spending more money on the effort to find and support them. They could cut back on lounges in the library and luxuries in the dorms—features of college life designed to please coddled students and attract more of the same. They could demand more from faculty and reward coaches and administrators less lavishly. And just as they scout for athletes across the nation and the world, they could hire more admissions professionals and assign them to inner-city and rural schools.

In the meantime, private philanthropies such as the New York Times Scholarship Program have intervened by identifying public school students "who have overcome exceptional hardship to achieve excellence," providing them with partial scholarships, mentoring, summer employment, and help with the admissions process. A few well-endowed or well-intentioned colleges and universities—among them, Amherst, Harvard, the University of North Carolina and the University of Virginia and, most recently, Princeton—have also made a start toward restoring some equity to the process.[4] The young president of Amherst College, Anthony Marx, is leading the effort to recruit aggressively from schools in poor neighborhoods, and Amherst is also seeking outstanding transfer students from local community colleges.[5] Other colleges have terminated their early admission programs, which work in favor of applicants from private and affluent suburban schools, while still others have replaced loans with grants for students from the lowest income bracket.[6] Bowen, former president of Princeton and of the Andrew W. Mellon Foundation, wants selective colleges to "put a thumb on the scale" to give explicit advantage to candidates from economically deprived backgrounds—candidates, that is, who have already overcome long odds to "get into the credible applicant pool."[7] He is calling, in effect, for an affirmative action program for the poor.

While these proposals are being debated by presidents and trustees—at least one hopes they are debating them—an odor of hypocrisy has gathered in the gap between academic rhetoric and academic reality. The American university tends to be described these days by foe and friend alike as the Alamo of the left—a last fortress for liberal holdouts in a society that has pretty much routed liberals from politics and public life. But how persuasive are testimonials of devotion to equity and democracy when they come from institutions that are usually beyond the reach of anyone without lots of money?

This question is taken up in a number of recent books about universities written in a spirit of sharp chastisement. Among them, Daniel Golden's *The Price of Admission: How America's Ruling Class Buys Its Way into Elite Colleges—and Who Gets Left Outside the Gates* is the angriest.[8] It exemplifies Bowen's point that

> the sense of democratic legitimacy is undermined if people believe that the rich are admitted to selective colleges and universities regardless of merit while able and deserving candidates from more modest backgrounds are turned away.

That is exactly what Golden, who writes about education for *The Wall Street Journal*, believes. To him, the odor of hypocrisy has become a stench. He thinks that elite universities make "room for the unexceptional rich" by turning "away brighter, upwardly mobile applicants" in a process that amounts to "affirmative action for rich white people."

To make his case, he has assembled an anthology of sordid stories intended to show how the rich rig the system to get what they want. It all reminds me of a story I have on good authority about a meeting at a New York City private school of high school seniors with their college counselor. The counselor, trying to help them prepare for their college interviews, asked what they would say about what special contribution they would bring to the college of their choice. "I'm very outgoing," said one. "I'm passionate about community service," said another. The discussion took an unexpected twist when one young man said, simply, "a library." "What do you mean, a library?" asked the counselor, a little taken aback. "Well, my dad said he'd give a library to whatever school I want to go to." Golden's book amounts to the charge that colleges are lining up to take Dad up on his offer.

He names names. Duke University comes off especially badly, followed by Brown, Harvard, and other Ivies. He also names a few recipients of these schools' favor—celebrities, politicians, investment bankers, venture capitalists who have been generous to their alma mater; all of them, according to Golden, get the quid pro quo of preferential treatment for their children or even the children of friends. Some cases are egregious, as when a command is handed down from the development office to the admissions office to accept a patently weak candidate.

But such commands are often refused, and though it is true that they are occasionally obeyed, it is also true that private colleges have a legitimate interest in securing a donor base of loyal alumni, which is essential to their fund-raising for, among other things, financial aid to help needy students. In view of the vast numbers of applications now flooding into the top schools (over 20,000 is no longer exceptional), it is more difficult than ever for the child of an alumnus or otherwise privileged family to get in.

At Yale, for instance, as late as the 1960s, more than two thirds of alumni sons who applied were accepted. Since then, that figure has dropped by over half, and all such institutions are now engaged in ferocious competition for bright and driven students.[9] Golden takes note of this trend, but only implicitly, by enumerating the high test scores and high school class ranks of most students today at places like Yale. In light of that information his cases of putative influence-peddling look strikingly anomalous. Rather than proving that "elites [are] mastering the art of perpetuating themselves," he has shown, in fact, how much harder it has become for families with old school ties, even the very rich, to get their children into colleges where they once would have walked in.

The Price of Admission is a muckraking morality tale with many villains and few heroes. One of the few is the California Institute of Technology, which "comes closer," Golden says, "than any other major American university to admitting its student body purely on academic merit."[10] Caltech is a great institution and its admissions standards are impressively pure. But its strong focus on training young scientists can hardly serve as a model for institutions with a broader mission.

As Golden himself points out, Caltech enrolled exactly one African-American student in its Class of 2008, and only 30 percent of its students are women. Its admissions officers, by their own account, find it painfully necessary to reject candidates who have passion and talent but who, having attended inferior high schools, lack the advanced placement courses and test scores proving strong science preparation. One purpose of a more flexible admissions policy is to give such students with "holes in the transcript" a chance—and while Caltech may not be the right place for them, it does not follow that they should be excluded from all highly selective institutions.

Moreover, if applicants to top colleges were admitted on the basis of grades and tests alone, this would simply ensure that they come overwhelmingly from prosperous families—precisely what Golden is against—since the close correlation of test scores and family income is well documented.[11] Golden is right that our current college admissions system has serious problems, but fixing it by making tests and grades count for even more than they already do is not the right fix.

Walter Benn Michaels, an English professor at the University of Illinois, is also angry, but he has a different view of where the problem begins. He directs his anger not so much at the admissions or development office as at the entire culture of academia, which, in his view, has settled somewhere between insouciance and hypocrisy with regard to the widening class divide. "Poor people," he writes in *The Trouble with Diversity: How We Learned to Love Identity and Ignore Inequality*,

> are an endangered species in elite universities not because the universities put quotas on them...and not even because they can't afford to go to them (Harvard will lend you or even give you the money you need to go there) but because they can't get into them.

This is basically true, as Bowen and his colleagues demonstrate. What Michaels adds to the discussion is the idea that many academic liberals have been deceiving themselves about this uncomfortable truth while—unwittingly, perhaps—abetting it.

What he means is that the academic left (which he tartly calls the "supposed left") expends its energy rallying against such phantom enemies as racism and sexism—erstwhile evils that he believes barely exist today, at least not in the narrow social stratum from which college students come. As a result, "progressive politics" too often "consists of disapproving of bad things that happened a long time ago." But Michaels does not stop at chiding the "supposed left" for indulging in nostalgia for battles already won. He thinks that by obscuring the real issue—the class divide—that persists behind all the smoke and noise over "diversity," the academic left has become complicit with the broader political right in rewarding the rich and penalizing the poor.

Michaels is fed up with the mantra of diversity, and it is hard to blame him. In the past, one obstacle that kept minority students out of college was patent racism—the asserted association between external physical characteristics (skin color, facial features, body type) and inherent mental capacities or tendencies.[12] Today, however, this kind of pseudoscience has been discredited, and the word "race" tends to be employed as a synonym for culture—an equivalence based on the dubious, or at least imperfect, premise that a person's ancestry tells us something important about how that person experiences the world. The problem with "this way of thinking about culture instead of race," Michaels says, "is that it just takes the old practice of racial stereotyping and renovates it in the form of cultural stereotyping."[13] People of African ancestry are expected to prefer blues to Brahms. People of Asian ancestry are lumped together in the category "Asian-American" even though they might identify themselves primarily as Laotians or Christians. In any event, they are supposed to prefer engineering to poetry.

Michaels argues that nothing much has changed by substituting the idea of particular cultures for the discredited idea of race. For pragmatic as well as analytical reasons, he wants the left to forget about this kind of diversity, whether we call it racial or cultural ("diversity, like gout, is a rich people's problem"), and focus instead on poverty. A satirical verse (quoted in another recent book by another English professor, Michael Berubé of Pennsylvania State University) nicely captures Michaels's point. It might be called the Song of the Abject Affluent, and a lot of people at elite colleges are singing it:

> I'm sorry for what my people did to your people
> It was a nasty job
> Please note the change of attitude
> On the bumper of my Saab.[14]

Quite apart from the question of who "my people" and "your people" are at a time when more and more Americans claim multiple racial descent, this mixture of guilt and pride is mostly for show, just like the car.

Along with racism, the other excoriated enemy of the academic left is sexism, as in the controversy provoked by former Harvard president Lawrence Summers, who posed the question of whether men and women may have different innate intellectual capacities. Michaels regards sexism, too, as a convenient phantom at a time when half the students in the Ivy League, four presidents (soon to include Summers's successor, the distinguished historian Drew Gilpin Faust), and an increasing percentage of faculty are women. In the transformed world of what was once an old boys club, "feminism," he writes, "is what you appeal to when you want to make it sound as if the women of Wall Street and the women of Wal-Mart are both victims of sexism." In fact, few of the former are victims of sexism and many of the latter are victims, first and foremost, of poverty. In short, Michaels thinks the academic left willfully misses the point—that the big obstacle to equal opportunity is not race or gender, but class.

Michaels is right to insist that in the triumvirate of social evils so often invoked in academic life—race, class, and gender—the middle term has all but dropped out of the discussion. But in trying to bring it back, he is too quick to dismiss the other two. He writes, for example, that "it's their lack of family wealth, not color of their skin, that disproportionately keeps blacks out of elite colleges." This is too pat. It fails to acknowledge the lingering and subtly pernicious effects of race not so much on institutional policy as on individual experience. Difficult as it is for students from poor families to reach and succeed in the privileged culture of elite colleges, it is all the more so for those who must cross a racial as well as a class divide. Yet he insists that "affirmative action...solves a problem that no longer exists." Bowen differs, wanting class-based admissions preferences to be a supplement, not a substitute, for race-based preferences.[15]

As for the mistreatment and disadvantages faced by women, Michaels argues that such problems as domestic abuse are overwhelmingly, if not exclusively, problems for poor women. Here too he overstates the case. He does not acknowledge the vestiges of male domination in university life, especially in certain scientific fields that have been slow to recruit and promote qualified women. Nor does he take into account how the demands of child care, for instance, can hold back even affluent women from professional advancement.[16]

Still, his main point is a fair one: campus liberals far prefer the soft issues of racial and gender diversity to such hard issues as the effect on American working families of cheap foreign labor or the gross inequities of a public school system funded by local property taxes, or, closer to home, the failure of their own institutions to recruit and support more talented students with no money. I have met very few faculty members who, even as they agitate for far-flung social causes, care to look closely at the admissions policies of their own institutions.[17]

Michaels has written a bracing polemic that should quicken the debate over what diversity really means, or should mean, in academia and beyond. He can be strident and even snide. But at his best, he recalls Irving Howe's exasperation with the "puerile" New Left as a movement of privileged children marching under the banner of revolution while the traditional constituency of the Old Left—people trying to make a decent life against the odds—watched the parade go by.

Whatever their differences of tone and authority, Bowen, Golden, and Michaels agree that our colleges and universities are following rather than resisting the national trend toward a widening disparity between rich and poor. This is true not only in how colleges admit their students, but in their internal structure (presidential compensation has crossed the million-dollar threshold in several cases), and in the wealth of leading institutions relative to their competitors (the annual return on Harvard's $30 billion endowment now exceeds the entire endowment of some of its Ivy League rivals).

The ideal—perhaps a better word is imaginary—university about which Harvard's great nineteenth-century president Charles W. Eliot remarked that "luxury and learning are ill bed fellows" is dying if not extinct. It has given way to a sprawling and diffuse new entity no longer adequately described by the term coined by University of California president Clark Kerr nearly fifty years ago, when he characterized his "multiversity" as "a series of individual faculty entrepreneurs held together by a common grievance over parking."[18] The multiversity has now become what the entrepreneurial president of Arizona State University, Michael Crow, calls a Comprehensive Knowledge Enterprise, or CKE—a network of corporations, governments, and universities in which the local campus is less and less central to the research, consulting, and international marketing that bring in money and prestige. To many faculty members, parking near the campus now matters less than airport access.

Meanwhile, new universities are emerging throughout the world, especially in China, and American institutions are expanding fiscally and physically in order to meet the challenge—from Harvard (which has acquired 250 acres across the Charles River in Allston) and Columbia (which is buying up a sparsely populated district in northern Manhattan) and the major state universities (a vast new "Centennial Campus" is under construction at North Carolina State University) to relatively small institutions like the University of Rochester and the University of California at Santa Cruz, once an outpost of post-Sixties counterculture.

Even in the richest institutions, the time-proven structures of liberal education—small-class discussion, personal mentors—are being distended if not destroyed, and the incentives of money and renown are pushing faculty toward research and away from teaching. In the shadow of all this growth and proliferation, books about college admissions properly put their emphasis on the question of where and how these institutions get their students; but it is also important to ask what happens to the students once they get in, no matter where they come from.

One thing that happens, especially at the most prestigious colleges, is that students acquire a strong sense of self-satisfaction. (Michaels speculates that one side effect of affirmative action is to reinforce the conviction of predominantly affluent white students "that they didn't get in just because they were white.") Former president Neil Rudenstine used to greet Harvard freshmen by telling them that, as nervous and unworthy as they might feel during their first days at college, Harvard would send them into the world proud and confident and ready for anyone and anything. Yet even successful applicants can be driven into anxiety and depression by the entire process of applying, which turns the high school years into a frantic scramble for distinction. And, in a terrible paradox, as our top colleges turn away more and more gifted students—a demographic fact that necessarily leaves many talented students outside the Ivy gates—the frenzy of competition makes the prize of admission worth more and more, leaving rejected applicants feeling wounded and unfit.

It will be difficult to adjust this system toward greater sanity and equity. As a start, it would help to recognize that the history of college admissions is a stark illustration of the law of unintended consequences. Today's system of personal essays, interviews, and recommendations, meant to ensure a diversity of temperaments and interests as well as racial and ethnic origins among admitted students, was invented early in the twentieth century for precisely the opposite reason: to detect and limit applicants with undesirable traits, notably Jewishness.[19] When the system of standardized testing was imposed a half-century ago it was originally intended to break the lock that children of privilege had on the elite colleges and to identify the best minds throughout the nation at a time when, to meet the Soviet threat, top American universities were transforming themselves from finishing schools for the rich into training schools for the bright.[20] Today, that system of standardized testing has become a tool of the wealthy, who have many means—expensive schools, private SAT tutors—to inflate the test scores of their children.

How much these ironies and contradictions are being discussed among presidents and trustees in their closed boardrooms is hard to say. Golden, Michaels, and even Bowen cannot tell us. One place to look for evidence of concern is in the steady stream of books by university presidents (or ex-presidents) and deans, of which examples have lately come from the present and former presidents of Duke, Yale, Princeton, Michigan, Wesleyan, Emory, and other leading universities. Typically collections of reworked speeches, such books tend to be hampered and cautious lest anything be said to upset the people—trustees, alumni, faculty, students, the impressionable public—whom presidents have to keep satisfied.[21]

There is very little about admissions in these books, but here and there one gets hints of discord or even of clashing passions. Harry Lewis, for instance, former dean of Harvard College (he was fired by Lawrence Summers), writes lyrically about college athletes as young prodigies living alongside their schoolmates "in a glorious parallel universe...detached from the banality of ordinary life," while Bowen, deploying damning statistics that show inferior academic performance by recruited athletes, believes that "college sports in their current form represent a distinct threat to academic values and educational excellence."[22] William Chace, former president of Wesleyan and Emory, has even published an argument with his former self—an Op-Ed piece in *The New York Times* billed as "the honest talk" he always wanted to deliver to incoming freshmen but never had the nerve to give. He writes, for example, that

> more than half of the freshmen at selective colleges, public and private, come from the highest-earning quarter of households. Tell me the ZIP code and I'll tell you what kind of college a high-school graduate most likely attends.[23]

The most substantive of the presidential books is *Our Underachieving Colleges: A Candid Look at How Much Students Learn and Why They Should be Learning More*, by Derek Bok, president of Harvard from 1971 to 1991 and currently its interim president. Bok paints a picture of colleges that, if not dysfunctional, are operating far below capacity. He questions the coherence and purpose of departmental majors, describes programs of study abroad as little more than recreational excursions, criticizes lecturers for their indifference to whether students learn anything, and, in general, holds faculty accountable for ignoring research about which teaching methods are most effective. Many of his points are cogent and timely, but when he tries to say what the fundamental aim of higher education ought to be, the best he can do is invoke today's reigning banality—"Critical Thinking"—a term that seems to mean something like the ability to think through difficult problems. There is nothing wrong with that goal, but it is a decidedly instrumental one that conceives of students as problem-solvers-in-training to be deployed into a society that needs them.

None of these books—whether by outside critics or inside administrators—has much to say about the interior lives of young people eager for intellectual and aesthetic excitement, learning to examine old ideas in light of new imperatives. If—as Bowen, Golden, and Michaels variously insist—it is a scandal that so few disadvantaged students are able to attend our most advantageous colleges, it is also urgent, in the words (the italics are his) of Donald Levine, former dean of the college at the University of Chicago, to notice that *the scandal of higher education in our time is that so little attention gets paid, in institutions that claim to provide an education, to what it is that college educators claim to be providing.*

In *Powers of the Mind: The Reinvention of Liberal Learning in America*, Levine has written a fascinating history of curricular debates at the University of Chicago, reaching back to its founding more than a century ago. It is a story of serious teachers responding to continuous change in the world and in their particular academic disciplines while always keeping in view the enduring goal of liberal education, which Levine succinctly calls "the cultivation of human powers." To reach this end requires first of all the recognition that it is unending, in the sense that "the purpose of school education," as John Dewey put it, "is to insure the continuance of education by organizing the powers that insure growth." It requires the student to become informed about past and present—to learn, that is, something substantial about history, science, and contemporary societies in order to bring that knowledge to bear on unforeseeable challenges of the future. It requires teachers and students collaboratively to develop (as Bok recommends) analytic problem-solving abilities, but also, as the great Chicago humanist Richard McKeon wrote, to study literature and the arts in order to cultivate "appreciation of artistic, cultural, and intellectual values, as opposed to the random associated reflections which frequently... pass for appreciation." And it requires the university to make clear to its students what it expects while expecting its faculty to work as educators as well as researchers.

Levine shows how one great research university has struggled to sustain and refresh these standards and goals. He describes how faculty from different disciplines have collaborated on "Big Problems" courses on themes such as "Evil," or "Language and Globalization." He discusses the University of Chicago's brief experiment with awarding degrees only upon successful completion of difficult comprehensive examinations rather than merely for the accumulation of course credits. And he describes how one famous Chicago professor, the biologist Joseph Schwab, in a course dealing with philosophical texts eschewed "class discussions where voice flits around the room while impulses of exhibitionism, excitement, or puzzlement jump from one student to another" in favor of "structured discussion" by putting "one student in the hot seat for a while and working that person as thoroughly and creatively as possible" before moving on to another.

In contemporary universities, this kind of intimate and intense education is threatened and already rare. One Chicago alumnus, Lee Shulman, president of the Carnegie Foundation for the Advancement of Teaching, recalls that sitting in Schwab's classes "fostered clammy hands, damp foreheads, and an ever-attentive demeanor." Today, a student with those symptoms would probably drop the class for fear of a poor grade, and the teacher would risk a poor score on the end-of-semester evaluations.[24] Moreover, if any "general education" program is to succeed, professors need to be tough not only on their students but on themselves—willing to plunge into subjects and texts with which they may not have engaged since they themselves were students, or which they may never have encountered at all.

Unfortunately, most incentives and rewards, especially in prestigious institutions, line up today against this kind of teaching and learning. Large classes are far more cost-efficient than small ones. An increasingly specialized faculty is likely to give only sporadic attention to general education, and is unlikely to reach consensus about what it should be. Even for those who care, spending time on undergraduate teaching is ill-advised in a world where publication and research are the routes to promotion and higher pay. For students, taking intellectual chances is risky as they compete for places in professional schools that regard grades as all-important. As Harvard's former dean Harry Lewis sums up the matter:

> Universities affect horror when students attend college in the hope of becoming financially successful, but they offer students neither a coherent view of the point of college education nor any guidance on how they might discover for themselves some larger purpose in life.

It is certainly a good thing that fresh attention is being paid in books such as Bowen's, Golden's, and Michaels's to the question of whom education is for. But there remains the fundamental question of what it is for and what it should consist of. One way to bring these questions together would be to ask how well our colleges reflect our best democratic traditions, in which individuals are not assessed by any group affiliation but are treated, regardless of their origins, as independent beings capable of responsible freedom.

Opening wider the admissions doors is a necessary step toward furthering that end, but it is by no means a sufficient one. Colleges will fulfill their responsibilities only when they confront the question of what students should learn—a question that most administrators, compilers of rank lists, and authors of books on higher education prefer to avoid.

Notes

1. Adam A. Solomon, "Give Us a Break: Harvard Students Should Not Have Class During Thanksgiving Week," *The Harvard Crimson*, November 21, 2006.

2. The figures are from William G. Bowen, Martin A. Kurzweil, and Eugene M. Tobin, *Equity and Excellence in American Higher Education*. The eleven institutions are Barnard, Columbia, Oberlin, Penn State, Princeton, Smith, Swarthmore, the University of Pennsylvania, Wellesley, Williams, and Yale. When the sample is broadened to include the "top 146 colleges," as reported in *The Chronicle of Higher Education* (Karin Fischer, "Elite Colleges Lag in Serving the Needy," May 12, 2006), the figure falls to 3 percent. Bowen also reports that only 3 percent of students at nineteen selective colleges and leading state universities are the first to attend college from a low-income family (p. 163).

3. For a devastating account of how poor children fall behind early in life, see Betty Hart and Todd R. Risley, "The Early Catastrophe: The 30 Million Word Gap by Age 3," *American Educator*, Spring 2003.

4. In January 2007, Princeton announced a one-year freeze on the price of tuition—a decision likely to prove more symbolic than substantive, since it was accompanied by a nearly 20 percent increase in the cost of lodging and board. And while this decision will make Princeton slightly more affordable for its (predominantly affluent) students, it may have a regressive effect at less wealthy institutions that feel compelled to match it. Tuition revenue is a main source of subsidy for students on financial aid, and freezing tuition therefore puts more demand on endowment, which is often restricted for use for other purposes. (See Scott Jaschik, "Princeton Freezes Tuition," InsideHigherEd.com, January 22, 2007, and David W. Breneman, "What Princeton Tuition Freeze Means— and Doesn't Mean," InsideHigherEd.com, January 29, 2007.)

5. See "Campus Revolutionary," *Business Week*, February 27, 2006. Mr. Marx's admirable initiative carries daunting costs (he estimates that about $1 million of endowment is required to support each student on full scholarship) and, ironically enough, risks hurting the college's reputation. By recruiting needy students—who are likely to have lower SAT scores—Amherst may see its ranking drop in such widely read publications as *U.S. News and World Report*.

6. Early admissions programs favor students from private or affluent suburban schools with skilled college counselors who lobby for their candidates at top colleges; and since applying early usually requires a commitment to attend if admitted, applicants cannot compare financial aid offers from multiple colleges—an essential process for needy students. Colleges have tended to deny that early admissions favors the wealthy, but when Harvard's interim president Derek Bok announced that Harvard would terminate its early admissions program, he conceded that "the existing process has been shown to advantage those who are already advantaged." See Alan Finder and Karen W. Arenson, "Harvard Ends Early Admission, Citing Barrier to Disadvantaged," *The New York Times*, September 12, 2006.

7. Based on numerical estimates of the advantages currently enjoyed (in descending order) by recruited athletes, racial minorities, early admission candidates, and "legacies" (children of alumni), Bowen proposes to give low-income applicants a boost roughly comparable to that of legacies.

8. I should say that Golden was a student of mine at Harvard nearly thirty years ago, and one whom I respected and admired.

9. This rate of acceptance still represents nearly triple the rate for nonlegacy candidates. Since children of Yale alumni tend to be well prepared academically, comparison with the whole applicant pool may be misleading.

10. Golden also admires Cooper Union in New York City, a distinguished art school that charges no tuition, and Berea College in the Appalachian region of Kentucky, a liberal arts college founded by an abolitionist minister that also charges no tuition and restricts admissions to students who are the first in their families to attend college. Berea defrays some of the cost by requiring students to work in campus maintenance and management operations. Both of these schools are excellent institutions but their admissions practices and distinctive missions would be difficult if not impossible for other institutions to emulate.

11. In 2004, for example, students from families earning over $100,000 had an average combined SAT score of 1115, while students from families earning between $30,000 and $40,000 had a combined score of 960. See Bowen et al. *Equality and Excellence in Higher Education*, p. 82, and Walter Benn Michaels, *The Trouble With Diversity*, p. 98.

12. The history of admissions quotas for Jews, for instance, who were once regarded as a distinctive race, is narrated in telling detail in Jerome Karabel, *The Chosen: The Hidden History of Admission and Exclusion at Harvard, Yale, and Princeton* (Houghton Mifflin, 2005). Golden cites anecdotal evidence and disparities in test scores to argue that at elite private colleges a quota system now exists for students of Asian ancestry, whom he calls the "New Jews."

13. Michaels traced the history of this transition from race to culture in an earlier book, *Our America: Nativism, Modernism, and Pluralism* (Duke University Press, 1995). In the present book, he says nothing about the rollback of affirmative action by recent referendums in states such as California and Michigan banning the consideration of race in admissions to public universities. While discounting the notion, suggested by Golden, that elite universities impose limits on the number of Asian-Americans they admit, he does not take a position on whether they are subject to de facto quotas.

14. Michael Berubé, *What's Liberal about the Liberal Arts?: Classroom Politics and "Bias" in Higher Education* (Norton, 2006), p. 93.

15. Race does still matter. African-American college students perform less well in college than their SAT scores predict, and "the *degree* of underperformance increases as SAT scores rise." See Douglas S. Massey, Camille Z. Charles, Garvey F. Lundy, and Mary J. Fischer, *The Source of the River: The Social Origins of Freshmen at America's Selective Colleges and Universities* (Princeton University Press, 2003), p. 16. This trend implies a shortfall between aptitude and achievement, for which explanations include "stereotype vulnerability—the disengagement from school work that stems from fears of living up to negative stereotypes of minority intellectual inferiority" (p. 206).

16. Mary Ann Mason and Marc Goulden, in "Marriage and Baby Blues: Re-defining Gender Equity in the Academy," *Annals of the American Academy of Political and Social Science*, Vol. 596 (November, 2004), find little evidence of systematic discrimination against academic women, but they do find a "pattern of low marriage and birth rates" among those who gain tenure, and a high attrition rate among tenure-track women who choose to marry and bear children.

17. Andrew Delbanco, "Where Is the Faculty in the Admissions Debates?," InsideHigherEd.com, October 12, 2006.

18. Eliot is quoted in Deborah L. Rhode, *In Pursuit of Knowledge: Scholars, Status, and Academic Culture* (Stanford University Press, 2006), p. 16; see also Clark Kerr, *The Uses of the University* (1963; Harvard University Press, 1995), p. 15.

19. See Karabel, *The Chosen*, especially Chapters 3 and 4.

20. The story of the SAT is told in Nicholas Lemann, *The Big Test: The Secret History of the American Meritocracy* (Farrar, Straus and Giroux, 1999).

21. In addition to those mentioned at the head of this article, other recent contributions to the genre include Nannerl O. Keohane, *Higher Ground: Ethics and Leadership in the Modern University* (Duke University Press, 2006); *A Larger Sense of Purpose: Higher Education and Society* (Princeton University Press, 2005) by former University of Michigan and Princeton president Harold T. Shapiro; and *The Work of the University* (Yale University Press, 2003), by current Yale president Richard C. Levin.

22. Bowen elaborates his argument in James L. Shulman and William G. Bowen, *The Game of Life: College Sports and Educational Values* (Princeton University Press, 2001).

23. William Chace, "A Little Learning Is an Expensive Thing," *The New York Times*, September 5, 2006. In Chace's academic memoir, *100 Semesters: My Adventures as Student, Professor, and University President, and What I Learned Along the Way* (Princeton University Press, 2006), he chronicles his increasing feeling as an English professor that he was little more than a "museum docent" giving students a tour of the galleries so they would have something elevated to chat about.

24. Recent studies of student evaluations have found that students tend to give good reviews "to instructors who are easy graders or who are good looking," and lesser reviews to women and instructors born outside the United States. The largest such study, at Ohio State University, finds "no correlation between professor evaluations and the learning that is actually taking place." See InsideHigherEd.com, January 29, 2007.

Andrew Delbanco, "Scandals of Higher Education," *The New York Review of Books*, Vol. 54, No. 5, March 29, 2007, pp. 42–47. Reprinted by permission.

Advertising's Fifteen Basic Appeals

Jib Fowles

Emotional Appeals

The nature of effective advertisements was recognized full well by the late media philosopher Marshall McLuhan. In his *Understanding Media*, the first sentence of the section on advertising reads, "The continuous pressure is to create ads more and more in the image of audience motives and desires."

By giving form to people's deep-lying desires, and picturing states of being that individuals privately yearn for, advertisers have the best chance of arresting attention and affecting communication. And that is the immediate goal of advertising: to tug at our psychological shirt sleeves and slow us down long enough for a word or two about whatever is being sold. We glance at a picture of a solitary rancher at work, and "Marlboro" slips into our minds.

Advertisers (I'm using the term as a shorthand for both the products' manufacturers, who bring the ambition and money to the process, and the advertising agencies, who supply the know-how) are ever more compelled to invoke consumers' drives and longings; this is the "continuous pressure" McLuhan refers to. Over the past century, the American marketplace has grown increasingly congested as more and more products have entered into the frenzied competition after the public's dollars. The economies of other nations are quieter than ours since the volume of goods being hawked does not so greatly exceed demand. In some economies, consumer wares are scarce enough that no advertising at all is necessary. But in the United States, we go to the other extreme. In order to stay in business, an advertiser must strive to cut through the considerable commercial hub-bub by any means available—including the emotional appeals that some observers have held to be abhorrent and underhanded.

The use of subconscious appeals is a comment not only on conditions among sellers. As time has gone by, buyers have become stoutly resistant to advertisements. We live in a blizzard of these messages and have learned to turn up our collars and ward off most of them. A study done a few years ago at Harvard University's Graduate School of Business Administration ventured that the average American is exposed to some 500 ads daily from television, newspapers, magazines, radio, billboards, direct mail, and so on. If for no other reason than to preserve one's sanity, a filter must be developed in every mind to lower the number of ads a person is actually aware of—a number this particular study estimated at about seventy-five ads per day. (Of these, only twelve typically produced a reaction—nine positive and three negative, on the average.) To be among the few messages that do manage to gain access to minds, advertisers must be strategic, perhaps even a little underhanded at times.

There are assumptions about personality underlying advertisers' efforts to communicate via emotional appeals, and while these assumptions have stood the test of time, they still deserve to be aired. Human beings, it is presumed, walk around with a variety of unfulfilled urges and motives swirling in the bottom half of their minds. Lusts, ambitions, tendernesses, vulnerabilities—they are constantly bubbling up, seeking resolution. These mental forces energize people, but they are too crude and irregular to be given excessive play in the real world. They must be capped with the competent, sensible behavior that permits individuals to get along well in society. However, this upper layer of mental activity, shot through with caution and rationality, is not receptive to advertising's pitches. Advertisers want to circumvent this shell of consciousness if they can, and latch on to one of the lurching, subconscious drives.

In effect, advertisers over the years have blindly felt their way around the underside of the American psyche, and by trial and error have discovered the softest points of entree, the places where their messages have the greatest likelihood of getting by consumers' defenses. As McLuhan says elsewhere, "Gouging away at the surface of public sales resistance, the ad men are constantly breaking through into the *Alice in Wonderland* territory behind the looking glass, which is the world of subrational impulses and appetites."

An advertisement communicates by making use of a specially selected image (of a supine female, say, or a curly-haired child, or a celebrity) which is designed to stimulate "subrational impulses and desires" even when they are at ebb, even if they are unacknowledged by their possessor. Some few ads have their emotional appeal in the text, but for the greater number by far the appeal is contained in the artwork. This makes sense, since visual communication better suits more primal levels of the brain. If the viewer of an advertisement actually has the importuned motive, and if the appeal is sufficiently well fashioned to call it up, then the person can be hooked. The product in the ad may then appear to take on the semblance of gratification for the summoned motive. Many ads seem to be saying, "If you have this need, then this product will help satisfy it." It is a primitive equation, but not an ineffective one for selling.

Thus, most advertisements appearing in national media can be understood as having two orders of content. The first is the appeal to deep-running drives in the minds of consumers. The second is information regarding the good[s] or service being sold: its name, its manufacturer, its picture, its packaging, its objective attributes, its functions. For example, the reader of a brassiere advertisement sees a partially undraped but blandly unperturbed woman standing in an otherwise commonplace public setting, and may experience certain sensations; the reader also sees the name "Maidenform," a particular brassiere style, and, in tiny print, words about the material, colors, price. Or, the viewer of a television commercial sees a demonstration with four small boxes labelled 650, 650, 650, and 800; something in the viewer's mind catches hold of this, as trivial as thoughtful consideration might reveal it to be. The viewer is also exposed to the name "Anacin," its bottle, and its purpose.

Sometimes there is an apparently logical link between an ad's emotional appeal and its product information. It does not violate common sense that Cadillac automobiles be photographed at country clubs, or that Japan Air Lines be associated with Orientalia. But there is no real need for the linkage to have a bit of reason behind it. Is there anything inherent to the connection between Salem cigarettes and mountains, Coke and a smile, Miller Beer and comradeship? The link being forged in minds between product and appeal is a pre-logical one.

People involved in the advertising industry do not necessarily talk in the terms being used here. They are stationed at the sending end of this communications channel, and may think they are up to any number of things—Unique Selling Propositions, explosive copywriting, the optimal use of demographics or psychographics, ideal media buys, high recall ratings, or whatever. But when attention shifts to the receiving end of the channel, and focuses on the instant of reception, then commentary becomes much more elemental: an advertising message contains something primary and primitive, an emotional appeal, that in effect is the thin end of the wedge, trying to find its way into a mind. Should this occur, the product information comes along behind.

When enough advertisements are examined in this light, it becomes clear that the emotional appeals fall into several distinguishable categories, and that every ad is a variation on one of a limited number of basic appeals. While there may be several ways of classifying these appeals, one particular list of fifteen has proven to be especially valuable.

Advertisements can appeal to:

1. The need for sex

2. The need for affiliation

3. The need to nurture

4. The need for guidance

5. The need to aggress

6. The need to achieve

7. The need to dominate

8. The need for prominence

9. The need for attention

10. The need for autonomy

11. The need to escape

12. The need to feel safe

13. The need for aesthetic sensations

14. The need to satisfy curiosity

15. Physiological needs: food, drink, sleep, etc.

Murray's List

Where does this list of advertising's fifteen basic appeals come from? Several years ago, I was involved in a research project which was to have as one segment an objective analysis of the changing appeals made in post-World War II American advertising. A sample of magazine ads would have their appeals coded into the categories of psychological needs they seemed aimed at. For this content analysis to happen, a complete roster of human motives would have to be found.

The first thing that came to mind was Abraham Maslow's famous four-part hierarchy of needs. But the briefest look at the range of appeals made in advertising was enough to reveal that they are more varied, and more profane, than Maslow had cared to account for. The search led on to the work of psychologist Henry A. Murray, who together with his colleagues at the Harvard Psychological Clinic has constructed a full taxonomy of needs. As described in *Explorations in Personality*, Murray's team had conducted a lengthy series of in-depth interviews with a number of subjects in order to derive from scratch what they felt to be the essential variables of personality. Forty-four variables were distinguished by the Harvard group, of which twenty were motives. The need for achievement ("to overcome obstacles and obtain a high standard") was one, for instance; the need to defer was another; the need to aggress was a third; and so forth.

Murray's list had served as the groundwork for a number of subsequent projects. Perhaps the best-known of these was David C. McClelland's extensive study of the need for achievement, reported in his *The Achieving Society*. In the process of demonstrating that a people's high need for achievement is predictive of later economic growth, McClelland coded achievement imagery and references out of a nation's folklore, songs, legends, and children's tales.

Following McClelland, I too wanted to cull the motivational appeals from a culture's imaginative product—in this case, advertising. To develop categories expressly for this purpose, I took Murray's twenty motives and added to them others he had mentioned in passing in *Explorations in Personality* but not included on the final list. The extended list was tried out on a sample of advertisements, and motives which never seemed to be invoked were dropped. I ended up with eighteen of Murrays' motives, into which 770 print ads were coded. The resulting distribution is included in the 1976 book *Mass Advertising as Social Forecast.*

Since that time, the list of appeals has undergone refinements as a result of using it to analyze television commercials. A few more adjustments stemmed from the efforts of students in my advertising classes to decode appeals; tens of term papers surveying thousands of advertisements have caused some inconsistencies in the list to be hammered out. Fundamentally, though, the list remains the creation of Henry Murray. In developing a comprehensive, parsimonious inventory of human motives, he pinpointed the subsurface mental forces that are the least quiescent and most susceptible to advertising's entreaties.

Fifteen Appeals

1. *Need for sex.* Let's start with sex, because this is the appeal which seems to pop up first whenever the topic of advertising is raised. Whole books have been written about this one alone, to find a large audience of mildly titillated readers. Lately, due to campaigns to sell blue jeans, concern with sex in ads has redoubled.

The fascinating thing is not how much sex there is in advertising, but how little. Contrary to impressions, unambiguous sex is rare in these messages. Some of this surprising observation may be a matter of definition: the Jordache ads with the lithe, blouse-less female astride a similarly clad male is clearly an appeal to the audience's sexual drives, but the same cannot be said about Brooke Shields in the Calvin Klein commercials. Directed at young women and their credit-card carrying mothers, the image of Miss Shields instead invokes the need to be looked at. Buy Calvins and you'll be the center of much attention, just as Brooke is, the ads imply; they do not primarily inveigle their target audience's need for sexual intercourse.

In the content analysis reported in *Mass Advertising as Social Forecast* only two percent of ads were found to pander to this motive. Even *Playboy* ads shy away from sexual appeals: a recent issue contained eighty-three full-page ads, and just four of them (or less than five percent) could be said to have sex on their minds.

The reason this appeal is so little used is that it is too blaring and tends to obliterate the product information. Nudity in advertising has the effect of reducing brand recall. The people who do remember the product may do so because they have been made indignant by the ad; this is not the response most advertisers seek.

To the extent that sexual imagery is used, it conventionally works better on men than women; typically a female figure is offered up to the male reader. A Black Velvet liquor advertisement displays an attractive woman wearing a tight black outfit, recumbent under the legend, "Feel the Velvet." The figure does not have to be horizontal, however, for the appeal to be present as National Airlines revealed in its "Fly me" campaign. Indeed, there does not even have to be a female in the ad; "Flick my Bic" was sufficient to convey the idea to many.

As a rule, though, advertisers have found sex to be a tricky appeal, to be used sparingly. Less controversial and equally fetching are the appeals to our need for affectionate human contact.

2. Need for affiliation. American mythology upholds autonomous individuals, and social statistics suggest that people are ever more going it alone in their lives, yet the high frequency of affiliative appeals in ads belies this. Or maybe it does not: maybe all the images of companionship are compensation for what Americans privately lack. In any case, the need to associate with others is widely invoked in advertising and is probably the most prevalent appeal. All sorts of goods and services are sold by linking them to our unfulfilled desires to be in good company.

According to Henry Murray, the need for affiliation consists of desires "to draw near and enjoyably cooperate or reciprocate with another; to please and win affection of another; to adhere and remain loyal to a friend." The manifestations of this motive can be segmented into several different types of affiliation, beginning with romance.

Courtship may be swifter nowadays, but the desire for pair-bonding is far from satiated. Ads reaching for this need commonly depict a youngish male and female engrossed in each other. The head of the male is usually higher than the female's, even at this late date; she may be sitting or leaning while he is standing. They are not touching in the Smirnoff vodka ads, but obviously there is an intimacy, sometimes frolicsome, between them. The couple does touch for Martell Cognac when "The moment was Martell." For Wind Song perfume they have touched, and "Your Wind Song stays on his mind."

Depending on the audience, the pair does not absolutely have to be young—just together. He gives her a DeBeers diamond, and there is a tear in her laugh lines. She takes Geritol and preserves herself for him. And numbers of consumers, wanting affection too, follow suit.

Warm family feelings are fanned in ads when another generation is added to the pair. Hallmark Cards brings grandparents into the picture, and Johnson and Johnson Baby Powder has Dad, Mom, and baby, all fresh from the bath, encircled in arms and emblazoned with "Share the Feeling." A talc has been fused to familial love.

Friendship is yet another form of affiliation pursued by advertisers. Two women confide and drink Maxwell House coffee together; two men walk through the woods smoking Salem cigarettes. Miller Beer promises that afternoon "Miller Time" will be staffed with three or four good buddies. Drink Dr. Pepper, as Mickey Rooney is coaxed to do, and join in with all the other Peppers. Coca-Cola does not even need to portray the friendliness; it has reduced this appeal to "a Coke and a smile."

The warmth can be toned down and disguised, but it is the same affiliative need that is being fished for. The blonde has a direct gaze and her friends are firm businessmen in appearance, but with a glass of Old Bushmill you can sit down and fit right in. Or, for something more up-beat, sing along with the Pontiac choirboys.

As well as presenting positive images, advertisers can play to the need for affiliation in negative ways, by invoking the fear of rejection. If we don't use Scope, we'll have the "Ugh! Morning Breath" that causes the male and female models to avert their faces. Unless we apply Ultra Brite or Close-Up to our teeth, it's good-bye romance. Our family will be cursed with "House-a-tosis" if we don't take care. Without Dr. Scholl's antiperspirant foot spray, the bowling team will keel over. There go all the guests when the supply of Dorito's nacho cheese chips is exhausted. Still more rejection if our shirts have ring-around-the-collar, if our car needs to be Midasized. But make a few purchases, and we are back in the bosom of human contact.

As self-directed as Americans pretend to be, in the last analysis we remain social animals, hungering for the positive, endorsing feelings that only those around us can supply. Advertisers respond, urging us to "Reach out and touch someone," in the hopes our monthly bills will rise.

3. *Need to nurture.* Akin to affiliative needs is the need to take care of small, defenseless creatures—children and pets, largely. Reciprocity is of less consequence here, though; it is the giving that counts. Murray uses synonyms like "to feed, help, support, console, protect, comfort, nurse, heal." A strong need it is, woven deep into our genetic fabric, for if it did not exist we could not successfully raise up our replacements. When advertisers put forth the image of something diminutive and furry, something that elicits the word "cute" or "precious," then they are trying to trigger this motive. We listen to the childish voice singing the Oscar Mayer weiner song, and our next hot-dog purchase is prescribed. Aren't those darling kittens something, and how did this Meow Mix get into our shopping cart?

This pitch is often directed at women, as Mother Nature's chief nurturers. "Make me some Kraft macaroni and cheese, please," says the elfin preschooler just in from the snowstorm, and mothers' hearts go out, and Kraft's sales go up. "We're cold, wet, and hungry," whine the husband and kids, and the little woman gets the Manwiches ready. A facsimile of this need can be hit without children or pets: the husband is ill and sleepless in the television commercial, and the wife grudgingly fetches the NyQuil.

But it is not women alone who can be touched by this appeal. The father nurses his son Eddie through adolescence while the John Deere lawn tractor survives the years. Another father counts pennies with his young son as the subject of New York Life Insurance comes up. And all over America are businessmen who don't know why they dial Qantas Airlines when they have to take a trans-Pacific trip; the koala bear knows.

4. *Need for guidance.* The opposite of the need to nurture is the need to be nurtured: to be protected, shielded, guided. We may be loath to admit it, but the child lingers on inside every adult—and a good thing it does, or we would not be instructable in our advancing years. Who wants a nation of nothing but flinty personalities?

Parent-like figures can successfully call up this need. Robert Young recommends Sanka coffee, and since we have experienced him for twenty-five years as television father and doctor, we take his word for it. Florence Henderson as the expert mom knows a lot about the advantages of Wesson oil.

The parent-ness of the spokesperson need not be so salient; sometimes pure authoritativeness is better. When Orson Welles scowls and intones, "Paul Masson will sell no wine before its time," we may not know exactly what he means, but we still take direction from him. There is little maternal about Brenda Vaccaro when she speaks up for Tampax, but there is a certainty to her that many accept.

A celebrity is not a necessity in making a pitch to the need for guidance, since a fantasy figure can serve just as well. People accede to the Green Giant, or Betty Crocker, or Mr. Goodwrench. Some advertisers can get by with no figure at all: "When E.F. Hutton talks, people listen."

Often it is tradition or custom that advertisers point to and consumers take guidance from. Bits and pieces of American history are used to sell whiskeys like Old Crow, Southern Comfort, Jack Daniel's. We conform to traditional male/female roles and age-old social norms when we purchase Barclay cigarettes, which informs us "The pleasure is back."

The product itself, if it has been around for a long time, can constitute a tradition. All those old labels in the ad for Morton salt convince us that we should continue to buy it. Kool-Aid says "You loved it as a kid. You trust it as a mother," hoping to get yet more consumers to go along.

Even when the product has no history at all, our need to conform to tradition and to be guided are strong enough that they can be invoked through bogus nostalgia and older actors. Country-Time lemonade sells because consumers want to believe it has a past they can defer to.

So far the needs and the ways they can be invoked which have been looked at are largely warm and affiliative; they stand in contrast to the next set of needs, which are much more egoistic and assertive.

5. *Need to aggress.* The pressures of the real world create strong retaliatory feelings in every functioning human being. Since these impulses can come forth as bursts of anger and violence, their display is normally tabooed. Existing as harbored energy, aggressive drives present a large, tempting target for advertisers. It is not a target to be aimed at thoughtlessly, though, for few manufacturers want their products associated with destructive motives. There is always the danger that, as in the case of sex, if the appeal is too blatant, public opinion will turn against what is being sold.

Jack-in-the-Box sought to abruptly alter its marketing by going after older customers and forgetting the younger ones. Their television commercials had a seventy-ish lady command, "Waste him," and the Jack-in-the-Box clown exploded before our eyes. So did public reaction until the commercials were toned down. Print ads for Club cocktails carried the faces of octogenarians under the headline, "Hit me with a Club"; response was contrary enough to bring the campaign to a stop.

Better disguised aggressive appeals are less likely to backfire: Triumph cigarettes has models making a lewd gesture with their uplifted cigarettes, but the individuals are often laughing and usually in close company of others. When Exxon said, "There's a Tiger in your tank," the implausibility of it concealed the invocation of aggressive feelings.

Depicted arguments are a common way for advertisers to tap the audience's needs to aggress. Don Rickles and Lynda Carter trade gibes, and consumers take sides as the name of Seven-Up is stitched on minds. The Parkay tub has a difference of opinion with the user; who can forget it, or who (or what) got the last word in?

6. *Need to achieve.* This is the drive that energizes people, causing them to strive in their lives and careers. According to Murray, the need for achievement is signalled by the desires "to accomplish something difficult. To overcome obstacles and attain a high standard. To excel one's self. To rival and surpass others." A prominent American trait, it is one that advertisers like to hook on to because it identifies their product with winning and success.

The Cutty Sark ad does not disclose that Ted Turner failed at his latest attempt at yachting's America Cup; here he is represented as a champion on the water as well as off in his television enterprises. If we drink this whiskey, we will be victorious alongside Turner. We can also succeed with O.J. Simpson by renting Hertz cars, or with Reggie Jackson by bringing home some Panasonic equipment. Cathy Rigby and Stayfree Maxipads will put people out front.

Sports heroes are the most convenient means to snare consumers' needs to achieve, but they are not the only one. Role models can be established, ones which invite emulation, as with the profiles put forth by Dewar's scotch. Successful, tweedy individuals relate they have "graduated to the flavor of Myer's rum." Or the advertiser can establish a prize: two neighbors play one-on-one basketball for a Michelob beer in a television commercial, while in a print ad a bottle of Johnnie Walker Black Label has been gilded like a trophy.

Any product that advertises itself in superlatives—the best, the first, the finest—is trying to make contact with our needs to succeed. For many consumers, sales and bargains belong in this category of appeals, too; the person who manages to buy something at fifty percent off is seizing an opportunity and coming out ahead of others.

7. *Need to dominate.* This fundamental need is the craving to be powerful—perhaps omnipotent, as in the Xerox ad where Brother Dominic exhibits heavenly powers and creates miraculous copies. Most of us will settle for being just a regular potentate, though. We drink Budweiser because it is the King of Beers, and here comes the powerful Clydesdales to prove it. A taste of Wolfschmidt vodka and "The spirit of the Czar lives on."

The need to dominate and control one's environment is often thought of as being masculine, but as close students of human nature advertisers know, it is not so circumscribed. Women's aspirations for control are suggested in the campaign theme, "I like my men in English Leather, or nothing at all." The females in the Chanel No. 19 ads are "outspoken" and wrestle their men around.

Male and female, what we long for is clout; what we get in its place is Mastercard.

8. *Need for prominence.* Here comes the need to be admired and respected, to enjoy prestige and high social status. These times, it appears, are not so egalitarian after all. Many ads picture the trappings of high position; the Oldsmobile stands before a manorial doorway, the Volvo is parked beside a steeplechase. A book-lined study is the setting for Dewar's 12, and Lenox China is displayed in a dining room chock full of antiques.

Beefeater gin represents itself as "The Crown Jewel of England" and uses no illustrations of jewels or things British, for the words are sufficient indicators of distinction. Buy that gin and you will rise up the prestige hierarchy, or achieve the same effect on yourself with Seagram's 7 Crown, which ambiguously describes itself as "classy."

Being respected does not have to entail the usual accoutrements of wealth: "Do you know who I am?" the commercials ask, and we learn that the prominent person is not so prominent without his American Express card.

9. *Need for attention.* The previous need involved being *looked up to*, while this is the need to be *looked at*. The desire to exhibit ourselves in such a way as to make others look at us is a primitive, insuppressible instinct. The clothing and cosmetic industries exist just to serve this need, and this is the way they pitch their wares. Some of this effort is aimed at males, as the ads for Hathaway shirts and Jockey underclothes. But the greater bulk of such appeals is targeted singlemindedly at women.

To come back to Brooke Shields: this is where she fits into American marketing. If I buy Calvin Klein jeans, consumers infer, I'll be the object of fascination. The desire for exhibition has been most strikingly played to in a print campaign of many years' duration, that of Maidenform lingerie.The woman exposes herself, and sales surge. "Gentlemen prefer Hanes" the ads dissemble, and women who want eyes upon them know what they should do. Peggy Fleming flutters her legs for L'eggs, encouraging females who want to be the star in their own lives to purchase this product.

The same appeal works for cosmetics and lotions. For years, the little girl with the exposed backside sold gobs of Coppertone, but now the company has picked up the pace a little: as a female, you are supposed to "Flash 'em a Coppertone tan." Food can be sold the same way, especially to the diet-conscious; Angie Dickinson poses for California avocados and says, "Would this body lie to you?" Our eyes are too fixed on her for us to think to ask if she got that way by eating mounds of guacomole.

10. *Need for autonomy.* There are several ways to sell credit card services, as has been noted: Mastercard appeals to the need to dominate, and American Express to the need for prominence. When Visa claims, "You can have it the way you want it," yet another primary motive is being beckoned forward—the need to endorse the self. The focus here is upon the independence and integrity of the individual; this need is the antithesis of the need for guidance and is unlike any of the social needs. "If running with the herd isn't your style, try ours," says Rotan-Mosle, and many Americans feel they have finally found the right brokerage firm.

The photo is of a red-coated Mountie on his horse, posed on a snowcovered ledge; the copy reads, "Windsor—One Canadian stands alone." This epitome of the solitary and proud individual may work best with male customers, as may Winston's man in the red cap. But one-figure advertisements also strike the strong need for autonomy among American women. As Shelly Hack strides for Charlie perfume, females respond to her obvious pride and flair; she is her own person. The Virginia Slims tale is of people who have come a long way from subservience to independence. Cachet perfume feels it does not need a solo figure to work this appeal, and uses three different faces in its ads; it insists, though, "It's different on every woman who wears it."

Like many psychological needs, this one can also be appealed to in a negative fashion, by invoking the loss of independence or self-regard. Guilt and regrets can be stimulated: "Gee, I could have had a V-8." Next time, get one and be good to yourself.

11. *Need to escape.* An appeal to the need for autonomy often co-occurs with one for the need to escape, since the desire to duck out of our social obligations, to seek rest or adventure, frequently takes the form of one-person flight. The dashing image of a pilot, in fact, is a standard way of quickening this need to get away from it all.

Freedom is the pitch here, the freedom that every individual yearns for whenever life becomes too oppressive. Many advertisers like appealing to the need for escape because the sensation of pleasure often accompanies escape, and what nicer emotional nimbus could there be for a product? "You deserve a break today," says McDonald's, and Stouffer's frozen foods chime in, "Set yourself free."

For decades men have imaginatively bonded themselves to the Marlboro cowboy who dwells untarnished and unencumbered in Marlboro Country some distance from modern life; smokers' aching needs for autonomy and escape are personified by that cowpoke. Many women can identify with the lady ambling through the woods behind the words, "Benson and Hedges and mornings and me."

But escape does not have to be solitary. Other Benson and Hedges ads, part of the same campaign, contain two strolling figures. In Salem cigarette advertisements, it can be several people who escape together into the mountaintops. A commercial for Levi's pictured a cloudbank above a city through which ran a whole chain of young people.

There are varieties of escape, some wistful like the Boeing "Some day" campaign of dream vacations, some kinetic like the play and parties in soft drink ads. But in every instance, the consumer exposed to the advertisement is invited to momentarily depart his everyday life for a more carefree experience, preferably with the product in hand.

12. *Need to feel safe.* Nobody in their right mind wants to be intimidated, menaced, battered, poisoned. We naturally want to do whatever it takes to stave off threats to our well-being, and to our families'. It is the instinct of self-preservation that makes us responsive to the ad of the St. Bernard with the keg of Chivas Regal. We pay attention to the stern talk of Karl Malden and the plight of the vacationing couples who have lost all their funds in the American Express travelers cheques commercials. We want the omnipresent stag from Hartford Insurance to watch over us too.

In the interest of keeping failure and calamity from our lives, we like to see the durability of products demonstrated. Can we ever forget that Timex takes a licking and keeps on ticking? When the American Tourister suitcase bounces all over the highway and the egg inside doesn't break, the need to feel safe has been adroitly plucked.

We take precautions to diminish future threats. We buy Volkswagen Rabbits for the extraordinary mileage, and MONY insurance policies to avoid the tragedies depicted in their black-and-white ads of widows and orphans.

We are careful about our health. We consume Mazola margarine because it has "corn goodness" backed by the natural food traditions of the American Indians. In the medicine cabinet is Alka-Seltzer, the "home remedy"; having it, we are snug in our little cottage.

We want to be safe and secure; buy these products, advertisers are saying, and you'll be safer than you are without them.

13. *Need for aesthetic sensations.* There is an undeniable aesthetic component to virtually every ad run in the national media: the photography or filming or drawing is near-perfect, the type style is well chosen, the layout could scarcely be improved upon. Advertisers know there is little chance of good communication occurring if an ad is not visually pleasing. Consumers may not be aware of the extent of their own sensitivity to artwork, but it is undeniably large.

Sometimes the aesthetic element is expanded and made into an ad's primary appeal. Charles Jordan shoes may or may not appear in the accompanying avant-grade photographs; Kohler plumbing fixtures catch attention through the high style of their desert settings. Beneath the slightly out of focus photograph, languid and sensuous in tone, General Electric feels called upon to explain, "This is an ad for the hair dryer."

This appeal is not limited to female consumers: J&B scotch says "It whispers" and shows a bucolic scene of lake and castle.

14. *Need to satisfy curiosity.* It may seem odd to list a need for information among basic motives, but this need can be as primal and compelling as any of the others. Human beings are curious by nature, interested in the world around them, and intrigued by tidbits of knowledge and new developments. Trivia, percentages, observations counter to conventional wisdom—these items all help sell products. Any advertisement in a question-and-answer format is strumming this need.

A dog groomer has a question about long distance rates, and Bell Telephone has a chart with all the figures. An ad for Porsche 911 is replete with diagrams and schematics, numbers and arrows. Lo and behold, Anacin pills have 150 more milligrams than its competitors; should we wonder if this is better or worse for us?

15. *Physiological needs.* To the extent that sex is solely a biological need, we are now coming around full circle, back toward the start of the list. In this final category are clustered appeals to sleeping, eating, drinking. The art

of photographing food and drink is so advanced, sometimes these temptations are wondrously caught in the camera's lens: the crab meat in the Red Lobster restaurant ads can start us salivating, the Quarterpounder can almost be smelled, the liquor in the glass glows invitingly. Imbibe, these ads scream.

Styles

Some common ingredients of advertisements were not singled out for separate mention in the list of fifteen because they are not appeals in and of themselves. They are stylistic features, influencing the way a basic appeal is presented. The use of humor is one, and the use of celebrities is another. A third is time imagery, past and future, which goes to several purposes.

For all of its employment in advertising, humor can be treacherous, because it can get out of hand and smother the product information. Supposedly, this is what Alka-Seltzer discovered with its comic commercials of the late sixties; "I can't believe I ate the whole thing," the sadfaced husband lamented, and the audience cackled so much it forgot the antacid. Or, did not take it seriously.

But used carefully, humor can punctuate some of the softer appeals and soften some of the harsher ones. When Emma says to the Fruit-of-the-Loom fruits, "Hi, cuties. Whatcha doing in my laundry basket?" we smile as our curiosity is assuaged along with hers. Bill Cosby gets consumers tickled about the children in his Jell-O commercials, and strokes the need to nurture.

An insurance company wants to invoke the need to feel safe, but does not want to leave readers with an unpleasant aftertaste; cartoonist Rowland Wilson creates an avalanche about to crush a gentleman who is saying to another, "My insurance company? New England Life, of course. Why?" The same tactic of humor undercutting threat is used in the cartoon commercials for Safeco when the Pink Panther wanders from one disaster to another. Often humor masks aggression: comedian Bob Hope in the outfit of a boxer promises to knock out the knockknocks with Texaco; Rodney Dangerfield, who "can't get no respect," invites aggression as the comic relief in Miller Lite commercials.

Roughly fifteen percent of all advertisements incorporate a celebrity, almost always from the fields of entertainment or sports. The approach can also prove troublesome for advertisers, for celebrities are human beings too, and fully capable of the most remarkable behavior. If anything distasteful about them emerges, it is likely to reflect on the product. The advertisers making use of Anita Bryant and Billy Jean King suffered several anxious moments. An untimely death can also react poorly on a product. But advertisers are willing to take risks because celebrities can be such a good link between producers and consumers, performing the social role of introducer.

There are several psychological needs these middlemen can play upon. Let's take the product class of cameras and see how different celebrities can hit different needs. The need for guidance can be invoked by Michael Landon, who plays such a wonderful dad on "Little House on the Prairie"; when he says to buy Kodak equipment, many people listen. James Garner for Polaroid cameras is put in a similar authoritative role, so defined by a mocking spouse. The need to achieve is summoned up by Tracy Austin and other tennis stars for Canon AE-1; the advertiser first makes sure we see these athletes playing to win. When Cheryl Tiegs speaks up for Olympus cameras, it is the need for attention that is being targeted.

The past and future, being outside our grasp, are exploited by advertisers as locales for the projection of needs. History can offer up heroes (and call up the need to achieve) or traditions (need for guidance) as well as art objects (need for aesthetic sensations). Nostalgia is a kindly version of personal history and is deployed by advertisers to rouse needs for affiliation and for guidance; the need to escape can come in here, too. The same need to escape is sometimes the point of futuristic appeals but picturing the avant-garde can also be a way to get at the need to achieve.

Analyzing Advertisements

When analyzing ads yourself for their emotional appeals, it takes a bit of practice to learn to ignore the product information (as well as one's own experience and feelings about the product). But that skill comes soon enough, as does the ability to quickly sort out from all the non-product aspects of an ad the chief element which is the most striking, the most likely to snag attention first and penetrate brains farthest. The key to the appeal, this element usually presents itself centrally and forwardly to the reader or viewer.

Another clue: the viewing angle which the audience has on the ad's subjects is informative. If the subjects are photographed or filmed from below and thus are looking down at you much as the Green Giant does, then the need to be guided is a good candidate for the ad's emotional appeal. If, on the other hand, the subjects are shot from above and appear deferential, as is often the case with children or female models, then other needs are being appealed to.

To figure out an ad's emotional appeal, it is wise to know (or have a good hunch about) who the targeted consumers are; this can often be inferred from the magazine or television show it appears in. This piece of information is a great help in determining the appeal and in deciding between two different interpretations. For example, if an ad features a partially undressed female, this would typically signal one appeal for readers of *Penthouse* (need for sex) and another for readers of *Cosmopolitan* (need for attention).

It would be convenient if every ad made just one appeal, were aimed at just one need. Unfortunately, things are often not that simple. A cigarette ad with a couple at the edge of a polo field is trying to hit both the need for affiliation and the need for prominence; depending on the attitude of the male, dominance could also be an ingredient in this. An ad for Chimere perfume incorporates two photos: in the top one the lady is being commanding at a business luncheon (need to dominate), but in the lower one she is being bussed (need for affiliation). Better ads, however, seem to avoid being too diffused; in the study of post-World War II advertising described earlier, appeals grew more focused as the decades passed. As a rule of thumb, about sixty percent have two conspicuous appeals; the last twenty percent have three or more. Rather than looking for the greatest number of appeals, decoding ads is most productive when the loudest one or two appeals are discerned, since those are the appeals with the best chance of grabbing people's attention.

Finally, analyzing ads does not have to be a solo activity and probably should not be. The greater number of people there are involved, the better chance there is of transcending individual biases and discerning the essential emotional lure built into an advertisement.

Do They Or Don't They?

Do the emotional appeals made in advertisements add up to the sinister manipulation of consumers?

It is clear that these ads work. Attention is caught, communication occurs between producers and consumers, and sales result. It turns out to be difficult to detail the exact relationship between a specific ad and a specific purchase, or even between a campaign and subsequent sales figures, because advertising is only one of a host of influences upon consumption. Yet no one is fooled by this lack of perfect proof; everyone knows that advertising sells. If this were not the case, then tight-fisted American businesses would not spend a total of fifty billion dollars annually on these messages.

But before anyone despairs that advertisers have our number to the extent that they can marshal us at will and march us like automatons to the check-out counters, we should recall the resiliency and obduracy of the American consumer. Advertisers may have uncovered the softest spots in minds, but that does not mean they have found truly gaping apertures. There is no evidence that advertising can get people to do things contrary to their self-interests. Despite all the finesse of advertisements, and all the subtle emotional tugs, the public resists the vast majority of the petitions. According to the marketing division of the A.C Nielsen Company, a whopping seventy-five percent of all new products die within a year in the marketplace, the victims of consumer disinterest which no amount of advertising could overcome. The appeals in advertising may be the most captivating there are to be had, but they are not enough to entrap the wiley consumer.

The key to understanding the discrepancy between, on the one hand, the fact that advertising truly works, and, on the other, the fact that it hardly works, is to take into account the enormous numbers of people exposed to an ad. Modern-day communications permit an ad to be displayed to millions upon millions of individuals; if the smallest fraction of that audience can be moved to buy the product, then the ad has been successful. When one percent of the people exposed to a television advertising campaign reach for their wallets, that could be one million sales, which may be enough to keep the product in production and the advertisements coming.

In arriving at an evenhanded judgment about advertisements and their emotional appeals, it is good to keep in mind that many of the purchases which might be credited to these ads are experienced as genuinely gratifying to the consumer. We sincerely like the goods or service we have bought, and we may even like some of the emotional drapery that an ad suggests comes with it. It has sometimes been noted that the most avid students of advertisements are the people who have just bought the product; they want to steep themselves in the associated imagery. This may be the reason that Americans, when polled, are not negative about advertising and do not disclose any sense of being misused. The volume of advertising may be an irritant, but the product information as well as the imaginative material in ads are partial compensation.

A productive understanding is that advertising messages involve costs and benefits at both ends of the communications channel. For those few ads which do make contact, the consumer surrenders a moment of time, has the lower brain curried, and receives notice of a product; the advertiser has given up money and has increased the chance of sales. In this sort of communications activity, neither party can be said to be the loser.

Jib Fowles, 1982, "Advertising's Fifteen Basic Appeals," *Etc.*, 39(3). Reprinted by permission.

Deborah Meier's Progressive Traditionalism

Gerald Graff

The teaching approach that I have been outlining in this book straddles the divide between traditional and progressive philosophies of education. If I had to nominate one educator whose work best exemplifies this "progressive traditionalism," my choice would be Deborah Meier, whose 1993 book *The Power of Their Ideas: Lessons for America from a Small School in Harlem* could be its manifesto. Meier's work as a writer, teacher, and school administrator provides a rich model of how schooling can be demystified.

Though Meier is politically on the Left, her educational thinking resists being categorized as Left or Right. On the one hand, Meier stands squarely in the progressive Deweyan tradition, arguing that "democratic community" is "the nonnegotiable purpose of good schooling,"[1] that schooling should enable all students to enter the culture's "political conversation across divisions of race, class, religion, and ideology" (7). Meier also embraces the central tenet of progressive education, that in order to move students to a higher intellectual level teachers have to begin from where the learner is and build from there. Meier has no use for conservative nostalgia, answering the charge that American students' performance has precipitously declined by reminding us that "until World War II the average American did not graduate from high school" (69), much less attain the high standards of literacy that are now fondly imagined to have been achieved at some earlier time.[2]

On the other hand, Meier is at one with traditional educators in stressing that schools and teachers need to provide strong models of intellectual authority. She rejects the view of some progressives that students can't become active learners unless teachers deny or soften their authority, getting themselves out of the students' way. Refusing to see classroom authority as a zero-sum game in which students can be "empowered" only if teachers relinquish control, Meier's central point is one that traditionalists should warm to: that schools must become intellectually challenging institutions instead of shopping malls, staging grounds for radical politics, or dispensers of feel-good therapy.

Meier recognizes that no model of educational reform can gain general acceptance unless it embraces both progressives and traditionalists, as well as others who are at odds on fundamental issues. As Meier puts it, changing schools "must be done by people who don't all like the same movies, vote for the same politicians, or raise their own kids in the same way" (38). Paradoxically, because Meier's vision of education welcomes and incorporates disagreement, it has greater power to produce consensus than do rival visions. Meier understands that making intellectual issues central in a curriculum means giving disagreements a prominent, positive role, partly because there is so much disagreement about such issues, but also because disagreement is clarifying. Though such a vision may sound divisive, its underlying premise is one that everyone committed to democracy on the Right, Left, and Center should be able to accept: that improving the quality of education depends on making the intellectual culture of schools more coherent, clear, and challenging. Meier gives educational primacy to those common skills of analysis, argument, and public conversation on which all the contending educational agendas depend for their articulation. She understands that which groups in our society get access to these intellectual skills has everything to do with politics and power, but for her these skills themselves are not the monopoly of any social class or political faction.

Meier understands that learning problems start with the fact that, to many students, the very concept of "education" is nebulous and is never explained. "Young people," she says, "have always had only the foggiest notion of what schools are all about once the 3 R's stage is completed. Even the 3 R's mostly have stood for skill at schooling, only loosely connected, if at all, to anything you do elsewhere" (162). Meier understands, in other words, that effective education involves clarifying the mysterious world of school knowledge and ideas and its connection with "anything you do elsewhere." She sees that in order for such clarification to occur, the world of school knowledge and ideas needs to be organized as a coherent and intelligible culture whose practices make sense.

Youth Culture Vs. School Culture

In *The Power of Their Ideas*, Meier describes how she (as principal) and her associates transformed the Central Park East Secondary School in Harlem (CPESS) into such a coherent intellectual environment, one that has proved remarkably effective in educating "disadvantaged" students (a label, as she notes, that her students reject). CPESS, which began in 1985, grew out of the Central Park East elementary school that Meier and her associates had founded 1974. Her vision of CPESS arose from her search for an alternative to the shopping mall high school, what Meier calls "the big, mindless high school" where the fact that "the capacity to educate is missing . . . seems almost beside the point" (31–32). Meier's account suggests that at CPESS, intellectual issues and debates have the central role occupied by sports and socializing in many high schools (though one infers that at CPESS sports and socializing themselves are grist for intellectual discussion). By 1993, when her book appeared, CPESS was serving 450 seventh-through-twelfth graders. In a city in which the average graduation rate was 50 percent, 90 percent of CPESS's students graduated from high school and another 90 percent "went directly on to college and stayed there" (16). In the mid-nineties Meier left New York for Boston, where she is now principal of the Mission Hill school in Roxbury. Meier says "the exact same principles apply" to all these schools.[3]

Meier's starting point is a key insight into the disabling separation of adolescence and adulthood in postwar America, one that echoes the writing of Paul Goodman in books of the '60s like *Growing Up Absurd and Compulsory Miseducation*.[4] As Meier puts it in a radio interview, "the average adolescent in this country has almost no relationship with anybody who is much different [from] themselves. I mean, they live in an enormously small world, and can't imagine belonging to the many other worlds around them. . . . there are no grown-ups in their little community." Meier observes that this isolation of adolescents from the grown-up world vastly increased in post–World War II consumer culture, which produced

> the first generation of adolescents in the history of the world that were expected to be irresponsible. Young people, who historically would have been expected to go to work, were cut off from adults, with more money for self-indulgent purposes than they are likely ever to have in their lives, and very little incentive then for growing up. Nor were there many models of why it was wonderful to be grown-up. So that we really have institutionalized the idea that just before you become a grown-up you're part of the most alienated and irresponsible subculture anyone could imagine creating.

To house this subculture, Meier continues, "we created this institution of the American high school, which also isolated kids from adults."[5]

Others have pointed to this isolation of the young from the adult world as a factor in school shootings of the 1990s like that at Littleton, Colorado, in which two high school students killed thirteen classmates and themselves. William Damon, director of the Stanford University Center on Adolescence observed that "there has never in the history of the civilized world been a cohort of kids that is so little affected by adult guidance and so attuned to a peer world."[6] Adults, Meier suggests, actually feel envy and resentment for the insularity and irresponsibility that our culture has granted adolescents, a backlash reflected in the post-Littleton trend toward "zero tolerance" policies.

For Meier, the trouble with such crackdowns is their failure to address the problem at its source, the estrangement of young people from adult culture, an estrangement schools must address in order to have a chance to be effective. At Central Park East School, she writes, "that's one of the central characteristics that's different, that the grown-ups and the kids belong to the same school. They don't just happen to bump into each other in classes and then go to their separate worlds. They really are part of the same community. I think that's a critical part of why the school's powerful" (39). Here Meier both follows and revises Dewey's argument in early books such as *The School and Society* and *The Child and the Curriculum*, books that became the blueprint for the Laboratory School at the University of Chicago and numerous other progressive schools.

Dewey had argued that to overcome the sterility and irrelevance of traditional education, the democratic school had to find a way to integrate the child into the adult world of labor and production. Dewey assumed that children harbored a natural curiosity about adult productive systems and vocations such as farming, transportation, and manufacturing. He reasoned that if "occupations are made the articulating centers of school life," students' interest in adult social practices will transform them from "passive and inert recipiency" to active interest.[7] Dewey's vision had nothing to do with vocationalism; the appeal of the occupational world for him lay in its expression of the heroic project of modernity, the progressive struggle of humanity "to master and use nature so as to make it tributary to the enrichment of human life."[8] What Dewey did not foresee, however, was that the appeal to children of this heroic project would be undermined by the rise of youth culture and consumerism, which alienate the young from the adult world of work and civic participation. Meier recognizes that the structural isolation of youth culture from school culture has greatly deepened since Dewey's time, and that a new organization of teaching and learning is necessary if this isolation is to be counteracted.

Meier argues that the school needs to become a kind of intellectual "counterculture" to counteract the anti-intellectualism of youth culture and the "mindless" shopping mall school. As Meier puts it, to counteract the usual school culture in which "students move about bereft of relationships with anyone but their exact age and grade peers," the school needs to become "a thick, complex and powerful counterculture to balance the one that has been developed for adolescents only," a culture that can act as a "counterforce representing serious adult ideas and concerns to which these novices might now and then apprentice themselves" (113). To become such a counterculture, the curriculum must be more than a series of good courses taught by caring individuals; it has to become a coherent, continuous intellectual community that makes intelligible sense to students. Good teaching is a given, but Meier stresses that to make a difference the key lies in how we *organize teaching and learning* (71). For good organization and teamwork can make teachers better by enabling students to see the relationship between one course, subject, and idea and another. Teachers working together make the world of ideas less mysterious than teachers working in isolation and often at cross-purposes.

It is here that Meier's ability to mesh progressive and traditional educational thinking gives her argument a power lacking in either alternative alone. Meier's stress on organization and community provides an alternative to the bad choice between traditional and progressive educational models, or between strong teachers' authority on the one hand and turning courses over to the students on the other. Meier argues that "teaching as telling" has its limits, that students have to play an active role in their learning (143). But Meier also suggests that, far from being silenced by intellectually aggressive teachers, students need such teachers to achieve intellectual authority themselves. Unlike Jane Tompkins, for example, who argues that students' "feelings and opinions won't surface, unless the teacher gets out of the way on a regular basis,"[9] Meier assumes that for those feelings and opinions to surface—or even to come into existence—students need to see the intellectual game clearly modeled by strong adults. As Meier puts it, the premise at CPESS has been that "adults had important things to teach children, not just a mission to get out of their way" (21).

Meier writes of seeing "children being driven into dumbness by a failure to challenge their curiosity, to build on their natural drive toward competence." Meier adds that nonwhite teachers and parents in particular are rightly frustrated at progressive teachers' "seeming avoidance of 'direct' instruction, as though if we waited long enough children would discover everything on their own." Meier observes that it's "no wonder many African American teachers and parents" see progressive education as a "cop-out, a way of avoiding, not confronting, the challenge" of actually teaching kids something (21). Meier here acknowledges a debt to Lisa Delpit (whose *Other People's Children* appeared the same year as Meier's book), who argues that the reluctance of teachers to be explicit about what is wanted has the effect of withholding secrets from the minority students who most need them.

The Importance Of Being Organized

Meier's stress on organization, which follows from her assumption of the clublike nature of intellectual socialization, represents a welcome corrective to the individualistic, great-teacher ideology that has long pervaded popular educational thinking. That thinking, as William Ayers points out, is dominated by the romantic idea of the "hero-teacher, the lone individual" who triumphs through sheer determination and grit over "the backward parents, the hopeless colleagues, and the sewer of society to redeem the good juvenile delinquent."[10] Ayers notes that this heroic teacher is idealized in films like *Stand and Deliver*, *Dangerous Minds*, and *Dead Poets Society*, which reinforce the belief that improving schooling is chiefly a matter of inspiring more dedication and passion in individual teachers, an outcome not likely to happen or to be sustained for long if it does. Meier, by contrast, recognizes that improving education means changing the culture of the schools, a feat that certainly requires inspired individual teaching (as does any educational model), but that also requires the school to become an organized intellectual community with clear goals and practices.

The success of Central Park East seems traceable to its creation of such a community based on several programmatic features, ones that again blur the distinction between the progressive and the traditional. CPESS replaced fifty-five-minute class periods and disconnected subjects with two-hour classes that combined disciplines. It "provided time during those two hours for presentations, seminars, group work, and independent study" (32); instead of short-answer tests, the school instituted demonstration projects. Following a model developed by Sizer's Coalition of Essential Schools, CPESS instituted portfolio-based graduation exercises, on the order of "a series of doctoral orals" (42) in which students publicly presented exhibitions, "tangible demonstrations of their knowledge and competence rather than accumulating 'seat time' (credits) or grades on multiple choice tests" (30). CPESS also enlisted the collaboration of "parents (or grandparents, aunts, older siblings)" in the school's operations and decision making (an approach that has been pioneered in the lower schools by James Comer of Yale University) (22).

At CPESS these innovations, which are usually identified with progressivism, served a solidly traditional emphasis on intellectual habits of mind. The school's curriculum was organized around "five major 'intellectual habits'—habits that should be internalized by every student, and used no matter what they are studying about, both in school and especially out of it!" (41) The five habits condense the moves of intellectual culture into a set of templates:

1. Concern for evidence (how do you know that?)

2. Viewpoint (who said it and why?)

3. Cause and effect (what led to it, what else happened?)

4. Hypothesizing (what if, supposing that)

5. Who cares? Knowing and learning take on importance only when we are convinced it matters, it makes a difference (41).

Asking why academic work should indeed "matter" to a fifteen-year old, Meier recognizes the wisdom of not getting bogged down in the old conflict between vocational and liberal justifications for learning. For CPFSS students a subject or issue might matter "because it will help get us ahead, get into a good college, hold a well-paying job," or because "it will also help save the world" (41). A school can keep both liberal and vocational justifications for education in play, making the tension and debate between them a focus of school discussion.

This creation of "a strong school culture" (24), in which the moves of the intellectual game are clarified, seems ultimately to have been the key to CPESS's success. As Meier describes it, it is an atmosphere in which intellectual issues matter and "the clash of ideas" (11) is central rather than marginal or nonexistent. Again Meier's crucial assumption is that becoming a literate person is like joining a social club, though one bent on expanding rather than restricting its membership. For most American students, joining such a club entails a profound change in their social affiliations and the way they think about themselves, a fact that explains why curricular prescriptions for more classic texts or more cultural literacy facts are inevitably superficial.

As Meier puts it in a passage I quoted earlier, the essential key for club members is learning "to say 'I've got a theory!'" and, for that to happen, "somewhere, young people need to join, if only part-time, the club we belong to. That's more critical than the particulars of what they learn" (157). In a talk entitled "Changing Our Habits of Schooling," Meier observes that most schools have been settings "in which few had reason to imagine themselves as members of the club that teachers belonged to. Children need to be members of a community that encourages youth to roam imaginatively across genders, nationalities, races, periods of history, and universes. Only in a community in which children and adults belong to the same club does such an imaginative life thrive." Meier adds that "seeing oneself as members of the same club is not a matter of liking or not liking one's teachers," but of wanting to be the kind of person they are: "It goes deeper. Young children select from the wide range available to them whom they will sound like, walk like, and so forth," and Meier mentions her brother, who, when he went to baseball games, "was watching as a make-believe ball player, an aspiring member of that club."[11] Schools fail when they do not inspire such emulative "watching" of the academic game, when the student body remains a youth club divorced from the adult club.

Meier knows that most students "resist membership" in the club of intellectuals—"either out of fear of rejection or because to join such a club means to reject their own community or peer clubs. Or because they just don't 'get it' yet, or 'who wants it!'" (158). Schools fail either because they do not represent the intellectual life at all, or they represent it only intermittently, as a set of dissociated courses and teachers— the mixed message curriculum—rather than as a connected conversation that students can understand and enter. Again, the crucial element is organization: changing "our accepted organization of schooling," Meier writes, is a prerequisite for "creating environments where all kids can experience the power of their ideas" (4) . The organization of CPESS involves an unusual degree of collaboration and coordination, primarily among the faculty, but also including parents. Meier notes that in the conventional schools in which she and her staff had previously worked, "we had grown accustomed to closing our [classroom] doors and secretly doing what we wanted," a separatism that is often seductive to progressive educators who are alienated from the established institution and have the freedom to do their own classroom thing (24). But the CPESS model also differs from traditional programs in which "core" subjects are so isolated that they obscure the critical conversation that gives them meaning. At CPESS Meier and her staff taught together in interactive courses, frequently airing their disagreements openly rather than keeping them hidden. Meier observes that since "our adult debates are not hidden from our students" (58), a "climate of diversity and disagreement" arises that "becomes enormously powerful over time" and draws students in (59).

This positive view of disagreement provided CPESS with a creative way of dealing with vexed political issues and their much disputed place in classrooms. For Meier bringing debates about politics into the curriculum is preferable either to teaching one political view exclusively or teaching a variety of views in isolation from one another, practices that conceal the adult conversation from students:

> Few young people (she writes) imagine that adults have intense discussions around ideas, that what they are studying is influenced by what their teachers read and debate: arguing over the impact of voluntary versus forced migrations, what constitutes "our" canon, hearing each other out on words like "Eurocentric" and "Afrocentric," and considering how the concepts we introduce help or hinder our capacity to imagine "the other." Such discussions surprise visitors to our school, but above all they influence our students for whom these matters would otherwise be "academic" (118).

Meier notes that "staunch 'lefties' occasionally berate us at CPE for not removing books with the 'wrong' beliefs, and they're not always satisfied with our solution: write an attack and we'll post it or even include it in the back of the book." As Meier writes, "ignoring the clash" of values—like that between religion and secularism—"won't resolve it. These questions are the stuff of a good democratic debate for the minds and hearts of Americans" (81).

Finally, in creating a *public* sphere of intellectual discussion and disagreement in the school, CPESS developed what is arguably a better model of "staff development" than the one that has become most popular in which a master teacher (or college professor) talks with teachers about how to teach or showcases "best practices." Meier writes that "because our adult debates are not hidden from our students, there is no sharp dividing line between 'staff development' activities and student educational activities" (58). In other words, teachers learn to teach not by watching or getting advice from master teachers, but by visiting "each other's classes, to reflect on their own and their colleagues' practice, and give each other feedback and support" in the process of the planning and teaching of their courses (56). Taking a page from Meier's model, college and high school teachers need to collaborate in designing courses together and adapting them for teaching at their different sites.[12]

Must Bigness Be Bad?

I have saved for last my one point of disagreement with Meier, on the issue of school size. Meier argues that in order to be effective, the kind of learning community she promotes and developed at CPESS has to be small: "Only in small schools can we reasonably speak of immersing students in a culture that adults have played a significant role in shaping" (113). "In schools," she maintains, "big doesn't work no matter how one slices the data. . . . Small school size is not only a good idea but an absolute prerequisite for qualitative change in deep-seated habits." "Only in a small school can deep ongoing discussion take place in ways that produce change and involve the entire faculty" (107–8). Only in small schools can "the accountability we owe to parents and the public" be "a matter of access, not of complex governing bodies or monitoring arrangements" (112).

I do not dispute the claim—which is now widely accepted by educators and public officials—that for many students to become motivated and to do their best work, they need to be in small groups for a significant portion of the school or college day. Nor do I dispute Meier's claim that the reforms she and her associates instituted at CPESS would have been impossible to implement in a large school. I want to argue, however, that the small vs. big dichotomy is another of those educational polarities that we are too quick to see as mutually exclusive. Like the dualisms that oppose traditional and progressive methods or academic and personal discourse, the choice between small vs. large schools (or small vs. large classes) is one that we should resist. It is possible, after all, for students to spend considerable time in classes of twelve to twenty-five while at other times working in larger groups. Though a major proportion of students' experience should be in small classes, not all classes need to be small all the time, nor do all schools.

Precisely because of what Meier herself so well points out—the magnitude and power of the youth culture that competes for students' attention with schooling—it's hard to imagine educational success on a mass democratic scale that tries to fight bigness with smallness. To put the point another way, the more we cut the process of education into smaller units, the harder we make it for that process to maintain consistency and quality control and to represent itself intelligibly to students. The smaller we make the units of education, the more we increase curricular fragmentation and decrease the amount of common focus that is necessary for intellectual clarity. The incoherence of the mixed-message curriculum that I examined in chapter 3 results from chopping the curriculum into small courses that do not communicate and therefore can't discover their latent common ground.

Like most of today's categorical arguments for educational smallness, Meier's seem to have arisen in reaction to bad versions of bigness. I believe that for school culture to gain the clarity that will enable it to counteract the youth culture "that has been developed for adolescents only," we need to rethink bigness in more imaginative ways. The very size and public reach of popular films, music, and sports, and the tremendous sense of commonly shared culture they produce, contributes to the excitement and interest generated by these media mega-spectacles. When it comes to education, however, we assume that large size has to mean alienation rather than excitement.

It should be possible for schools to learn from the media's success at mega-communication without replicating the media's worst aspects. Large assembly meetings could coexist with small classes the way the best college lecture courses combine with small discussion sections. Indeed, in many cases, the quality of discussion in small classes would itself improve if larger meetings provided the common intellectual reference point that those small classes now lack. Chicago's North Side College Prep has instituted such a weekly all-school colloquium based on general intellectual and cultural issues. North Side is a magnet school that attracts mostly high-achieving students, but its all-school colloquium is potentially adaptable to the student bodies and problems of more troubled schools. New electronic technologies should also help us reimagine school and class size, for a wired classroom can be both small and big at the same time, physically small while connecting with larger groups.[13]

At times, Meier's small-is-beautiful bias betrays a certain romantic localism, as in her contribution to a recent Boston Review Symposium, published as a book under the title *Will Standards Save Higher Education?* In reacting against standardized testing, Meier tends to confuse common intellectual standards with standardization. Thus she questions whether "it is possible and desirable to agree on a single definition of what constitutes a well-educated eighteen year old and demand that every school be held to the same definition."[14] This attack on "single definitions" seems strange coming from Meier, since in *The Power of Their Ideas* she herself advances a single definition of the well-educated student. As I noted above, Meier calls the "five major 'intellectual habits'" central to the CPESS curriculum "habits that *should be internalized by every student*" at CPESS, "*and used no matter what they are studying about, both in school and especially out of it!*" (41; emphasis mine). I do not often find myself on the same side as the conservative Abigail Thernstrom in any dispute, but Thernstrom seems to me quite right in a response included in *Will Standards Save Higher Education?* when she wonders if Meier would "label the insistence that kids learn to read abhorrent 'standardization.'" Does Meier, Thernstrom asks, "really want to argue about the worth of learning geometry or the importance of understanding why we fought a civil war?"[15]

But however we may feel about Meier's localist bias, it does not vitiate the value of her educational ideas and her example. Meier is a great educator and educational thinker because she has synthesized the best lessons of both progressivism and traditionalism. She understands that the problem of education has to be thought through from the viewpoint not of the already educated, but of the clueless student for whom the very words "education" and "academic" are opaque. But she also understands that such students have the ability to join an intellectual community that makes sense to them. In the demystification of academia that we need, thinkers and teachers like Deborah Meier will lead the way.

Notes

1.   Deborah Meier, *The Power of Their Ideas: Lessons for America from a Small School in Harlem* (Boston: Beacon Press, 1995), 20. Page references to this book are henceforth given in the text.

2.   To refute this nostalgia, Meier cites the statistical research of Richard Rothstein in his Century Foundation Report, *The Way We Were? The Myths and Realities of America's Student Achievement* (New York: Century Foundation Press, 1998). For other debunkings of the alleged decline in performance of American students, see Leon Botstein, Jefferson's *Children: Education and the Promise of American Culture* (New York: Doubleday, 1997), 22–23 and passim, and my own *Beyond the Culture Wars: How Teaching the Conflicts Can Revitalize American Education* (New York: W. W. Norton, 1992), 87–92.

3.   Meier, private correspondence. CPESS is a public pilot school, which Meier (in correspondence) calls "an attempt to demonstrate that charters were not needed." At the same time, Meier defends school choice if it can be made to promote community rather than free marketeering:

> We need to examine whether public chartering is part of a trend to wards everybody-out.for-themselves or is a wider way of looking at community. It could be either. The question is, what kind of public policy could make charters a vehicle for democratic life rather than a vehicle for running away from democratic life? …

The geographic neighborhood school can be a way of isolating us from our fellow citizens, or it can be a way of creating strong communities. In that sense, these labels sometimes hide what's really happening underneath them … Some schools of choice, I think, are simply vehicles for creating class segregation within cities, and enabling people to go to private schools with a public subsidy (Interview with David Cayley, in *The Education Debates*, ed. David Cayley [transcripts of the Canadian Broadcasting Corp., Toronto, Ontario, 1998–99], 40–41).

See also Meier, "Choice Can Save Public Education," *The Power of Their Ideas*, 81.

4. Paul Goodman, *Compulsory Miseducation and the Community of Scholars* (New York: Vintage Books, 1966).

5. Meier, radio interview with David Cayley, *The Education Debates*, 45.

6. William Damon, quoted by Ethan Bronner, "Rethinking America's Schools of Hard Knocks," *New York Times* (May 3 1999): 3.

7. John Dewey, *The School and Society* (Chicago: University of Chicago Press, 1990; first published, 1900, 1902), 15.

8. Dewey, 152.

9. Jane Tompkins, *A Life in School: What the Teacher Learned* (New York: Addison-Wesley, 1996), 147. For another writer who makes a case for teachers getting out of their students' way, see Donald Finkel, *Teaching with Your Mouth Shut* (Portsmouth, N.H.: Heinemann Boynton Cook, 2000).

10. William Ayers, *A Kind and Just Parent: The Children of Juvenile Court* (Boston: Beacon Press, 1997), 78.

11. Meier, "Changing Our Habits of Schooling," Marianne Amerel Memorial Lecture (East Lansing, Mich.: The Holmes Group, 1993), 12–3.

12. For an example of a kind of staff development project in which teachers at different levels work together in course design and delivery teams—a kind of *vertical* learning community—see Gerald Graff, "Working with the Schools: Project Tempest," *Publications of the Modern Language Association*, 115, no. 7 (December 2000): 1968–71.

13. Herbert W. Simons, a professor of rhetoric and communications at Temple University, has experimented with an adaptation of the talk-show format in a program of public debates he has developed there called the "Temple Issues Forum," which has a student arm, the Temple Debate and Discussion Club. Simons argues that the talk-show format is more successful than the single-person lecture in engaging the interest of today's young people. Simons's is the kind of thinking that is needed for imagining educational bigness in more arresting ways. "The Temple Issues Forum," unpublished talk delivered at the *Rhetoric Society* of America Conference, May 2002.

14. Meier, "Educating a Democracy," in *Will Standards Save Higher Education?*, ed. Deborah Meier (Boston: Beacon Press, 2000), 7.

15. Abigail Themstrom, "No Excuses," in *Will Standards Save Higher Education?*, 37.

Thank You, Esther Forbes

George Saunders

It began, like so many things in those days, with a nun. Unlike the other nuns at St. Damian School, who, it seemed, had been born nuns, Sister Lynette seemed to have been born an adorable, sun-dappled Kansas girl with an Audrey Hepburn smile, who was then kidnapped by a band of older, plumper, meaner nuns who were trying to break her. I was a little in love with Sister Lynette, with her dry wit and good-heartedness and the wisp of hair that snuck out from under her wimple. I thought of a convent as a place of terrific rigor, where prospective nuns were given access to esoteric knowledge, which they were then to secretly disseminate among select students in Middle America, to save the culture. Hoping to be so identified, I would linger in Sister Lynette's classroom after school (both of us covered in chalk dust, my wool pants smelling like Distressed Sheep) as she told me stories about her Kansas girlhood. I entertained rescue fantasies, in which Sister realized that the best way for her to serve God was to quit the nuns, marry me, and start wearing jeans as we traveled around the country making antiwar speeches. Since I was only in third grade, these fantasies required a pre-fantasy, in which pacifist aliens placed me in a sort of Aging Apparatus.

One afternoon, Sister Lynette handed me a book: *Johnny Tremain*, by Esther Forbes. This is the story of an arrogant apprentice silversmith in Boston during the Revolutionary War, whose prospects are cut short by a tragic accident until he finds a new sense of purpose in the war. The cover was a picture of a young Johnny, looking a bit like Twiggy. On it there was a shiny gold medallion: the Newbery Medal.

It was an award-winner.

Sister Lynette had given me an award-winner.

I was soon carrying it around twenty-four hours a day, the Newbery Medal facing out, as if I, and not Esther Forbes, had written *Johnny Tremain*.

"I think you can handle this," Sister had said as she handed me the book (she'd checked it out of the library), but what I heard was: "Only you, George, in this entire moronic class, can handle this. There is a spark in you, and it is that spark that keeps me from fleeing back to Kansas."

I imagined the scene at the convent—everyone in nun gear, sitting around a TV that was somehow always tuned to *The Flying Nun*. And then Sister Lynette makes her announcement:

"I'm thinking of giving Saunders *Johnny Tremain*."

A tense silence.

"Isn't that...," asks Sister Humiline, the principal, "an award-winner?"

"It is," says Sister Lynette. "But I think he's ready."

"Well, then. . . ," says Sister Humiline. Clearly this is important. Denied this, Sister Lynette might make her break for Kansas. "Let him give it a try, then. But, truly, I wonder if he's got it in him. That book is hard, and he is only a third-grader."

"Even I had trouble with it," pipes up a junior nun.

"I think he can handle it," says Sister Lynette.

And the wonderful thing was: I could. I loved the language, which was dense and seemed not to care that it sounded mathematically efficient ("On rocky islands gulls woke"). The sentences somehow had got more life in them than normal sentences had. They were not merely sentences but compressed moments that burst when you read them. I often left the book open on the kitchen table, so that my mother and her friends could see how at home I was with phrases like "too cripple-handed for chopping open sea chests" or "Isannah drank herself sick and silly on sillabubs."

A sentence, Forbes seemed to believe, not only had to say something, it had to say it uniquely, with verve. A sentence was more than just a fact-conveyor; it also made a certain sound, and could have a thrilling quality of being over-full, saying more than its length should permit it to say. A sequence of such sentences exploding in the brain made the invented world almost unbearably real, each sentence serving as a kind of proof.

The tragic accident that happens early in the book ends Johnny's silversmithing: his right thumb is melded to the palm of his hand by molten silver. During recess, I started holding my hand like his in the pocket of my coat, trying to get through the entire period without uncrippling myself. There was a sweetness in the bitterness I felt as I imagined that I was Johnny and the whole world had turned against me, even my fiancée, Cilia, and her real-life corollary, Susan Pusateri. Had Susan smiled? She would marry me in spite of my deformity. Was she talking energetically to Joey Cannarozzi? She preferred his fully opposable thumb, and I would therefore have to lay siege to the British armory.

After a while, because I liked the idea of being wounded, but didn't much like the idea of actually having that pink flipperlike thing flapping around on my arm, a world-famous surgeon from France would arrive in the Boston in my head and fix my hand, and I would go back to class, face chapped from the wind, holding the book in my now-perfect hand, Newbery Medal facing outward.

"Good book?" Sister Lynette would say from her desk.

"Good book," I would say.

Before *Johnny Tremain*, writers and writing gave me the creeps. In our English book, which had one of those 1970s titles that connoted nothing (*Issues and Perspectives*, maybe, or *Amalgam 109*), the sentences

("Larry, aged ten, a tow-headed heavyset boy with a happy smile for all, meandered down to the ballfield, hoping against hope he would at last be invited to join some good-spirited game instigated by the other lads of summer") repulsed me the way a certain kind of moccasin-style house slipper then in vogue among my father's friends repulsed me. I would never, I swore, wear slippers like that. Only old people who had given up on life could wear slippers like that. Likewise the sentences in *Amalgam 109* or *Polyglot Viewpoints* seemed to have given up on life, or to never have taken life sufficiently personally. They weren't lies, exactly, but they weren't true either. They lacked will. They seemed committee-written, seemed to emanate from no-person, to argue against the intimate actual feeling of minute-to-minute life.

Forbes suggested that the sentence was where the battle was fought. With enough attention, a sentence could peel away from its fellows and be, not only from you, but *you*. I later found the same quality in Hemingway, in Isaac Babel, Gertrude Stein, Henry Green: sentences that had been the subject of so much concentration, they had become things in the world instead of attempts to catalog it.

A person can write: "There were, out in the bay, a number of rocks, islands of a sort, and upon these miniature islands, there resided a number of gulls, which, as the sun began to rise, gradually came to life, ready to begin another day of searching for food."

Or she can write: "On rocky islands gulls woke."

The first sentence is perfectly correct. There is, strictly speaking, more information in it than in the second. But is the increased information justified by the greater number of words? The second sentence credits our intelligence. Where else would the islands be, but in a bay? The plural "islands" implies that there are "a number" of them. If the rocks are "islands of a sort," let's call them "islands." Gulls search for food every day, no need to point it out.

The second sentence has been loved by its creator. She has given it her full attention. That missing comma? She meant it. There was, to Forbes, I expect, a world of difference between, "On rocky islands, gulls woke," and "On rocky islands gulls woke."

Standing around the school yard, I tried out sentences meant to describe, with Forbes-like precision, whatever I happened to be seeing: "Sister Lynette was eating lunch in the doorway while watching the third- and fourth-grade kids running around in the parking lot at recess and as she watched them, she thought of her home in Kansas." That wasn't very Forbes-ish. Sister Lynette wasn't actually standing in the doorway at all. She was…she was "standing on the sidewalk that ran between the school building itself and the parking lot on which the children played." Or actually, she was "standing with one foot on that sidewalk and one foot in the parking lot." Did we need all that? Was her exact position worth the resulting sentence-bulk? Why did we care where she was standing anyway? Did it affect what came next? Also, she wasn't watching "the third- and fourth- grade kids." She was watching *some* of them. Actually, on closer inspection, she wasn't. She was looking across the street, at a run-down house. What did I mean by "run-down"? What were the specific characteristics of the house that might cause me to think of it as "run-down"?

I remember those times with great affection: the bitter Chicago cold, the vast parking lot, the world, suddenly and for the first time, transformed into something describable, with me, the Potential Describer, at its center.

The world, I started to see, was a different world, depending on what you said about it, and how you said it. By honing the sentences you used to describe the world, you changed the inflection of your mind, which changed your perceptions.

The difference between Esther Forbes and the authors of *Polyglot 141* was that Forbes had fully invested herself in her sentences. She had made them her own, agreed to live or die by them, taken total responsibility for them. How had she done this? I didn't know. But I do now: she'd revised them. She had abided long enough with each of them to push past the normal into what we might call the *excessive-meaningful*; had held the prose up to sufficient scrutiny to turn it into something iconic, something that sounded like her and only like her.

What happens when this attention is not paid?

Well, *Polyglot 141* happens.

But worse things can happen than *Polyglot 141*.

A petty bureaucrat writes to his superior: "The lighting must be better protected than now. Lights could be eliminated, since they apparently are never used. However, it has been observed that when the doors are shut, the load always presses hard against them as soon as darkness sets in. This is because the load naturally rushes toward the light when darkness sets in, which makes closing the door difficult. Also, because of the alarming nature of darkness, screaming always occurs when the doors are closed. It would therefore be useful to light the lamp before and during the first moments of the operation." The bureaucrat was the ironically named "Mr. Just," his organization the SS, the year 1942.

What Mr. Just did not write—what he would have written, had he been taking full responsibility for his own prose—is: "To more easily kill the Jews, leave the lights on." But writing this would have forced him to admit what he was up to. To avoid writing this, what did he have to do? Disown his prose. Pretend his prose was not him. He may have written a more honest version, and tore it up. He may have intuitively, self-protectively, skipped directly to this dishonest, passive-voice version. Either way, he accepted an inauthentic relation to his own prose, and thereby doomed himself to hell.

Working with language is a means by which we can identify the bullshit within ourselves (and others). If we learn what a truthful sentence looks like, a little flag goes up at a false one. False prose can mark an attempt to evade responsibility ("On structures not unlike rock masses, it was observed that certain animals perhaps prone to flight slept somewhat less aggressively than previously"), or something more diabolical ("The germ-ridden avatars of evil perched on their filthy black rocks in the otherwise pure bay, daring the clear-souled inhabitants of the city to do what was so obviously necessary: kill them before they could infest the city's hopeful, innocent children"); the process of improving our prose disciplines the mind, hones the logic, and, most important of all, tells us what we really think. But this process takes time, and immersion in prior models of beautiful compression.

Forbes was my first model of beautiful compression. She did for me what one writer can do for another: awoke a love for sentences. Behind her prose I sensed the loving hand of an involved human maker. Her thirst for direct, original language seemed like a religion of sorts, a method of orientation, and a comfort, in all countries and weathers, in happiness and sadness, in sickness and in health. Reading *Johnny Tremain*, I felt a premonition that immersion in language would enrich and bring purpose to my life, which has turned out to be true.

So thank you, Esther Forbes. I never knew you, it turned out your Boston never existed, but that nonexistent town, and that boy made out of words, changed things for me forever.

The Complexity of Identity
"Who am I?"

Beverly Daniel Tatum

The concept of identity is a complex one, shaped by individual characteristics, family dynamics, historical factors, and social and political contexts.
Who am I? The answer depends in large part on who the world around
me says I am. Who do my parents say I am? Who do my peers say I am?
What message is reflected back to me in the faces and voices of my teachers, my neighbors, store clerks? What do I learn from the media about
myself? How am I represented in the cultural images around me? Or am
I missing from the picture altogether? As social scientist Charles Cooley
pointed out long ago, other people are the mirror in which we see ourselves.[1]

This "looking glass self" is not a flat one-dimensional reflection,
but multidimensional. Because the focus of this book is racial identity in
the United States, race is highlighted in these pages. Yet, how one's racial
identity is experienced will be mediated by other dimensions of oneself:
male or female; young or old; wealthy, middle-class, or poor; gay, lesbian,
bisexual, transgender, or heterosexual; able-bodied or with disabilities;
Christian, Muslim, Jewish, Buddhist, Hindu, or atheist.

Abigail Stewart and Joseph Healy's research on the impact of historical periods on personality development raises the question, Who is my
cohort group?[2] Am I a child of the Depression, a survivor of World War II,
the Holocaust, the U.S. internment of Japanese Americans? A product of
the segregation of the 1940s and 1950s, or a beneficiary of the Civil Rights
era? Did I serve in the Vietnam War, or am I a refugee of it? Did I come of
age during the conservatism of the Reagan years? Did I ride the wave of the
Women's Movement? Was I born before or after Stonewall and the emer-
gence of gay activism? What historical events have shaped my thinking?

What has my social context been? Was I surrounded by people like
myself, or was I part of a minority in my community? Did I grow up
speaking standard English at home or another language or dialect? Did I
live in a rural county, an urban neighborhood, a sprawling suburb, or on
a reservation?

Who I am (or say I am) is a product of these and many other factors. Erik Erikson, the psychoanalytic theorist who coined the term
identity crisis, introduced the notion that the social, cultural, and historical context is the ground in which individual identity is embedded.
Acknowledging the complexity of identity as a concept, Erikson writes,

> We deal with a process "located" *in the core of the individual* and yet also *in the core of his communal culture*.... In psychological terms, identity formation employs a process of simultaneous reflection and observation, a process taking place on all levels of mental functioning, by which the individual judges himself in the light of what he perceives to be the way in which others judge him in comparison to themselves and to a typology significant to them; while he judges their way of judging him in the light of how he perceives himself in comparison to them and to types that have become relevant to him. This process is, luckily, and necessarily, for the most part unconscious except where inner conditions and outer circumstances combine to aggravate a painful, or elated, "identity-consciousness."[3]

Triggered by the biological changes associated with puberty, the maturation of cognitive abilities, and changing societal expectations, this process of simultaneous reflection and observation, the self-creation of one's identity, is commonly experienced in the United States and other Western societies during the period of adolescence.[4] Though the foundation of identity is laid in the experiences of childhood, younger children lack the physical and cognitive development needed to reflect on the self in this abstract way. The adolescent capacity for self-reflection (and resulting self: allows one to ask, "Who am I now?" "Who was I before?" "Who will I become?" The answers to these questions will influence choices about who one's romantic partners will be, what type of work one will do, where one will live, and what belief system one will embrace. Choices made in adolescence ripple throughout the lifespan.

Who Am I? Multiple Identities

Integrating one's past, present, and future into a cohesive, unified sense of self is a complex task that begins in adolescence and continues for a lifetime. The complexity of identity is made clear in a collection of autobiographical essays about racial identity called *Names We Call Home*.[5] The multiracial, multiethnic group of contributors narrate life stories highlighting the intersections of gender, class, religion, sexuality, race, and historical circumstance, and illustrating that "people's multiple identifications defy neat racial divisions and unidimensional political alliances."[6] My students' autobiographical narratives point to a similar complexity; but the less developed narratives of the late adolescents that I teach highlight the fact that our awareness of the complexity of our own identity develops over time. The salience of particular aspects of our identity varies at different moments in our lives. The process of integrating the component parts of our self-definition is indeed a lifelong journey.

Which parts of our identity capture our attention first? While there are surely idiosyncratic responses to this question, a classroom exercise I regularly use with my psychology students reveals a telling pattern. I ask my students to complete the sentence, "I am _____," using as many descriptors as they can think of in sixty seconds. All kinds of trait descriptions are used—friendly, shy, assertive, intelligent, honest, and so on—but over the years I have noticed something else. Students of color usually mention their racial or ethnic group: for instance, I am Black, Puerto Rican, Korean American. White students who have grown up in strong ethnic enclaves occasionally mention being Irish or Italian. But in general, White students rarely mention being White. When I use this exercise in coeducational settings, I notice a similar pattern in terms of gender, religion, and sexuality. Women usually mention being female, while men don't usually mention their maleness. Jewish students often say they are Jews, while mainline Protestants rarely mention their religious identification. A student who is comfortable revealing it publicly may mention being gay, lesbian, or bisexual. Though I know most of my students are heterosexual, it is very unusual for any one to include their heterosexuality on their list.

Common across these examples is that in the areas where a person is a member of the dominant or advantaged social group, the category is usually not mentioned. That element of their identity is so taken for granted by them that it goes without comment. It is taken for granted by them because it is taken for granted by the dominant culture. In Eriksonian terms, their inner experience and outer circumstance are in harmony with one another, and the image reflected by others is similar to the image within. In the absence of dissonance, this dimension of identity escapes conscious attention.

The parts of our identity that *do* capture our attention are those that other people notice, and that reflect back to us. The aspect of identity that is the target of others' attention, and subsequently of our own, often is that which sets us apart as exceptional or "other" in their eyes. In my life I have been perceived as both. A precocious child who began to read at age three, I stood out among my peers because of my reading ability. This "gifted" dimension of my identity was regularly commented upon by teachers and classmates alike, and quickly became part of my self-definition. But I was also distinguished by being the only Black student in the class, an "other," a fact I grew increasingly aware of as I got older.

While there may be countless ways one might be defined as exceptional, there are at least seven categories of "otherness" commonly experienced in U.S. society. People are commonly defined as other on the basis of race or ethnicity, gender, religion, sexual orientation, socioeconomic status, age, and physical or mental ability. Each of these categories has a form of oppression associated with it: racism, sexism, religious oppression/anti-Semitism,[7] heterosexism, classism, ageism, and ableism, respectively. In each case, there is a group considered dominant (systematically advantaged by the society because of group membership) and a group considered subordinate or targeted (systematically disadvantaged). When we think about our multiple identities, most of us will find that we are both dominant and targeted at the same time. But it is the targeted identities that hold our attention and the dominant identities that often go unexamined.

In her essay, "Age, Race, Class, and Sex: Women Redefining Difference," Audre Lorde captured the tensions between dominant and targeted identities co-existing in one individual. This self-described "forty-nine-year-old Black lesbian feminist socialist mother of two" wrote,

> Somewhere, on the edge of consciousness, there is what I call a *mythical norm*, which each one of us within our hearts knows "that is not me." In america, this norm is usually defined as white, thin, male, young, heterosexual, christian, and financially secure. It is with this mythical norm that the trappings of power reside within society. Those of us who stand outside that power often identify one way in which we are different, and we assume that to be the primary cause of all oppression, forgetting other distortions around difference, some of which we ourselves may be practicing.[8]

Even as I focus on race and racism in my own writing and teaching, it is helpful to remind myself and my students of the other distortions around difference that I (and they) may be practicing. It is an especially useful way of generating empathy for our mutual learning process. If I am impatient with a White woman for not recognizing her White privilege, it may be useful for me to remember how much of my life I spent oblivious to the fact of the daily advantages I receive simply because I am heterosexual, or the ways in which I may take my class privilege for granted.

Domination and Subordination

It is also helpful to consider the commonality found in the experience of being dominant or subordinate even when the sources of dominance or subordination are different. Jean Baker Miller, author of *Toward a New Psychology of Women*, has identified some of these areas of commonality.[9]

Dominant groups, by definition, set the parameters within which the subordinates operate. The dominant group holds the power and authority in society relative to the subordinates and determines how that power and authority may be acceptably used. Whether it is reflected in determining who gets the best jobs, whose history will be taught in school, or whose relationships will be validated by society, the dominant group has the greatest influence in determining the structure of the society.

The relationship of the dominants to the subordinates is often one in which the targeted group is labeled as defective or substandard in significant ways. For example, Blacks have historically been characterized as less intelligent than Whites, and women have been viewed as less emotionally stable than men. The dominant group assigns roles to the subordinates that reflect the latter's devalued status, reserving the most highly valued roles in the society for themselves. Subordinates are usually said to be innately incapable of being able to perform the preferred roles. To the extent that the targeted group internalizes the images that the dominant group reflects back to them, they may find it difficult to believe in their own ability.

When a subordinate demonstrates positive qualities believed to be more characteristic of dominants, the individual is defined by dominants as an anomaly. Consider this illustrative example: Following a presentation I gave to some educators, a White man approached me and told me how much he liked my ideas and how articulate I was. "You know," he concluded, "if I had had my eyes closed, I wouldn't have known it was a Black woman speaking." (I replied, "This is what a Black woman sounds like.")

The dominant group is seen as the norm for humanity. Jean Baker Miller also asserts that inequitable social relations are seen as the model for "normal human relationships." Consequently, it remains perfectly acceptable in many circles to tell jokes that denigrate a particular group, to exclude subordinates from one's neighborhood or work setting, or to oppose initiatives which might change the power balance.

Miller points out that dominant groups generally do not like to be reminded of the existence of inequality. Because rationalizations have been created to justify the social arrangements, it is easy to believe everything is as it should be. Dominants "can avoid awareness because their explanation of the relationship becomes so well integrated in other terms; they can even believe that both they and the subordinate group share the same interests and, to some extent, a common experience."[10]

The truth is that the dominants do not really know what the experience of the subordinates is. In contrast, the subordinates are very well informed about the dominants. Even when firsthand experience is limited by social segregation, the number and variety of images of the dominant group available through television, magazines, books, and newspapers provide subordinates with plenty of information about the dominants. The dominant world view has saturated the culture for all to learn. Even the Black or Latino child living in a segregated community can enter White homes of many kinds daily via the media. However, dominant access to information about the subordinates is often limited to stereotypical depictions of the "other." For example, there are many images of heterosexual relations on television, but very few images of gay or lesbian domestic partnerships beyond the caricatures of comedy shows. There are many images of White men and women in all forms of media, but relatively few portrayals of people of color.

Not only is there greater opportunity for the subordinates to learn about the dominants, there is also greater need. Social psychologist Susan Fiske writes, "It is a simple principle: People pay attention to those who control their outcomes. In an effort to predict and possibly influence what is going to happen to them, people gather information about those with power."[11]

In a situation of unequal power, a subordinate group has to focus on survival. It becomes very important for the subordinates to become highly attuned to the dominants as a way of protecting themselves from them. For example, women who have been battered by men often talk about the heightened sensitivity they develop to their partners' moods. Being able to anticipate and avoid the men's rage is important to survival.

Survival sometimes means not responding to oppressive behavior directly. To do so could result in physical harm to oneself, even death. In his essay "The Ethics of Living Jim Crow," Richard Wright describes eloquently the various strategies he learned to use to avoid the violence of Whites who would brutalize a Black person who did not "stay in his place."[12] Though it is tempting to think that the need for such strategies disappeared with Jim Crow laws, their legacy lives on in the frequent and sometimes fatal harassment Black men experience at the hands of White police officers.[13]

Because of the risks inherent in unequal relationships, the subordinates often develop covert ways of resisting or undermining the power of the dominant group. As Miller points out, popular culture is full of folk tales, jokes, and stories about how the subordinate—whether the woman, the peasant, or the sharecropper—outwitted the "boss."[14] In his essay "I Won't Learn from You," Herbert Kohl identifies one form of resistance, "not-learning," demonstrated by targeted students who are too often seen by their dominant teachers as "others."

> Not-learning tends to take place when someone has to deal with unavoidable challenges to her or his personal and family loyalties, integrity, and identity. In such situations, there are forced choices and no apparent middle ground. To agree to learn from a stranger who does not respect your integrity causes a major loss of self. The only alternative is to not-learn and reject their world.[15]

The use of either strategy, attending very closely to the dominants or not attending at all, is costly to members of the targeted group. Not-learning may mean there are needed skills which are not acquired. Attending closely to the dominant group may leave little time or energy to attend to one's self. Worse yet, the negative messages of the dominant group about the subordinates may be internalized, leading to self-doubt or, in its extreme form, self-hate. There are many examples of subordinates attempting to make themselves over in the image of the dominant group—Jewish people who want to change the Semitic look of their noses, Asians who have cosmetic surgery to alter the shape of their eyes, Blacks who seek to lighten their skin with bleaching creams, women who want to smoke and drink "like a man." Whether one succumbs to the devaluing pressures of the dominant culture or successfully resists them, the fact is that dealing with oppressive systems from the underside, regardless of the strategy, is physically and psychologically taxing.

Breaking beyond the structural and psychological limitations imposed on one's group is possible, but not easily achieved. To the extent that members of targeted groups do push societal limits—achieving unexpected success, protesting injustice, being "uppity"—by their actions they call the whole system into question. Miller writes, they "expose the inequality, and throw into question the basis for its existence. And they will make the inherent conflict an open conflict. They will then have to bear the burden and take the risks that go with being defined as 'troublemakers.'"[16]

The history of subordinate groups is filled with so-called troublemakers, yet their names are often unknown. Preserving the record of those subordinates and their dominant allies who have challenged the status quo is usually of little interest to the dominant, culture, but it is of great interest to subordinates who search for an empowering reflection in the societal mirror.

Many of us are both dominant and subordinate. Clearly racism and racial identity are at the center of discussion in this book, but as Audre Lorde said, from her vantage point as a Black lesbian, "There is no hierarchy of oppression." The thread and threat of violence runs through all of the isms. There is a need to acknowledge each other's pain, even as we attend to our own.

For those readers who are in the dominant racial category, it may sometimes be difficult to take in what is being said by and about those who are targeted by racism. When the perspective of the subordinate is shared directly, an image is reflected to members of the dominant group which is disconcerting. To the extent that one can draw on one's own experience of subordination—as a young person, as a person with a disability, as someone who grew up poor, as a woman—it may be easier to make meaning of another targeted group's experience. For those readers who are targeted by racism and are angered by the obliviousness of Whites sometimes described in these pages, it may be useful to attend to your experience of dominance where you may find it—as a heterosexual, as an able-bodied person, as a Christian, as a man—and consider what systems of privilege you may be overlooking. The task of resisting our own oppression does not relieve us of the responsibility of acknowledging our complicity in the oppression of others.

Our ongoing examination of who we are in our full humanity, embracing all of our identities, creates the possibility of building alliances that may ultimately free us all. It is with that vision in mind that I move forward with an examination of racial identity in the chapters to follow. My goal is not to flatten the multidimensional self-reflection we see of ourselves, but to focus on a dimension often neglected and discounted in the public discourse on race.

Notes

1. See C. Cooley, *Human Nature and the Social Order* (New York: Scribner, 1922). George H. Mead expanded on this idea in his book, *Mind, Self, and Society* (Chicago; University of Chicago Press, 1934).

2. A.J. Stewart and J.M. Healy, "Linking Individual Development and Social Changes," *American Psychologist* 44, no. 1 (1989): 30–42.

3. E.H. Erikson, *Identity, Youth, and Crisis* (New York: W.W. Norton, 1968). p. 22.

4. For a discussion of the Western biases in the concept of the self and individual identity, see A. Roland, "Identity, Self, and Individualism in a Multi-Cultural Perspective," pp. 11–23 in E.P. Salett and D.R. Koslow (Eds.), *Race, Ethnicity, and Self: Identity in Multicultural Perspective* (Washington, DC: National MultiCultural Institute, 1994).

5. B. Thompson and S. Tyagi (Eds.), *Names We Call Home: Autobiography on Racial Identity* (New York: Routledge, 1996).

6. Ibid., p. xi.

7. *Anti-Semitism* is a term commonly used to describe the oppression of Jewish people. However, other Semitic peoples (Arab Muslims, for example) are also subject to oppressive treatment on the basis of ethnicity as well as religion. For that reason, the terms *Jewish oppression* and *Arab oppression* are sometimes used to specify the particular form of oppression under discussion.

8. A. Lorde, "Age, Race, Class, and Sex: Women Redefining Difference," pp. 445–51 in P. Rothenberg (Ed.) *Race, Class, and Gender in the United States: An Integrated Study,* 3rd ed. (New York: St. Martin's Press, 1995), p. 446.

9. J.B. Miller, "Domination and Subordination," pp. 3–9 in *Toward a New Psychology of Women* (Boston: Beacon Press, 1976).

10. Ibid., p. 8.

11. S.T. Fiske, "Controlling Other People: The Impact of Power on Stereotyping," *American Psychologist* 48, no. 6 (1993): 621–28.

12. R. Wright, "The Ethics of Living Jim Crow" (1937), reprinted in P. Rothenberg (Ed.) *Race, Class, and Gender in the United States: An Integrated Study,* 3rd ed. (New York: St. Martin's Press, 1995).

13. An article in the popular weekly magazine *People* chronicled the close encounters of famous black men with White police officers. Despite their fame, these men were treated as potential criminals. Highlighted in the article is the story of Johnny Gammage, who was beaten to death by White police officers following a routine traffic stop in Pittsburgh. T. Fields-Meyer, "Under Suspicion," *People (*January 15, 1996); *40–47.*

14. Miller, "Domination and Subordination," p. 10.

15. H. Kohl, "I won't learn from you: Confronting student resistance,: pp. 134–35 in *Rethinking Our Classrooms: Teaching for Equity and Justice* (Milwaukee: Rethinking Our Schools, 1994), p. 134.

16. Miller, "Domination and Subordination," p. 12.

Beverly Daniel Tatum, "The Complexity of Identity," from *Why are All the Black Kids Sitting Together in the Cafeteria?: And Other Conversations About Race.* New York: Basic Books, 1997, pp. 18-28. Reprinted by permission of Basic Books, a member of Perseus Books Group.

CRITIQUE: DEVELOPING A CRITICAL APPROACH THROUGH RESEARCH AND ARGUMENTATION

Introduction

Critique: Developing a Critical Approach through Research and Argumentation

This final sequence of assignments asks you to engage in research in order to develop a critical approach to your topic. Your job will be to design a research approach, which you will then implement as you investigate your subject. The writing you produce should make an argument about your researched topic, supporting your views with well-documented reasons and evidence. This sequence builds on your practice in the previous sequence, where you analyze and use texts, consider audience and purpose, and incorporate others' ideas into your own writing.

The kind of writing you produce will be shaped by a number of factors. What is your purpose? Who is your audience? What kinds of evidence or other supporting material will be effective in making your argument? As you will see in the variety of essays included in this section, there are a variety of ways to make your argument and/or communicate information. Howard Gardner's essay, "A Rounded Version: The Theory of Multiple Intelligences," is similar to the kind of scholarly essay that you might write in the university, identifying a key question or idea for investigation, surveying the research or discussions about this idea, analyzing and discussing data or evidence, and forwarding an argument and new understanding of the idea. Gerald Graff also writes a scholarly essay, but his object of analysis—student writing—may differ from the kind of evidence or data that you may typically expect. However, Graff still summarizes, analyzes, and synthesizes the ideas in these texts just as he does when he discusses Deborah Meier's ideas. Finally, the essays by Thomas Frank, Eric Schlosser, and Ginger Strand are also examples of argument but they rely more readily on analyses of experiences, places, people, culture, events, or other kinds of "social texts." These types of texts can also be evidence but you should pay close attention to the way these writers carefully analyze, unpack, and document these texts just as they would source materials from scholarly journals, books, or other "traditional" materials.

Alternative to What?

Thomas Frank

It's Not Your Father's Youth Movement

There are few spectacles corporate America enjoys more than a good counterculture, complete with hairdos of defiance, dark complaints about the stifling "mainstream," and expensive accessories of all kinds. So it was only a matter of months after the discovery of "Generation X" that the culture industry sighted an all-new youth movement, whose new looks, new rock bands, and menacing new 'tude quickly became commercial shorthand for the rebel excitement associated with everything from Gen X ads and TV shows to the information revolution. Consumers have been treated to what has undoubtedly been the swiftest and most profound shift of imagery to come across their screens since the 1960s. New sound-tracks, new product design, new stars, new ads. "Alternative," they call it. Out with the old, in with the new.

Before this revelation, punk rock and its descendents had long been considered commercially unviable in responsible business circles because of their incorrigible angriness, their implacable hostility to the cultural climate that the major record labels had labored so long to build, as well as because of their difficult sound. Every one knows pop music is sup-posed to be simple and mass-producible, an easy matter of conforming to simple genres, of acting out the standard and instantly recognizable cultural tropes of mass society: *I love love, I'm sad sometimes, I like cars, I'm my own person, I'm something of a rebel, I'm a cowboy on a steel horse I ride.* All through the seventies and eighties the culture industry knew instinctively, that the music that inhabited the margins couldn't fit, didn't even merit consideration. So back in 1977, at the dawn of punk, the American media, whose primary role has long been the uncritical promo-tion of whatever it is that Hollywood, the record labels, or the networks are offering at the time, lashed out at this strange, almost unfathomable movement. "Rock Is Sick," announced the cover of *Rolling Stone* in 1977. The national news magazines pronounced the uprising to be degeneracy of the worst variety, then proceeded to ignore it all through the eighties. Its listeners were unmentionable on TV, film, and radio except as quasi-criminals, and in the official channels of music-industry discourse—ra-dio, MTV, music magazines—this music and the tiny independent labels that supported it simply didn't exist.

Of course we all know what happened next. Thanks to the turn-ing of generations and the inexorable logic of the market—and the wild success of Nirvana in 1991—the industry was forced to reconsider, and it descended in a ravenous frenzy on the natural habitats of those it once shunned. Within weeks high-powered executives were offering contracts to bands they had seen—only once, college radio playlists became the objects of intense corporate scrutiny, and longstanding independent labels were swallowed whole. *Rolling Stone* magazine began making pious reference to the pioneering influence of defunct bands like Big Black and Mission of Burma, whose records they ignored when new, and MTV hastily abandoned its pop origins to push "alternative" bands round the clock. By 1993, the mass media had risen as one and proclaimed itself in solidarity with the rebels, anxious to don flannel, head out to Lollapalooza on the weekend and "mosh" with the kids. The pinnacle came when *Time* magazine finally smelled green in the music, too. In its issue of October 2 1993, *Time* sent Christopher John Farley headlong into the kind of reckless celebrationism the magazine usually reserved only for the biggest-budget movies and the most successful TV shows. Salivating over the "anxious rebels" of "a young, vibrant alternative scene," Farley breathlessly detailed every aspect of the youngsters' deliciously ingenuous insurrection: They're "defiant," they're concerned with "purity and anticommercialism," they sing about "homes breaking," and— tastiest of all—they're upset about "being copied or co-opted by the mainstream."

Strangely, though, Farley's *Time* story on "alternative" rock barely mentioned a band that is not a "co-optation," that still produces records on an actual independent label. As per the usual dictates of American culture, only money counts, and indie labels don't advertise in *Time*. So Pearl Jam, the major-label band that has made a career out of imitating the indie sounds of the late eighties, won the magazine's accolades as the "demigod" of the new "underground," leading the struggle for "authenticity" and against "selling out."

Of course this is poor reporting, but journals like *Time* have always been more concerned with industry boosterism and the hard, profitable facts of making credible the latest packaging of youth culture than with a vague undefinable like "news." Thus while we read almost nothing about the still unmentionable world of independent rock, we are bombarded with insistences that Pearl Jam is the real rebel thing, the maximum leaders of America's new youth counterculture—assertions that are driven home by endless descriptions of the band going through all the varieties of insurgent posturing. They have a "keen sense of angst," and singer Eddie Vedder feels bad about the family problems of his youth. He rose to success from nowhere, too: He was a regular guy with a taste for living on the edge (much like the people in ads for sneakers and cars and jeans), a "gas station attendant and high school dropout," who thought up the band's lyrics while surfing. But Eddie's real sensitive also, a true Dionysian like Mick Jagger, with a "mesmerizing stage presence" that "reminded fans of an animal trying to escape from a leash." In fact, he's so sensitive that certain of the band's lyrics aren't included with the others on the album sleeve because "the subject matter is too painful for Vedder to see in print."

The gushing of official voices like *Time* make necessary a clarification that would ordinarily go without saying: Among the indie rock circles, which they mimic and from which they pretend to draw their credibility, bands like Pearl Jam are almost universally recognized to suck. Almost without exception, the groups and music that are celebrated as "alternative" are watery, derivative, and strictly second-rate; so uniformly bad, in fact, that one begins to believe that shallowness is a precondition of their marketability. Most of them play predigested and predictable versions of formulaic heavy guitar rock, complete with moronic solos and hoarse masculine poutings. There is certainly nothing even remotely "alternative" about this sound, since music like this has long been the favorite of teenage boys everywhere; it's just the usual synthetic product, repackaged in a wardrobe of brand new imagery made up of thousands of fawning articles and videos depicting them as "rebel" this or "twentysomething" that. The sole remarkable feature of these otherwise stunningly mediocre bands is their singers' astonishing ability to warble the shallowest of platitudes with an earnestness that suggests they have actually internalized their maudlin, Hallmark-worthy sentimentality.

As ever, the most interesting aspect of the industry's noisy clamoring and its self-proclaimed naughtiness is not the relative merits of the "alternative" culture products themselves, but the shift of imagery they connote. Forget the music; what we are seeing is just another overhaul of the rebel ideology that has fueled business culture ever since the 1960s, a new entrant in the long parade of "countercultural" entrepreneurship. Look back at the ads and the records and the artists of the pre-Nirvana period: all the same militant protestations of nonconformity are there, just as they are in the ads and records and artists of the seventies and the sixties. Color Me Badd and Wham! once claimed to be as existentially individualist, as persecuted a group of "anxious rebels" as Bush now does. But by the years immediately preceding 1992, these figures' claims to rebel leadership had evaporated, and American business faced a serious imagery crisis. People had at long last tired of such obvious fakery, grown unconvinced and bored. No one except the most guileless teeny-boppers and the most insecure boomers fell for the defiant posturing of Duran Duran or Vanilla Ice or M.C. Hammer or Bon Jovi; especially when the ghettos began to burn, especially when the genuinely disturbing sounds of music that was produced without benefit of corporate auspices were finding wider audiences.

By the beginning of the new decade, the patina of daring had begun to wear thin on the eighties' chosen crop of celebrity-rebels. Entire new lines of insolent shoes would have to be designed and marketed; entire new looks and emblems of protest would have to be found somewhere. Consumerism's traditional claim to be the spokesman for our inchoate disgust with consumerism was hemorrhaging credibility, and independent rock, with its Jacobin "authenticity" obsession, had just the things capital required.

Out went the call for an "alternative" from a thousand executive suites, and overnight everyone even remotely associated with independent rock in Seattle—and Minneapolis, Chapel Hill, Champaign, Lawrence, and finally Chicago—found themselves the recipients of unsolicited corporate attention. Only small adjustments were required to bring the whole universe of corporate-sponsored rebellion up to date, to give us Blind Melon instead of Frankie Goes to Hollywood; 10,000 Maniacs instead of Sigue Sigue Sputnik. And suddenly we were propelled into an entirely new hip paradigm, a new universe of cool, with all new stars and all new relationships between the consumer, his celebrities, and his hair.

And now Pepsi is no longer content to cast itself as the beverage of Michael Jackson or Ray Charles or even Madonna: These figures' hip has been outdated suddenly, convincingly, and irreparably. Instead we watch a new and improved, an even more anti-establishment Pepsi Generation, cavorting about to what sounds like "grunge" rock, engaged in what appears to be a sort of oceanside slam dance. *Vanity Fair*, a magazine devoted strictly to the great American pastime of celebrating celebrity, hires the editors of a noted "alternative" 'zine to overhaul its hipness; *Interview*, the great, stupid voice of art as fashion, runs a lengthy feature on college radio, the site of the juiciest, most ingenuously "alternative" lifestyle innovations in the land. Ad agencies and record labels compete with each other in a frenzied scramble to hire leading specimens of the "alternative" scene they have ignored for fifteen years. Even commercial radio stations have seen the demographic writing on the wall and now every city has one that purports to offer an "alternative" format, featuring musical hymns to the various rebellious poses available to consumers at malls everywhere.

But the most revealing manifestation of the new dispensation is something you aren't supposed to see: an ad for MTV that ran in the business sections of a number of newspapers. "Buy this 24-year-old and get all his friends absolutely free," its headline reads. Just above these words is a picture of the 24-year-old referred to, a quintessential "alternative" boy decked out in the rebel garb that the executives who read this ad will instantly recognize from their market reports to be the costume of the "twentysomethings": beads and bracelets, a vest and t-shirt, torn jeans, Doc Martens, and a sideways haircut like the Jesus and Mary Chain wore in 1985. His pose: insolent, sprawled insouciantly in an armchair, watching TV of course. His occupation: consumer. "He watches MTV," continues the ad, "which means he knows a lot. More than just what CDs to buy and what movies to see. He knows what car to drive and what credit cards to use. And he's no loner. What he eats, his friends eat. What he wears, they wear. What he likes, they like."

Thus with the "alternative" face-lift, "rebellion" continues to perform its traditional function of justifying the economy's ever-accelerating cycles of obsolescence with admirable efficiency. Since our willingness to load up our closets with purchases depends upon an eternal shifting of the products paraded before us, upon our being endlessly convinced that the new stuff is better than the old, we must be persuaded over and over again that the "alternatives" are more valuable than the existing or the previous. Ever since the 1960s hip has been the native tongue of advertising, "antiestablishment" the vocabulary by which we are taught to cast off our old possessions and buy whatever they have decided to offer this year. And over the years the rebel has naturally become the central image of this culture of consumption, symbolizing endless, directionless change, an eternal restlessness with "the establishment"—or, more correctly, with the stuff "the establishment" convinced him to buy last year.

Not only did the invention of "alternative" provide capital with a new and more convincing generation of rebels, but in one stroke it outdated all the rebellions of the past ten years, rendered our acid-washed jeans, our Nikes, our DKNYs meaningless. Are you vaguely pissed off at the world? Well, now you get to start proving it all over again, with flannel shirts, a different brand of jeans, and big clunky boots. And in a year or two there will be an "alternative" to that as well, and you'll get to do it yet again.

It's not only the lure of another big Nirvana-like lucre-glut that brings label execs out in droves to places like Seattle, or hopes of uncovering the new slang that prompts admen to buy journals like *The Baffler*. The culture industry is drawn to "alternative" by the more general promise of finding the eternal new, of tapping the very source of the fuel that powers the great machine. As *Interview* affirms, "What still makes the genre so cool is not its cash potential or hype factor but the attendant drive and freedom to create and discover fresh, new music." Fresh new music, fresh new cars, fresh new haircuts, fresh new imagery.

Thus do capital's new dancing flunkeys appear not in boater hat and ingratiating smile, but in cartoonish postures of sullen angst or teen frustration: dyed hair, pierced appendages, flannel shirt around the waist. Everyone in advertising remembers how frightening and enigmatic such displays were ten years ago when they encountered them in TV stories about punk rock, and now their time has come to be deployed as the latest signifiers of lifestyle savvy. Now it's executives themselves on their days off, appearing in their weekend roles as kings of the consumer hill, who flaunt such garb, donning motorcycle jackets and lounging around the coffeehouses they imagine to be frequented by the latest generation of angry young men. Of course every other persecuted-looking customer is also an advertising account exec or a junior vice president of something-or-other; of course nobody would ever show up to see a band like, say, the New Bomb Turks or Prisonshake in a costume like this.

So on we plod through the mallways of our lives, lured into an endless progression of shops by an ever-changing chorus of manic shaman-rebels, promising existential freedom—sex! ecstasy! liberation!—from the endless trudge. All we ever get, of course, are some more or less baggy trousers or a hat that we can wear sideways. Nothing works, we are still entwined in vast coils of tawdriness and idiocy, and we resolve not to be tricked again. But lo! Down the way is a new rebel-leader, doing hand-stands this time, screaming about his untrammeled impertinence in an accent that we know could *never* be co-opted, and beckoning us into a shoe store. Marx's quip that the capitalist will sell the rope with which he is hanged begins to seem ironically incomplete. In fact, with its endless ranks of beautifully coiffed, fist-waving rebel boys to act as barker, business is amassing great sums by charging admission to the ritual simulation of its own lynching.

Come Around to My Way of Thinking

Perhaps the only good thing about the commodification of "alternative" is that it will render obsolete, suddenly, cleanly, and inexorably, that whole flatulent corpus of "cultural studies" that seeks to appreciate Madonna as some sort of political subversive. Even though the first few anthologies of writings on the subject only appeared in 1993, the rise of a far more threatening generation of rock stars has ensured that this singularly annoying pedagogy will never become a full-fledged "discipline," with its own lengthy quarterly issued by some university press, with annual conferences where the "subaltern articulations" of *Truth or Dare* are endlessly dissected and debated.

Looking back from the sudden vantage point that only this kind of image-revolution affords, the scholarship of academia's Madonna fans now appears as predictable in its conclusions as it was entertaining in its theoretical pyrotechnics. After careful study of the singer's lyrics and choreography, the professors breathlessly insisted, they had come upon a crucial discovery: Madonna was a gender-questioning revolutionary of explosive potential, a rule-breaking avatar of female empowerment, a person who disliked racism! One group of gaping academics hailed her "ability to tap into and disturb established hierarchies of gender and sexuality." Another celebrated her video "Vogue" as an "attempt to enlist us in a performance that, in its kinetics, deconstructs gender and race," an amusing interpretation, to be sure, but also one that could easily have been translated into academese directly from a Madonna press kit.

The problem is not that academics have abandoned their sacred high-culture responsibilities for a channel changer and a night at the disco, but that in so doing they have uncritically reaffirmed the mass media's favorite myths about itself. Discovering, after much intellectual twisting and turning, that Madonna is exactly the rebel that she and her handlers imagine her to be, is more an act of blithe intellectual complicity than of the "radicalism" to which the Madonna analysts believe they are contributing. After all, it was Madonna's chosen image as liberator from established mores that made her so valuable to the culture industry in the first place. It doesn't take a genius to realize that singing the glories of pseudo-rebellion remains to this day the monotone anthem of advertising, film, and TV sitcom, or that the pseudo-rebel himself—the defier of repressive tradition, ever overturning established ways to make way for the new; the self-righteous pleasure-monad, changing identity, gender, hair color, costume, and shoes on a whim—is more a symbol of the machine's authority than an agent of resistance. But academics seem to have missed the point. For years the culture industry has held up for our admiration an unending parade of such self-proclaimed subverters of middle-class tastes, and certain scholars have been only too glad to play their part in the strange charade, studying the minutiae of the various artists' rock videos and deciding, after long and careful deliberation, that yes, each one is, in fact, a bona fide subversive. How thoroughly had they come around to the Industry's way of thinking; how desperately did they want to, *want to* get along!

But thanks to the rise of "alternative," with its new and vastly improved street cred, sneers, and menacing hairdos, the various postmodern courses by which each scribbler arrived at his or her conclusion that Madonna is "subverting" from within, and the particular costly academic volume in which they presented their "findings" are now, thankfully, finally, and irresistibly made irrelevant. Just as Madonna's claims to rebel authenticity have been made suddenly laughable by an entirely new package of much more rebellious rebel imagery, so their works are consigned to the same fate. Academia's Madonna fans have built their careers by performing virtually the same task, with a nice intellectual finish, as the toothy hosts of *Entertainment Tonight*, and now they are condemned to the same rubbish bin of instant forgetting. Their embrace of corporate culture has brought them face to face with *its* unarguable conclusions, the steel logic of *its* unprotestable workings: obsolescence.

In at least one sense, then, the triumph of Urge Overkill is a liberation. At least we will never, ever have to hear this favorite Paglian (or, should we say, all-American) platitude chanted for the thousand-and-first time: "I admire Madonna because she's a woman who's totally in control of her career." And since it will take at least three years for the first close readings of the "Sister Havana" video to appear in assigned texts, let us enjoy the respite and ponder the strange twists of history that brought academia so closely into line with the imperatives of mass culture.

In this spirit I offer the following observation.

Perhaps the saddest aspect of all this is not scholars' gullible swallowing of some industry publicist's line, or even their naïve inability to discern Madonna's obvious labor-fakery. The real disappointment lies in their abject inability to recognize "popular culture" anywhere but in the officially-sanctioned showplaces of corporate America; their utter dependence on television to provide them with an imagery of car miracles qua dissidence. Even as they delved deeper and deeper into the esoterica of poststructuralist theory, investing countless hours scrutinizing bad rock videos frame by frame, they remained hopelessly ignorant of the actual insurgent culture that has gone on all around them for fifteen years, for the simple reason that it's never made MTV. And academics, the wide-eyed, well-scrubbed sons and daughters of the suburbs, cannot imagine a "counterculture" that exists outside of their full-color, 36-inch screens. So in TV-land as well as the academy, Madonna was as "radical" as it got. Thus did the role of criticism become identical to that of the glossy puff magazines, with their well-practiced slavering over the latest products of the Culture Industry: to celebrate celebrity, to find an epiphany in shopping, a happy heteroglossia in planned obsolescence. As for their interpretations, the professorial class might just as well have been proclaiming the counter-hegemonic undercurrents of *Match Game* or the patriarchy-resisting profundity of Virginia Slims advertising.

Imagine what they could do if they only knew about Borbe-tomagus or Merzbow!

Fuck You and Your Underground

At the center of the academics' intricate webs of Madonna-theories lay the rarely articulated but crucial faith that the workings of the culture industry, the stuff that comes over our TV screens and through our stereos, are profoundly *normal*. The culture-products that so unavoidably define our daily lives, it is believed, are a given—a natural expression of the tastes of "the people." This has long been a favorite sophistry of the industry's *paid* publicity flacks as well: mass culture is fundamentally democratic. The workings of the market ensure that the people get what the people want; that sitcoms and Schwarzenegger and each of the various sneering pop stars are the embodiment of the general will. Thus, as the academic celebrators of Madonna were always careful to assert, those who insist on criticizing Madonna are deeply suspicious, affected adherents of an elitist and old-fashioned aesthetic that unfairly dismisses "low" culture in favor of such insufferably stuffy pastimes as ballet and opera.

This anti-elitist theme is, quite naturally, also a favorite in sitcoms and movies, which establish their hegemony over the public mind by routinely bashing various stock snobs and hapless high-brow figures. Advertising repeatedly strikes the same note: a drink called "Somers" is to gin, one ad asserts, as a bright green electric guitar, implement of transgressive cool, is to an old brown violin, squeaky symbol of the slow-moving. A Pizza Hut commercial similarly juxtaposes a moralizing, old-fashioned, stuffed-shirt man who is filmed in black and white, with a full-color, rock 'n' roll rendition of the restaurant of revolt. And when the straw man of "cultural elitism" is conjured up by the academics for its ritual stomping, the feeling is exactly the same. There is only the dry, spare, highbrow of the privileged and the lusty, liberated, lowbrow of the masses, and between these two the choice is clear.

This, then, is the culture of "the people." Never mind all the openly conducted machinations of the culture industry—the mergers: and acquisitions, the "synergy," the admen's calculations of "penetration" and "usage pull," the dismantling of venerable publishing operations for reasons of fiscal whimsy. What the corporations have decided we will watch and read and listen to has somehow become the grassroots expressions of the nation. The Cultural Studies verdict is crucial financially as well, since the primary business of business is no longer, say, making things or exploiting labor, but manufacturing culture, finding the means to persuade you of the endless superiority of the new over the old, that the solution to whatever your unhappiness may be lies in a few new purchases. It is a truism of the business world that Coke and Pepsi don't make soda pop, they make advertising. Nike may pay Indonesian laborers absurdly low wages, but their most important concern is convincing us that it is meaningful, daring, and fulfilling to spend over one hundred dollars for a pair of sneakers. If you feel a burning need to understand "culture," get out of the coffeehouse and buy yourself a subscription to *Advertising Age*.

The media-flurry over the definition of the "twentysomethings" provides an interesting example of the ways in which "popular culture" is made, not born. Between the multitude of small presses and independent record labels that were founded, produced, and distributed by young people over the last decade, we have been an unusually voluble group. But this is not what was meant when the various lifestyle journalists and ad agency hacks went looking for "Generation X." The only youth culture that concerned them was the kind that's prefabricated for us in suites on Sunset Strip and Madison Avenue, and the only question that mattered was how to refine this stuff so that the young be lured into the consumer maelstrom. Take a look at the book *13th Gen* by Neil Howe and

Bill Strauss, the most baldfaced attempt to exploit the culture industry's confusion about how to pigeonhole us. What matters and what deserves to be reported are the movies, TV sitcoms, and major-label records that are targeted our way. The book's press kit explicitly cast *13th Gen* as a useful guide for executives in the advertising, public-relations, and election-winning industries. We are to be sold, not heard.

Under no condition is "popular culture" something that we make ourselves, in the garage with electric guitars and second-hand amplifiers, on the office photocopier when nobody's looking. It is, strictly and exclusively, the stuff produced for us in a thousand corporate boardrooms and demographic studies. "Popular culture" sells us stuff, convinces us to buy more soap or a different kind of shirt, assures us of the correctness of business paternalism, offers us a rebel fantasy world in which to drown our never-to-be-realized frustration with lives that have become little more than endless shopping trips, marathon filing sessions.

"Popular culture" is the enemy; rock 'n' roll is the health of the state.

The true culture war has nothing to do with the clever *pas de deux* of affected outrage acted out by sputtering right-wingers and their blustering counterparts in Soho and Hollywood. It is not fought out over issues like "family values" or "cultural elitism," but with a much more basic concern: the power of each person to make his own life without the droning dictation of business interests. If we must have grand, sweeping cultural judgments, only one category seems to matter anymore: the adversarial. The business of business is our minds, and the only great divide that counts anymore is whether or not we comprehend, we resist, we evade the all-invasive embrace.

But between the virtual monopoly of business interests over the stuff you spend all day staring at and the decision of the academics to join the burgeoning and noisy legion of culture industry cheerleaders, very little that is adversarial is allowed to filter through. Our culture has been hijacked without a single cry of outrage. However we may fantasize about Madonna's challenging of "oppressive tonal hierarchies," however we may drool over Pearl Jam's rebel anger, there is, quite simply, almost no dissent from the great cultural project of corporate America, no voice to challenge television's overpowering din. You may get a different variety of shoes this year, but there is no "alternative," ever.

We may never be able to dismantle the culture of consumption nor achieve any sort of political solution to the problems of this botched civilization. The traditional organs of resistance, enfeebled by decades of legislative attack and a cultural onslaught they do not comprehend, have either made their peace with consumerism or cling to outdated political goals.

But through the deafening mechanical yammering of a culture long since departed from the rails of meaning or democracy, through the excited hum of the congregation gathered for celebrity-worship, there is one promising sound. Its scream of torment is this country's only mark of health; the sweet shriek of outrage is the only sign that sanity survives amid the stripmalls and hazy clouds of Hollywood desire. It is proof that just beyond the silence of suburban stupidity, the confusion of the parking lots, the aggression, display, and desperate supplication of the city streets, the possibility of a worthy, well-screamed *no* survives. That just behind the stupefying smokescreens of authorized "popular culture" seethes something *real*, thriving, condemned to happy obscurity both by the marketplace, to whose masters (and consumers) its violent negation will be forever incomprehensible, and by the academic arbiters of "radicalism," by whom the "culture of the people" is strictly understood to be whatever the corporate donors *say* it is. Unauthorized and unauthorizable, it clamors in disgust amid the pseudo-rebel propriety of the cultural avenues of the empire. For official America it's fantasies of the comfortable cul-de-sac with state-of-the-art security equipment, the fine car, the airborne curfew enforcement unit, the Lake Forest estate, the Westchester commute; for us it's the secession, the internal exile, the thrashing release, the glorious never never never.

For this expression of dissent there has been no Armory show, no haughty embrace by aesthetes or editors. The only recognition it has garnered is the siege equipment of the consumer age, a corporate-sponsored shadow movement that seeks to mine it for marketable looks, imitable sounds, menacing poses. A travelling youth circus patterned, of course, after the familiar boomer originals of Woodstock and Dead shows, is invented to showcase the new industry dispensations. With their bottomless appetite for new territory to colonize, the executives have finally come around to us. For years they were too busy to be bothered, but now what we have been building has begun to look marketable.

But we will not be devoured easily. Few among us are foolish enough to believe that "the music industry" is just a bigger version of the next-door indie label, just a collection of simple record companies gifted mysteriously with gargantuan budgets and strange powers to silence criticism. We inhabit an entirely different world, intend entirely different outcomes. They seek fresh cultural fuel so that the machinery of stupidity may run incessantly; we cry out from under that machine's wheels. They manufacture lifestyle; we live lives.

So as they venture into the dark new world of hip, they should beware: The natives in these parts are hostile, and we're armed with flamethrowers. We will refuse to do their market research for them, to provide them amiably with helpful lifestyle hints and insider trend know-how. We are not a convenient resource available for exploitation whenever they require a new transfusion of rebel street cred; a test-market for "acts" they can someday unleash on the general public. And as they canvass the college radio stations for tips on how many earrings and in which nostril, or for the names of the "coolest" up-and-coming acts, they will, find themselves being increasingly misled, embarrassed by bogus slang, deceived by phantom blips on the youth-culture futures index, anticipating releases from nonexistent groups. It has taken years to win the tiny degree of autonomy we now enjoy. No matter which way they cut their hair or how weepily Eddie Vedder reminisces about his childhood, we aren't about to throw it open to a process that in just a few years would leave us, too, jaded and spent, discarded for yet a newer breed of rebels, an even more insolent crop of imagery, looks, and ads.

Baffler #5, 1993

A Rounded Version:
The Theory of Multiple Intelligences

Howard Gardner
Coauthored by Joseph Walters

Two eleven-year-old children are taking a test of "intelligence." They sit at their desks laboring over the meanings of different words, the interpretation of graphs, and the solutions to arithmetic problems. They record their answers by filling in small circles on a single piece of paper. Later these completed answer sheets are scored objectively: the number of right answers is converted into a standardized score that compares the individual child with a population of children of similar age.

The teachers of these children review the different scores. They notice that one of the children has performed at a superior level; on all sections of the test, she answered more questions correctly than did her peers. In fact, her score is similar to that of children three to four years older. The other child's performance is average—his scores reflect those of other children his age.

A subtle change in expectations surrounds the review of these test scores. Teachers begin to expect the first child to do quite well during her formal schooling, whereas the second should have only moderate success. Indeed these predictions come true. In other words, the test taken by the eleven-year-olds serves as a reliable predictor of their later performance in school.

How does this happen? One explanation involves our free use of the word "intelligence": the child with the greater "intelligence" has the ability to solve problems, to find the answers to specific questions, and to learn new material quickly and efficiently. These skills in turn play a central role in school success. In this view, "intelligence" is a singular faculty that is brought to bear in any problem-solving situation. Since schooling deals largely with solving problems of various sorts, predicting this capacity in young children predicts their future success in school.

"Intelligence," from this point of view, is a general ability that is found in varying degrees in all individuals. It is the key to success in solving problems. This ability can be measured reliably with standardized pencil-and-paper tests that, in turn, predict future success in school.

What happens after school is completed? Consider the two individuals in the example. Looking further down the road, we find that the "average" student has become a highly successful mechanical engineer who has risen to a position of prominence in both the professional community of engineers as well as in civic groups in his community. His success is no fluke—he is considered by all to be a talented individual. The

181

"superior" student, on the other hand, has had little success in her chosen career as a writer; after repeated rejections by publishers, she has taken up a middle management position in a bank. While certainly not a "failure," she is considered by her peers to be quite "ordinary" in her adult accomplishments. So what happened?

This fabricated example is based on the facts of intelligence testing. IQ tests predict school performance with considerable accuracy, but they are only an indifferent predictor of performance in a profession after formal schooling.[1] Furthermore, even as IQ tests measure only logical or logical-linguistic capacities, in this society we are nearly "brain-washed" to restrict the notion of intelligence to the capacities used in solving logical and linguistic problems.

To introduce an alternative point of view, undertake the following "thought experiment." Suspend the usual judgment of what constitutes intelligence and let your thoughts run freely over the capabilities of humans—perhaps those that would be picked out by the proverbial Martian visitor. In this exercise, you are drawn to the brilliant chess player, the world-class violinist, and the champion athlete; such outstanding performers deserve special consideration. Under this experiment, a quite different view of *intelligence* emerges. Are the chess player, violinist, and athlete "intelligent" in these pursuits? If they are, then why do our tests of "intelligence" fail to identify them? If they are not "intelligent," what allows them to achieve such astounding feats? In general, why does the contemporary construct "intelligence" fail to explain large areas of human endeavor?

In this chapter we approach these problems through the theory of multiple intelligences (MI). As the name indicates, we believe that human cognitive competence is better described in terms of a set of abilities, talents, or mental skills, which we call "intelligences." All normal individuals possess each of these skills to some extent; individuals differ in the degree of skill and in the nature of their combination. We believe this theory of intelligence may be more humane and more veridical* than alternative views of intelligence and that it more adequately reflects the data of human "intelligent" behavior. Such a theory has important educational implications, including ones for curriculum development.

What Constitutes An Intelligence?

The question of the optimal definition of intelligence looms large in our inquiry. Indeed, it is at the level of this definition that the theory of multiple intelligences diverges from traditional points of view. In a traditional view, intelligence is defined operationally as the ability to answer items on tests of intelligence. The inference from the test scores to some underlying ability is supported by statistical techniques that compare

---

*veridical: Telling the truth.

responses of subjects at different ages; the apparent correlation of these test scores across ages and across different tests corroborates the notion that the general faculty of intelligence, *g*, does not change much with age or with training or experience. It is an inborn attribute or faculty of the individual.

Multiple intelligences theory, on the other hand, pluralizes the traditional concept. An intelligence entails the ability to solve problems or fashion products that are of consequence in a particular cultural setting or community. The problem-solving skill allows one to approach a situation in which a goal is to be obtained and to locate the appropriate route to that goal. The creation of a *cultural* product is crucial to such functions as capturing and transmitting knowledge or expressing one's views or feelings. The problems to be solved range from creating an end for a story to anticipating a mating move in chess to repairing a quilt. Products range from scientific theories to musical compositions to successful political campaigns.

MI theory is framed in light of the biological origins of each problem-solving skill. Only those skills that are universal to the human species are treated. Even so, the biological proclivity to participate in a particular form of problem solving must also be coupled with the cultural nurturing of that domain. For example, language, a universal skill, may manifest itself particularly as writing in one culture, as oratory in another culture, and as the secret language of anagrams in a third.

Given the desire of selecting intelligences that are rooted in biology, and that are valued in one or more cultural settings, how does one actually identify an "intelligence"? In coming up with our list, we consulted evidence from several different sources: knowledge about normal development and development in gifted individuals; information about the breakdown of cognitive skills under conditions of brain damage; studies of exceptional populations, including prodigies, idiots savants, and autistic children; data about the evolution of cognition over the millennia; cross-cultural accounts of cognition; psychometric studies, including examinations of correlations among tests; and psychological training studies, particularly measures of transfer and generalization across tasks. Only those candidate intelligences that satisfied all or a majority of the criteria were selected as bona fide intelligences. A more complete discussion of each of these criteria for an "intelligence" and the seven intelligences that have been proposed so far, is found in *Frames of Mind*.[2] This book also considers how the theory might be disproven and compares it to competing theories of intelligence.

In addition to satisfying the aforementioned criteria, each intelligence must have an identifiable core operation or set of operations. As a neutrally based computational system, each intelligence is activated or "triggered" by certain kinds of internally or externally presented information. For example, one core of musical intelligence is the sensitivity to pitch relations, whereas one core of linguistic intelligence is the sensitivity to phonological features.

An intelligence must also be susceptible to encoding in a symbol system—a culturally contrived system of meaning, which captures and conveys important forms of information. Language, picturing, and mathematics are but three nearly worldwide symbol systems that are necessary for human survival and productivity. The relationship of a candidate intelligence to a human symbol system is no accident. In fact, the existence of a core computational capacity anticipates the existence of a symbol system that exploits that capacity. While it may be possible for an intelligence to proceed without an accompanying symbol system, a primary characteristic of human intelligence may well be its gravitation toward such an embodiment.

The Seven Intelligences

Having sketched the characteristics and criteria of an intelligence, we turn now to a brief consideration of each of the seven intelligences. We begin each sketch with a thumbnail biography of a person who demonstrates an unusual facility with that intelligence. These biographies illustrate some of the abilities that are central to the fluent operation of a given intelligence. Although each biography illustrates a particular intelligence, we do not wish to imply that in adulthood intelligences operate in isolation. Indeed, except for abnormal individuals, intelligences always work in concert, and any sophisticated adult role will involve a melding of several of them. Following each biography we survey the various sources of data that support each candidate as an "intelligence."

Musical Intelligence

When he was three years old, Yehudi Menuhin was smuggled into the San Francisco Orchestra concerts by his parents. The sound of Louis Persinger's violin so entranced the youngster that he insisted on a violin for his birthday and Louis Persinger as his teacher. He got both. By the time he was ten years old, Menuhin was an international performer.[3]

Violinist Yehudi Menuhin's musical intelligence manifested itself even before he had touched a violin or received any musical training. His powerful reaction to that particular sound and his rapid progress on the instrument suggest that he was biologically prepared in some way for that endeavor. In this way evidence from child prodigies supports our claim that there is a biological link to a particular intelligence. Other special populations, such as autistic children who can play a musical instrument beautifully but who cannot speak, underscore the independence of musical intelligence.

A brief consideration of the evidence suggests that musical skill passes the other tests for an intelligence. For example, certain parts of the brain play important roles in perception and production of music. These areas are characteristically located in the right hemisphere, although musical skill is not as clearly "localized," or located in a specifiable area, as language. Although the particular susceptibility of musical ability to brain damage depends on the degree of training and other individual differences, there is clear evidence for "amusia" or loss of musical ability.

Music apparently played an important unifying role in Stone Age (Paleolithic) societies. Birdsong provides a link to other species. Evidence from various cultures supports the notion that music is a universal faculty. Studies of infant development suggest that there is a "raw" computational ability in early childhood. Finally, musical notation provides an accessible and lucid symbol system.

In short, evidence to support the interpretation of musical ability as an "intelligence" comes from many different sources. Even though musical skill is not typically considered an intellectual skill like mathematics, it qualifies under our criteria. By definition it deserves consideration; and in view of the data, its inclusion is empirically justified.

Bodily-Kinesthetic Intelligence

Fifteen-year-old Babe Ruth played third base. During one game his team's pitcher was doing very poorly and Babe loudly criticized him from third base. Brother Mathias, the coach, called out, "Ruth, if you know so much about it, YOU pitch!" Babe was surprised and embarrassed because he had never pitched before, but Brother Mathias insisted. Ruth said later that at the very moment he took the pitcher's mound, he KNEW he was supposed to be a pitcher and that it was "natural" for him to strike people out. Indeed, he went on to become a great major league pitcher (and, of course, attained legendary status as a hitter).[4]

Like Menuhin, Babe Ruth was a child prodigy who recognized his "instrument" immediately upon his first exposure to it. This recognition occurred in advance of formal training.

Control of bodily movement is, of course, localized in the motor cortex, with each hemisphere dominant or controlling bodily movements on the contra-lateral side. In right-handers, the dominance for such movement is ordinarily found in the left hemisphere. The ability to perform movements when directed to do so can be impaired even in individuals who can perform the same movements reflexively or on a nonvoluntary basis. The existence of specific apraxia constitutes one line of evidence for a bodily-kinesthetic intelligence.

The evolution of specialized body movements is of obvious advantage to the species, and in humans this adaptation is extended through the use of tools. Body movement undergoes a clearly defined developmental schedule in children. And there is little question of its universality across cultures. Thus it appears that bodily-kinesthetic "knowledge" satisfies many of the criteria for an intelligence.

The consideration of bodily-kinesthetic knowledge as "problem solving" may be less intuitive. Certainly carrying out a mime sequence or hitting a tennis ball is not solving a mathematical equation. And yet, the ability to use one's body to express an emotion (as in a dance), to play a game (as in a sport), or to create a new product (as in devising an invention) is evidence of the cognitive features of body usage. The specific computations required to solve a particular bodily-kinesthetic *problem*, hitting a tennis ball, are summarized by Tim Gallwey:

> At the moment the ball leaves the server's racket, the brain calculates approximately where it will land and where the racket will intercept it. This calculation includes the initial velocity of the ball, combined with an input for the progressive decrease in velocity and the effect of wind and after the bounce of the ball. Simultaneously, muscle orders are given: not just once, but constantly with refined and updated information. The muscles must cooperate. A movement of the feet occurs, the racket is taken back, the face of the racket kept at a constant angle. Contact is made at a precise point that depends on whether the order was given to hit down the line or crosscourt, an order not given until after a split-second analysis of the movement and balance of the opponent.
>
> To return an average serve, you have about one second to do this. To hit the ball at all is remarkable and yet not uncommon. The truth is that everyone who inhabits a human body possesses a remarkable creation.[5]

Logical-Mathematical Intelligence

In 1983 Barbara McClintock won the Nobel Prize in medicine or physiology for her work in microbiology. Her intellectual powers of deduction and observation illustrate one form of logical-mathematical intelligence that is often labeled "scientific thinking." One incident is particularly illuminating. While a researcher at Cornell in the 1920s McClintock was faced one day with a problem: while *theory* predicted 50-percent pollen sterility in corn, her research assistant (in the "field") was finding plants that were only 25- to 30-percent sterile. Disturbed by this discrepancy, McClintock left the cornfield and returned to her office, where she sat for half an hour, thinking:

> Suddenly I jumped up and ran back to the (corn) field. At the top of the field (the others were still at the bottom) I shouted "Eureka, I have it! I know what

the 30% sterility is!". . . They asked me to prove it. I sat down with a paper bag and a pencil and I started from scratch, which I had not done at all in my laboratory. It had all been done so fast; the answer came and I ran. Now I worked it out step by step—it was an intricate series of steps—and I came out with [the same result]. [They] looked at the material and it was exactly as I'd said it was; it worked out exactly as I had diagrammed it. Now, why did I know, without having done it on paper? Why was I so sure?[6]

This anecdote illustrates two essential facts of the logical-mathematical intelligence. First, in the gifted individual, the process of problem solving is often remarkably rapid—the successful scientist copes with many variables at once and creates numerous hypotheses that are each evaluated and then accepted or rejected in turn.

The anecdote also underscores the *nonverbal* nature of the intelligence. A solution to a problem can be constructed *before* it is articulated. In fact, the solution process may be totally invisible, even to the problem solver. This need not imply, however, that discoveries of this sort—the familiar "Aha!" phenomenon—are mysterious, intuitive, or unpredictable. The fact that it happens more frequently to some people (perhaps Nobel Prize winners) suggests the opposite. We interpret this as the work of the logical-mathematical intelligence.

Along with the companion skill of language, logical-mathematical reasoning provides the principal basis for IQ tests. This form of intelligence has been heavily investigated by traditional psychologists, and it is the archetype of "raw intelligence" or the problem-solving faculty that purportedly cuts across domains. It is perhaps ironic, then, that the actual mechanism by which one arrives at a solution to a logical-mathematical problem is not as yet properly understood.

This intelligence is supported by our empirical criteria as well. Certain areas of the brain are more prominent in mathematical calculation than others. There are idiots savants who perform great feats of calculation even though they remain tragically deficient in most other areas. Child prodigies in mathematics abound. The development of this intelligence in children has been carefully documented by Jean Piaget and other psychologists.

Linguistic Intelligence

At the age of ten, T. S. Eliot created a magazine called "Fireside" to which he was the sole contributor. In a three-day period during his winter vacation, he created eight complete issues. Each one included poems, adventure stories, a gossip column, and humor. Some of this material survives and it displays the talent of the poet.[7]

As with the logical intelligence, calling linguistic skill an "intelligence" is consistent with the stance of traditional psychology. Linguistic intelligence also passes our empirical tests. For instance, a specific area of the brain, called "Broca's Area," is responsible for the production of grammatical sentences. A person with damage to this area can understand words and sentences quite well but has difficulty putting words together in anything other than the simplest of sentences. At the same time, other thought processes may be entirely unaffected.

The gift of language is universal, and its development in children is strikingly constant across cultures. Even in deaf populations where a manual sign language is not explicitly taught, children will often "invent" their own manual language and use it surreptitiously! We thus see how an intelligence may operate independently of a specific input modality or output channel.

Spatial Intelligence

Navigation around the Caroline Islands in the South Seas is accomplished without instruments. The position of the stars, as viewed from various islands, the weather patterns, and water color are the only sign posts. Each journey is broken into a series of segments; and the navigator learns the position of the stars within each of these segments. During the actual trip the navigator must envision mentally a reference island as it passes under a particular star and from that he computes the number of segments completed, the proportion of the trip remaining, and any corrections in heading that are required. The navigator cannot see the islands as he sails along; instead he maps their locations in his mental "picture" of the journey.[8]

Spatial problem solving is required for navigation and in the use of the notational system of maps. Other kinds of spatial problem solving are brought to bear in visualizing an object seen from a different angle and in playing chess. The visual arts also employ this intelligence in the use of space.

Evidence from brain research is clear and persuasive. Just as the left hemisphere has, over the course of evolution, been selected as the site of linguistic processing in right-handed persons, the right hemisphere proves to be the site most crucial for spatial processing. Damage to the right posterior regions causes impairment of the ability to find one's way around a site, to recognize faces or scenes, or to notice fine details.

Patients with damage specific to regions of the right hemisphere will attempt to compensate for their spacial deficits with linguistic strategies. They will try to reason aloud, to challenge the task, or even make up answers. But such nonspatial strategies are rarely successful.

Blind populations provide an illustration of the distinction between the spatial intelligence and visual perception. A blind person can recognize shapes by an indirect method: running a hand along the object translates into length of time of movement, which in turn is translated into the size of the object. For the blind person, the perceptual system of the tactile modality parallels the visual modality in the seeing person. The analogy between the spatial reasoning of the blind and the linguistic reasoning of the deaf is notable.

There are few child prodigies among visual artists, but there are idiots savants such as Nadia.[9] Despite a condition of severe autism, this preschool child made drawings of the most remarkable representational accuracy and finesse.

Interpersonal Intelligence

With little formal training in special education and nearly blind herself, Anne Sullivan began the intimidating task of instructing a blind and deaf seven-year-old Helen Keller. Sullivan's efforts at communication were complicated by the child's emotional struggle with the world around her. At their first meal together, this scene occurred:

> Annie did not allow Helen to put her hand into Annie's plate and take what she wanted, as she had been accustomed to do with her family. It became a test of wills—hand thrust into plate, hand firmly put aside. The family, much upset, left the dining room. Annie locked the door and proceeded to eat her breakfast while Helen lay on the floor kicking and screaming, pushing and pulling at Annie's chair. [After half an hour] Helen went around the table looking for her family. She discovered no one else was there and that bewildered her. Finally, she sat down and began to eat her breakfast, but with her hands. Annie gave her a spoon. Down on the floor it clattered, and the contest of wills began anew.[10]

Anne Sullivan sensitively responded to the child's behavior. She wrote home: "The greatest problem I shall have to solve is how to discipline and control her without breaking her spirit. I shall go rather slowly at first and try to win her love."

In fact, the first "miracle" occurred two weeks later, well before the famous incident at the pumphouse. Annie had taken Helen to a small cottage near the family's house, where they could live alone. After seven days together, Helen's personality suddenly underwent a profound change—the therapy had worked:

> My heart is singing with joy this morning. A miracle has happened! The wild little creature of two weeks ago has been transformed into a gentle child.[11]

It was just two weeks after this that the first breakthrough in Helen's grasp of language occurred; and from that point on, she progressed with incredible speed. The key to the miracle of language was Anne Sullivan's insight into the *person* of Helen Keller.

Interpersonal intelligence builds on a core capacity to notice distinctions among others; in particular, contrasts in their moods, temperaments, motivations, and intentions. In more advanced forms, this intelligence permits a skilled adult to read the intentions and desires of others, even when these have been hidden. This skill appears in a highly sophisticated form in religious or political leaders, teachers, therapists, and parents. The Helen Keller–Anne Sullivan story suggests that this interpersonal intelligence does not depend on language.

All indices in brain research suggest that the frontal lobes play a prominent role in interpersonal knowledge. Damage in this area can cause profound personality changes while leaving other forms of problem solving unharmed—a person is often "not the same person" after such an injury.

Alzheimer's disease, a form of presenile dementia, appears to attack posterior brain zones with a special ferocity, leaving spatial, logical, and linguistic computations severely impaired. Yet, Alzheimer's patients will often remain well groomed, socially proper, and continually apologetic for their errors. In contrast, Pick's disease, another variety of presenile dementia that is more frontally oriented, entails a rapid loss of social graces.

Biological evidence for interpersonal intelligence encompasses two additional factors often cited as unique to humans. One factor is the prolonged childhood of primates, including the close attachment to the mother. In those cases where the mother is removed from early development, normal interpersonal development is in serious jeopardy. The second factor is the relative importance in humans of social interaction. Skills such as hunting, tracking, and killing in prehistoric societies required participation and cooperation of large numbers of people. The need for group cohesion, leadership, organization, and solidarity follows naturally from this.

Intrapersonal Intelligence

In an essay called "A Sketch of the Past," written almost as a diary entry, Virginia Woolf discusses the "cotton wool of existence"—the various mundane events of life. She contrasts this "cotton wool" with three specific and poignant memories from her childhood: a fight with her brother, seeing a particular flower in the garden, and hearing of the suicide of a past visitor:

> These are three instances of exceptional moments. I often tell them over, or rather they come to the surface unexpectedly. But now for the first time I have written them down, and I realize something that I have never realized before. Two of these moments ended in a state of despair. The other ended, on the contrary, in a state of satisfaction.

The sense of horror (in hearing of the suicide) held me powerless. But in the case of the flower, I found a reason; and was thus able to deal with the sensation. I was not powerless.

Though I still have the peculiarity that I receive these sudden shocks, they are now always welcome; after the first surprise, I always feel instantly that they are particularly valuable. And so I go on to suppose that the shock-receiving capacity is what makes me a writer. I hazard the explanation that a shock is at once in my case followed by the desire to explain it. I feel that I have had a blow; but it is not, as I thought as a child, simply a blow from an enemy hidden behind the cotton wool of daily life; it is or will become a revelation of some order; it is a token of some real thing behind appearances; and I make it real by putting it into words.[12]

This quotation vividly illustrates the intrapersonal intelligence—knowledge of the internal aspects of a person: access to one's own feeling life, one's range of emotions, the capacity to effect discriminations among these emotions and eventually to label them and to draw upon them as a means of understanding and guiding one's own behavior. A person with good intrapersonal intelligence has a viable and effective model of himself or herself. Since this intelligence is the most private, it requires evidence from language, music, or some other more expressive form of intelligence if the observer is to detect it at work. In the above quotation, for example, linguistic intelligence is drawn upon to convey intrapersonal knowledge; it embodies the interaction of intelligences, a common phenomenon to which we will return later.

We see the familiar criteria at work in the intrapersonal intelligence. As with the interpersonal intelligence, the frontal lobes play a central role in personality change. Injury to the lower area of the frontal lobes is likely to produce irritability or euphoria; while injury to the higher regions is more likely to produce indifference, listlessness, slowness, and apathy—a kind of depressive personality. In such "frontal-lobe" individuals, the other cognitive functions often remain preserved. In contrast, among aphasics who have recovered sufficiently to describe their experiences, we find consistent testimony: while there may have been a diminution of general alertness and considerable depression about the condition, the individual in no way felt himself to be a different person. He recognized his own needs, wants, and desires and tried as best he could to achieve them.

The autistic child is a prototypical example of an individual with impaired intrapersonal intelligence; indeed, the child may not even be able to refer to himself. At the same time, such children often exhibit remarkable abilities in the musical, computational, spatial, or mechanical realms.

Evolutionary evidence for an intrapersonal faculty is more difficult to come by, but we might speculate that the capacity to transcend the satisfaction of instinctual drives is relevant. This becomes increasingly important in a species not perennially involved in the struggle for survival.

In sum, then, both interpersonal and intrapersonal faculties pass the tests of an intelligence. They both feature problem-solving endeavors with significance for the individual and the species. Interpersonal intelligence allows one to understand and work with others; intrapersonal intelligence allows one to understand and work with oneself. In the individual's sense of self, one encounters a melding of inter- and intrapersonal components. Indeed, the sense of self emerges as one of the most marvelous of human inventions—a symbol that represents all kinds of information about a person and that is at the same time an invention that all individuals construct for themselves.

SUMMARY: THE UNIQUE CONTRIBUTIONS OF THE THEORY

As human beings, we all have a repertoire of skills for solving different kinds of problems. Our investigation has begun, therefore, with a consideration of these problems, the contexts they are found in, and the culturally significant products that are the outcome. We have not approached "intelligence" as a reified* human faculty that is brought to bear in literally any problem setting; rather, we have begun with the problems that humans solve and worked back to the "intelligences" that must be responsible.

Evidence from brain research, human development, evolution, and cross-cultural comparisons was brought to bear in our search for the relevant human intelligences: a candidate was included only if reasonable evidence to support its membership was found across these diverse fields. Again, this tack differs from the traditional one: since no candidate faculty is *necessarily* an intelligence, we could choose on a motivated basis. In the traditional approach to "intelligence," there is no opportunity for this type of empirical decision.

We have also determined that these multiple human faculties, the intelligences, are to a significant extent *independent*. For example, research with brain-damaged adults repeatedly demonstrates that particular faculties can be lost while others are spared. This independence of intelligences implies that a particularly high level of ability in one intelligence, say mathematics, does not require a similarly high level in another intelligence, like language or music. This independence of intelligences contrasts sharply with traditional measures of IQ that find high correlations among test scores. We speculate that the usual correlations among subtests of IQ tests come about because all of these tasks in fact measure the

---

*__reified__: Regarding an abstraction (e.g., intelligence) as if it were a concrete thing.

ability to respond rapidly to items of a logical-mathematical or linguistic sort; we believe that these correlations would be substantially reduced if one were to survey in a contextually appropriate way the full range of human problem-solving skills.

Until now, we have supported the fiction that adult roles depend largely on the flowering of a single intelligence. In fact, however, nearly every cultural role of any degree of sophistication requires a combination of intelligences. Thus, even an apparently straightforward role, like playing the violin, transcends a reliance on simple musical intelligence. To become a successful violinist requires bodily-kinesthetic dexterity and the interpersonal skills of relating to an audience and, in a different way, choosing a manager; quite possibly it involves an intrapersonal intelligence as well. Dance requires skills in bodily-kinesthetic, musical, interpersonal, and spatial intelligences in varying degrees. Politics requires an interpersonal skill, a linguistic facility, and perhaps some logical aptitude. Inasmuch as nearly every cultural role requires several intelligences, it becomes important to consider individuals as a collection of aptitudes rather than as having a singular problem-solving faculty that can be measured directly through pencil-and-paper tests. Even given a relatively small number of such intelligences, the diversity of human ability is created through the differences in these profiles. In fact, it may well be that the "total is greater than the sum of the parts." An individual may not be particularly gifted in any intelligence; and yet, because of a particular combination or blend of skills, he or she may be able to fill some niche uniquely well. Thus it is of paramount importance to assess the particular combination of skills that may earmark an individual for a certain vocational or avocational niche.

Notes

1. Jencks, C. (1972). *Inequality*. New York: Basic Books.

2. Gardner, H. (1983). *Frames of Mind: The Theory of Multiple Intelligences*. New York: Basic Books.

3. Menuhin, Y. (1977). *Unfinished Journey*. New York: Knopf.

4. Connor, A. (1982). *Voices from Cooperstown*. New York: Collier. (Based on a quotation taken from *The Babe Ruth Story*, Babe Ruth & Bob Considine. New York: Dutton, 1948.)

5. Gallwey, T. (1976). *Inner Tennis*. New York: Random House.

6. Keller, E. (1983). *A Feeling for the Organism* (p. 104). Salt Lake City: W. H. Freeman.

7. Soldo, J. (1982). Jovial juvenilia: T. S. Eliot's first magazine. *Biography*, 5, 25–37.

8. Gardner, H. (1983). *Frames of Mind: The Theory of Multiple Intelligences*. New York: Basic Books.

9. Selfe, L. (1977). *Nadia: A Case of Extraordinary Drawing in an Autistic Child*. New York: Academic Press.

10. Lash, J. (1980). *Helen and Teacher: The Story of Helen Keller and Anne Sullivan Macy* (p. 52). New York: Delacorte.

11. Lash (p. 54).

12. Woolf, V. (1976). *Moments of Being* (pp. 69–70). Sussex: The University Press.

Howard Gardner, "A Rounded Version: The Theory of Multiple Intelligences," from *Multiple Intelligences*. Cambridge, MA: Basic Books, 1993, pp. 13-34. Reprinted by permission of Basic Books, a member of Perseus Books Group.

Why Johnny Can't Argue

Gerald Graff

In fact, this chapter title has it wrong. Johnny can argue competently when he is in a real conversation that requires him to be persuasive. As I have pointed out, children learn to argue as soon as they are old enough to lobby parents or babysitters to let them stay up late or buy them an ice cream cone, a bike, or a skateboard like the one the kid across the street has. But Johnny—and Susie—do often run into problems when it comes to the kind of argumentation that is recognized and rewarded by academic institutions. School argument seems so remote from arguing with your parents or friends that there seems little carryover in these practices.

Schools should be tapping far more than they do into students' youthful argument cultures, which are not as far removed as they look from public forms of argument. I observed earlier that twelve-year-olds debating the merits of a Michael Jackson concert or a Mariah Carey video are making the same kinds of claims, counterclaims, and value judgments as those made by published book reviewers and media critics; there's even a continuity between the shrugging adolescent who says, "It sucks" or "That's cool," and the scholar or journalist who uses more sophisticated language. Instead of taking advantage of the bridges between youthful argument worlds and those of public discourse, schools generally make it hard for students to recognize their argumentative practices in those of academia. At worst, students get the impression that to do well in school or college they have to check whatever argumentative inclinations they have at the classroom door. I have heard high school teachers say that they've given up teaching argument because their students find it "boring." And in a post-Columbine High School age, anxieties about school violence can lead educators to discourage contentiousness in students. This is short-sighted, however, for arguably the real prescription for violence is to bottle up youthful passions and give them no legitimate outlet. Properly channeled, argument can be a substitute for violence rather than an incitement to it. As Deborah Meier has said, "Fighting with ideas rather than fists or guns or nasty sound bites could be a welcome relief." [1]

To be sure, students' problems with academic argument are often traceable to academic subject matter, which may have little connection with what they care about. But even when we change the subject and invite students to write about what personally interests them, if making an argument is part of the assignment the quality of students' writing doesn't necessarily improve. Once students have to translate their personal interests and experience into the formalized conventions of written Arguespeak, their interests and experience no longer seem their own.

There are ways, however, to make Arguespeak less foreign—and less boring—and the first step is to make clear to students that this language is an extension of everyday conversation. In the real world, we make arguments within some motivating conversation, whether we are chatting about last week's party or writing a letter to the newspaper in response to an editorial. Countless expository essays launch themselves by constructing a version of the "standard view" move, as it might be called: "The standard view of X runs like this. Here, by contrast, is what I think." In making the standard view move, we write a conversational partner into our text in order to set up our response. This summary-and-response pattern represents the deep structure of most written argument. In casual conversation, students unconsciously follow this structure, obeying what the linguistic philosopher Paul Grice calls "the conversational principle," which enjoins that we make our speech responsive to what our interlocutors have just said. [2] Academic assignments, however, often violate this conversational structure, asking students to come up with a thesis in a vacuum rather than to draw on their tacit conversational knowledge. I am thinking especially of the traditional five-paragraph theme in which students are asked to state a thesis and back it up. The five-paragraph theme does give students useful practice in stating a thesis and supporting it, but it fails to reproduce the conditions of real-world argument, where writers form their thesis in response to other writers or speakers.

What Conversation Are You In?

I want to suggest in this chapter how a more conversational view of argumentation can demystify academic writing and help high school and college students write better. The first step is to recognize that when student writing is flat and unfocused, the reason often lies in a failure to provide students with a conversation to argue *in*. I come to this conclusion the hard way, after teaching argument badly for many years. During that time, my most frequent critical comment on student papers was, "What's your argument?" or "What's your point?" My students' lack of improvement suggested that the exhortation to get an argument or a point is about as helpful as advising someone to "Get a life." Eventually it dawned on me that what counts as a makable "point" or "argument" is not as simple a matter as it seems. How do you go about finding a point if you haven't already got one? How do you know you've got one when you see it?

I thought back on my own writing struggles—how did I know when something I said qualified to be a main point or argument? I realized that it had as much to do with what other people were saying or thinking as it did with the intrinsic qualities of my text. Without those others out there and the conversations they were having I had no chance to have an argument of my own, even if—especially if—I wanted to change that conversation. Any hope I had of being original depended on others, since without them and their conversation my writing would literally be point-less. Here was a clue to why the student writing I was seeing often lacked a clear point: my students were trying to make a point without having a conversation in which to make it, an impossible feat.

Their difficulty was doubtless increased by the nebulous nature of the conversations of the academic humanities, where the kinds of arguments typically made are often mystifying. The problem, however, also arises in other academic disciplines, whose central conversations are often kept from students on the ground that they don't yet know the fundamentals of the subject, when in fact those conversations are the most fundamental thing of all. But if we can let students in on the secret that intellectual writing and discussion are extensions of their normal conversational practices, much of the mystification can be dissipated and the struggling students have a shot at catching up.

The point I make in this chapter, that students write better when they have conversations to enter, is implicit in much current composition and rhetorical theory, where conversation has become a central concept. The idea that discourse is inherently "dialogical," that we internalize external conversation in virtually everything we say, has been developed in various ways by influential thinkers such as Bakhtin, Rorty, Derrida, McIntyre, and Vygotsky. The idea is implicit in Kenneth Burke's celebrated depiction of intellectual history as an endless parlor conversation into which as individuals we drop in and out. My effort in this chapter will be to reduce "conversationalism" to its essential elements, making it more user-friendly for writing instructors and students than existing writing textbooks have done. The key point is that in order to make your own argument you have to write someone else's voice into your text.

Planting A Naysayer In Your Text

Let's try to apply this principle. Here is a typically flat piece of student prose by an eleventh-grader, Ellen, writing on Chinua Achebe's novel *Things Fall Apart*: "In the novel *Things Fall Apart* by Chinua Achebe, an African man known as Okonkwo struggles with Ibo life and traditions. He can be characterized as a tragic hero and was acknowledged as the man with title and honor. Okonkwo was portrayed as a hero because of the way he defended and what he tried to prove to his village and for his village."[3] Note that Ellen has no problem with the mechanics of grammar, punctuation, and syntax. Nor does she lack a clear thesis; she argues that Okonkwo, the main character of Achebe's novel, is a tragic hero. Why, then, does her writing seem flat and one-dimensional, lacking force and emphasis?

What is missing, I submit, is not an argument but an indication of *why* Ellen thinks her argument needs to be made at all. Her opening fails to survive the "So what?" or "Who cares?" test: Achebe's Okonkwo is a tragic hero. So what Who cares? Why say it? Who needs to hear it? Who would argue otherwise? I hasten to add that high school students are not the only writers who fail this "So what?" test. Is there anyone who has attended talks at a professional conference who has not wished that certain speakers had asked themselves the "So what?" and "Who cares?" questions?

Ellen's failure to address these questions helps explain why her writing sounds as if it is not addressed to anybody, why it doesn't give the impression that Ellen thinks there is anyone out there who needs to know that Okonkwo is a tragic hero. I don't know the assignment Ellen was responding to, but her writing sounds like the kind that tends to be elicited by instructions like "Discuss Okonkwo as a tragic hero," assignments that ask students to do something without knowing why it could be worth doing. The goal of this kind of assignment is usually to check up on whether Ellen has read the novel, knows basic information such as the standard definition of a tragic hero, or can write coherent sentences. Such assignments assume that Ellen needs *first* to master these elementary operations of reading and summarizing a narrative before she is ready to enter a higher-level conversation in which she engages with real issues and readers. Unfortunately, this kind of an assignment not only fails to prepare Ellen for that next step of engaging with real issues and readers; it probably will convince her that academic paper writing has nothing to do with engaging with real issues and readers.

Some will argue that the unimpassioned quality of Ellen's writing is a result of her not really *caring* about abstract literary questions like whether Okonkwo is a tragic hero or not. This could be true, and asking Ellen to write about something closer to her own experience may draw more engaged writing from her, though it also may not. My point, however, is that asking Ellen to write about such questions in a conversational vacuum itself helps ensure that she won't care. She may find it easier to care, however, if we provide her with a sense of the kinds of conversations that can take place about tragic heroes.

Others will argue that what Ellen lacks is a real reader, who could be supplied if she were asked to write the paper to her classmates, or perhaps to a small group within the class. This standard tactic is certainly worth trying, but it isn't likely to make a significant difference in Ellen's writing. For what Ellen needs is not just a real audience, but the understanding that she has to write that audience into her text. This is not something Ellen has to worry about when she engages in face-to-face conversations with her friends, family, and classmates, for in such oral situations the agenda is set by what others present have just said. In written discourse, however, which is implicitly addressed to an audience not present, the agenda (or context) has to be constructed explicitly by the writer.[4] To give point to what she says in writing, Ellen has to construct a conversation in which to say it.

In order to write a conversation into her text, Ellen needs to do something that can be hard for everyone but especially hard for young people: to imagine a person whose beliefs are different from her own. In order to motivate her argument that Okonkwo is a tragic hero, Ellen needs to imagine someone who doesn't already think what she thinks and then write that person into her text. That is, Ellen needs to imagine a person who is sufficiently "other" to her that that person needs to hear what Ellen wants to say. In other words, Ellen needs to think about her thesis in a contrastive or counterfactual way, something that means asking herself, *tragic hero as opposed to what*? To give point to her essay, Ellen needs to plant a hypothetical naysayer into her text, someone who would argue that Okonkwo is not a tragic hero but something else.

Now for reasons I suggested earlier, planting a naysayer in your text, a move in which you deliberately make trouble for yourself, is likely to seem counterintuitive if you have been socialized to think of school as a place you get through by *staying out* of trouble. The five-paragraph theme and other typical assignments reinforce this view by influencing students to think of writing (and academic study generally) as a business of stringing together true statements, statements that can't be challenged. Teachers need to help students see why this apparent common sense is not only misleading, but a sure-fire recipe for dull writing and student boredom. Unless we produce some problem, trouble, or instability, we have no excuse for writing at all.

How, then, can Ellen plant a naysayer in her text, and thereby produce a motivating problem? The easiest way is to imagine other plausible readings of the text besides hers. If you've read *Things Fall Apart* you'll recall that it's tempting to regard Okonkwo as an unqualified villain rather than a tragic hero. In fact, teachers who have taught the book tell me that students tend to find Okonkwo so repulsive that it's a challenge to get them to take him seriously. Okonkwo is rigid, overbearing, and unyielding with other tribal members, he behaves brutally to his wife and his mistress, and among the tribal traditions he defends and carries out is the ritual slaying of a child. Reflecting on these plot details and the negative views of her classmates might enable Ellen to construct the naysaying conversational partner whose counterfactual voice of otherness her argument needs to give it point, someone who sees Okonkwo as a simple villain.

If Ellen can think along these lines, she might eventually rewrite her opening in this way: "For many readers of Chinua Achebe's *Things Fall Apart*, the novel's main character Okonkwo may be so clearly repulsive as to seem a simple villain. Yet it is important to recognize that Achebe presents Okonkwo not as a mere villain but a tragic hero. Okonkwo, after all, is honored by his village for defending its traditions, however offensive those traditions may seem to us." By constructing a hypothetical reader who finds Okonkwo "so clearly repulsive as to seem a simple villain," this revision furnishes the naysayer whose "as opposed to what?" perspective would justify Ellen's argument. Someone could still ask, "Who cares if Okonkwo is a tragic hero?" or "So what?" but at least now Ellen's text anticipates and implicitly answers these questions: "Some readers care—those who think Okonkwo is just a straight villain; they care, so my claim is consequential."[5]

Of course if the naysaying, counterfactual reading is not plausible, then Ellen will seem to be creating a straw man. This would happen, for example, if readers could not plausibly see Okonkwo as *anything but* a tragic hero, as might be the case if, say, Achebe had repeatedly described Okonkwo in the text as a tragic hero, or had subtitled the novel *An Ibo Tragedy*. Ellen would either have to find another alternative reading to contrast with hers or change her thesis. Then, too, we can imagine more sophisticated critical conversations Ellen might try to enter—trying to get her essay published or submitting it as a master's thesis—that would require her to write a more complicated set of other voices into her text: "Though in obvious ways an evil man, Okonkwo nevertheless achieves a kind of tragic stature in the colonialist setting of the novel. As a residual African tribesman whose culture is being destroyed by the forces of colonialism and modernization that arrive in the novel's final chapters, Okonkwo is as much the tragic victim as the victimizer of others. On the other hand, though Okonkwo might be a victim to most postcolonial readers, he would certainly be a victimizer to feminists."

Instructing students to write a naysayer into their text is the single most effective device I have come up with in teaching writing. (Supplying lists of standard transitional words and phrases—*but, therefore, thus, on the other hand*, etc.—and requiring students to use them comes in second.) This device works even more effectively when I borrow the "argument templates" designed by my wife, Cathy Birkenstein-Graff, which we will look at in a moment, templates that give students standard formulas like "At this point my reader will probably object that…" and "Now I do not mean to suggest that…" In my experience, instructing students to write a naysayer into a text as part of the assignment and providing templates for doing so enables them right away to make argument moves they have never made before. This technique is far more effective than explaining in the abstract processes like how to have a point.

But what if students have trouble inventing the naysaying conversational partner they need in order to write argument? Constructing such a reader may be too hypothetical and abstract a process for inexperienced students. It becomes easier if you can refer to a specific person who says something you can respond to. After all, even experienced writers of argument often find their task easier when they come upon an article or book that serves as a foil for what they wish to say. In fact, it's probably by engaging with real people in this way that writers learn to construct hypothetical interlocutors. Furthermore, when the interlocutor is real rather than imagined, writers gain a leg up in answering the "Who cares?" question and warding off charges of creating a straw man, since they can point to at least one person who cares. We tend to write better, in short, when we are in conversation with actual others.

Conversationalism Tested

As you can see, I am steering toward making a case for assigning secondary commentary—criticism—especially in the humanities, where primary texts have ruled the roost. (I make this case at greater length in the next chapter.) My argument was informally field-tested by my former student and collaborator, Andrew Hoberek, when he taught English as a visiting instructor at the University of Puget Sound. In a course on the fiction of Flannery O'Connor, Hoberek assigned a paper in which each student was to choose an O'Connor short story from the reading list and do a close reading of it. Students were given the option of addressing specific questions such as "What is the meaning of the monkey at Red Sammy's BBQ restaurant in 'A Good Man is Hard to Find'?" On reading the papers, Hoberek found that most of the class had difficulty with the assignment, producing unfocused and disorganized essays.

Hoberek decided to follow up with a second assigned essay. As in the first, students were to perform a close reading of an O'Connor story of their own choosing. This time, however, they were to compose their reading in response to one of O'Connor's published critics. As Hoberek put it in a handout, "Choose an article or book chapter on the Flannery O'Connor short story you have chosen, summarize its argument, then disagree with it." To make sure the students' disagreements with their chosen critic led back to rather than away from the literary work itself, Hoberek also stipulated that the students must make specific reference to the story in question.

The two assignments thus constituted a fair, if unscientific, test of how having an actual critical conversation to enter affects student writing. Hoberek found that his students' writing in the second assignment was discernibly better focused and more sharply argued than in the first. Entering a conversation with a critic gave his students a clearer sense of what they wanted to say and why it needed saying. Hoberek also thought that the conversational second assignment lessened the distance between the struggling students and those who had been doing best in the class.

Whereas the open-ended invitation to explicate a text had left the strugglers at sea (even when given explicit suggestions like "explain the symbol of the monkey"), being asked to summarize and respond to a critic gave them dearer guidance on how to produce an explication. This result shouldn't surprise us, seeing that these students had little experience discoursing about the deep meaning of monkeys and other literary symbols, but they had plenty of experience conversing with other people. Having a specific critic's claims to respond to helped them write with more authority about symbolism. It also helped them begin to produce a bridge discourse that mingled the critics' analytic language with their own.

To let you judge these claims for yourself, here are two excerpts from Hoberek's student papers. Granting the inevitable degree of subjectivity in judgments on these matters, I think the examples show that the two students did write better when presented with critical conversations for them to enter:

In the first assignment, one student, Zach, opened his essay as follows:

"You might as well put those up," she told him.. "I don't want one."

"I appreciate your honesty," he said. "You don't see any more real honest people unless you go way out in the country" (O'Connor, CW, p. 271).

In this passage from "Good Country People," Manly Pointer has just learned that Mrs. Hopewell has no intention to buy a bible from her. She comes flat out and tells him that she does not plan to buy one. He appreciates her honesty and touches on his belief that the only real, good honest people live way out in the country.

What Pointer says here could be interpreted in a couple of different ways, depending on how the tone of the statement is taken....

Zach here does hint at a conversation that his paper will try to enter—one between readers who interpret a statement by Pointer in "Good Country People" in "a couple of different ways" that Zach presumably will arbitrate. He leaves unclear, however, how the possibility of several interpretations of Pointer's statement is a problem and what the stakes are if it is. He leaves the reader groping, I think, to get a handle on what Zach thinks the issue is.

Here is how Zach approached the second assignment, where he was asked to put himself explicitly into conversation with a critic:

Jon Lance Bacon, in chapter eleven of his book *Flannery O'Connor and Cold War Culture*, links the issues of modernization in the south and a loss of heterogeneous culture, with that of conformity and mass consumption....

> At one point in his chapter, Bacon looks at this issue specifically in regards to Coca-Cola. He mentions instances where Coke appears in O'Connor's work to "indicate the reach of American consumer culture within the region (Bacon, p. 120)."…
>
> I disagree with this, however. Coca-Cola, while representing "the American way of life" is still by and large a product of the South…."

The second version shows a clear gain in focus and rhetorical purpose. For one thing, it is easier to summarize Zach's argument: Bacon claims that Coca-Cola functions for O'Connor as a symptom of the invasion of Southern culture by American mass consumerism, but this can't be right since O'Connor shows Coca-Cola itself to be a Southern product.

Not only is it clearer in #2 than in #1 to whom and to what claim Zach is responding, but the stakes are also clearer: it matters if O'Connor shows Coca-Cola coming from outside the South or not since she would be suggesting in the first instance that the South is being destroyed by external social forces, but in the second that it is contributing to its own destruction. Zach still needs to work on sharpening his points and making himself more reader-friendly. For example, his statement that Coke "is still by and large a product of the South" would become more pointed if he added, "—and is not something imposed on the South from outside, as Bacon would claim." But he and his instructor are now in a better position to address such surface-level problems, since Zach's argument now has a firm conversational structure and setting.

In a second example, a student named Danielle opened her first paper as follows:

> In Flannery O'Connor's short story, *Good Country People*, Mrs. Hopewell found herself very disturbed by some of the literature her daughter Hulga was reading. She noticed words that had been underlined in blue pencil in a random book, amongst them: "We know it by wishing to know nothing of nothing" (269). The question of believing in nothing came up frequently in the story and each character had their own interpretation of belief. However, the outcomes for the characters who believed in something were more of a negative experience than for those who believed in nothing. In other words, the characters who believed in something in *Good Country People* were the ones who ultimately were led to disappointment, disillusionment, and pain. O'Connor portrayed belief and faith as negative experiences.

Danielle here has the makings of a conversation that would open a space for her claim: since we would normally think of "belief and faith" as positive things, why does O'Connor portray them as "negative experiences"? But since Danielle is not quite able to construct such a conversation, her opening flunks the "So what?" test: so what if O'Connor portrays belief and faith as negative? Why is that important and to whom?

Here is Danielle in the second paper writing with the benefit of a real critic as interlocutor:

> In Chapter 2 of Dorothy McFarland's studies of Flannery O'Connor, she says that O'Connor intended that both the peacock and Mr. Guizac be identified with Christ in her short story "The Displaced Person." McFarland asserts that this identification is clear and sees Mrs. Mcintyre's responses to both the peacock and Guizac as symbolic of her attitude toward Christ (indifference and rejection). Mr. Guizac is killed in the end like a sacrificial Christ and the peacock lives on "symbolizing the glorified Christ" (35). Although this view of Guizac and the peacocks is highly interesting, I assert that both can be seen outside of a Christian context and still give light to "The Displaced Person." Both the peacock and Mr. Guizac can be seen beyond the Christ symbols, as symbols of change which bring about reactions from Mrs. McIntyre and Mrs. Shortley ultimately displacing them.

Again, it seems evident that being in conversation with a critic has enabled the student to give clearer focus and consequentiality to her writing: after conceding McFarland's claim that the story's symbolism may refer to Christian beliefs, Danielle argues that it can just as plausibly be read as a comment on social change and displacement. Who cares? Well, at least one critic does.

Someone could still ask, "But who cares about *that*?" So what if some professor can squeeze Christ symbolism out of a story that somebody else can use to squeeze out something else? Would anyone care about such intramural debates who wasn't an academic or trying to get a grade from one? It is certainly true that claims and disputes that academics consider significant often seem trivial and petty to those outside the club. If we really value tolerance and respect for others' views, we can't be reminded too often that what seems manifestly weighty to ourselves and our circle may not amount to a hill of beans to others. "Let there be light" might draw a "So what?" from an atheist. This is precisely why it is always important when reading student work—or one's own—to keep asking "So what?" with a range of different possible audiences in mind.

Zach's and Danielle's examples help answer the objection that being asked to read literary criticism can only distract students from primary works of art. This is a risk, to be sure, but it is one that teachers can anticipate and correct for, as Hoberek did when he required his students to refer closely to their chosen short story while disagreeing with its critic. Responding to a critic does not draw Zach and Danielle's attention from the particulars of the work, but actually helps them focus on those particulars in a more pointed and purposeful way than they did in their first effort.

Granted, Hoberek's students were well-motivated college English majors who could be turned loose in the library to find critical articles they could understand and use. This is not an assignment that all undergraduates and certainly most high school and elementary students can do, though I suspect many would rise to the challenge if they had to. As I argue in the next chapter, even beginning students (and even students in the elementary grades) can engage with expert commentary if that commentary is made simple and accessible enough. Again, students are already engaging in spirited conversations outside school about films, music, sports, and other subjects. If we teachers can configure expert conversations in accessible ways, we can draw students into them.

Argument Templates

But before students can effectively enter intellectual conversations, many will need help to produce the conventional formalizations that characterize written argument. When Hoberek's Puget Sound undergraduates took issue with Flannery O'Connor interpreters, they had to perform sophisticated operations such as gracefully negotiating the transition from quoting or paraphrasing a critic to generating their own formulations. These moves seem disarmingly simple, but they are often hellishly perplexing for inexperienced writers and sometimes even for experienced ones. Yet as educators we often shy away from giving students explicit instruction on such moves, partly in order to avoid overemphasizing surface features of language, partly out of the recognition that students learn better when they discover things on their own rather than have them told to them.

The problem is that we will probably wait forever for some students on their own to produce formulations like "Whereas X argues that…, I contend that…" or "My reader will probably object…" Most of us learned to imitate such Arguespeak by osmosis through our reading, but many students don't read in that imitative way, in which one identifies with the voice of persuasive authorities whom one wants to be like. For such students, not to provide explicit help in using Arguespeak amounts to concealing secrets from them and then punishing them with low grades when they fail. In other words, withholding crucial formulas from students is at least as disabling as teaching such formulas too mechanically. It is simply condescending for educators to withhold tricks that they themselves have mastered.

In an earlier chapter, I mentioned compositionist David Bartholomae's suggestion (cited approvingly by Mike Rose) that "when stuck, student writers should try the following 'machine': 'While most readers of_____ have said _____, a close and careful reading shows that _____.'" Cathy Birkenstein-Graff, who has taught composition at Loyola and DePaul Universities in Chicago, has actually developed a version of such an argument machine. Birkenstein-Graff found that her struggling students wrote better when she provided them with the following argument template:

Title: _____

The general argument made by author X in her/his work,

_____, is that _____. More specifically, X argues that _____. She/He writes, "_____." In this passage, X is suggesting that _____. In conclusion, X's belief is that _____.

In my view, X is wrong/right, because _____. More specifically, I believe that _____. For example, _____. Although X might object that _____. I maintain that _____. Therefore, I conclude, that

_____.

Birkenstein-Graff's template gives students a sense of what it feels like to live inside the language of written argument, to hear what they would sound like using a voice of intellectual authority that most have never tried.

Birkenstein-Graff anticipates the objection that such templates squelch creativity. In an explanatory handout, she notes that the template in no way dictates or limits students' *thinking*, only the conventional forms for it. She argues that the template actually facilitates creative thinking by helping students negotiate stumbling blocks that often prevent them from doing justice to their best ideas. Once students get the hang of the argumentative moves—quoting and summarizing others' arguments, restating them in the students' own language, framing a response—they are free to deviate from the template as they choose. Birkenstein-Graff recognizes that there are many different forms of argument, that a formula like "Whereas X says, I argue…" is only one (though one that is pervasive). She believes, however, that students will gain more from mastering this basic form than from trying to learn many forms all at once and thereby learning none. She and I are currently at work on a book on how to write argument that will make central use of her argument templates.

In a freshman composition course that Jane Tompkins and I co-taught at UIC this year, we devised the following template to help our students make arguments out of their personal experiences:

In *A Life in School: What the Teacher Learned*, Jane Tompkins tells the story of her experience as a student and a teacher, emphasizing [HERE STATE THE THEME YOU WANT TO DEAL WITH] _____.

Tompkins believes/describes/asserts [HERE ELABORATE ON THE THEME] _____. My own experience as a student was very much the same/ both similar and different/quite different. Whereas Tompkins _____, I _____. [NOW ILLUSTRATE YOUR POINT WITH AN INCIDENT FROM YOUR OWN LIFE.]

Here is another templatelike device devised by Paul Fortunato, a graduate teaching assistant at UIC. Asking his students to respond to a critical essay on the literary work they chose to write about, Fortunato provides the following:

There are various ways and combinations of ways to respond, including:

- *disagree* with some key statement

- *agree* with something the critic says and then say even more about it than he or she did

- point to something the critic says that seems *to go contrary* to something else he or she says

- point to something the critic says and give a *counter example* from the text

- argue with the critic by showing that he or she is *leaving out* some key aspect of the story or some key issue or argument

- blow your critic out of the water by showing that he or she is *totally wrong*

- praise your critic for making an extremely important point, and *add something* important to that point

A final example of an argument template comes from the National Academy of Education postdoctoral fellowship program, which contains the following question, designed by Howard Gardner:

In fifty words or less, complete this sentence: Most scholars in the field now believe…as a result of my study…

Incorporating such templates into standardized tests for high school students might help raise the intellectual level of such tests while making them less confusing:

In fifty words or less, complete this sentence: The author of this [set] passage argues…I, however, would argue…

There is always the risk that teachers will use such templates in a mechanical and sterile way, just as there is a risk that prescriptions like "write a naysayer into your text," "enter a conversation with a critic," or "summarize a critic and then disagree" will turn students into robots. But I hope this chapter has persuaded you that these are risks that need to be taken, especially if you agree that the alternative is to keep students in the dark, desperately trying to guess what the teacher "wants," a predicament that produces its own kind of robotic response. Ultimately it seems better to give students the frameworks they need than to leave them to figure everything out on their own. It is better for teachers to be up front about what we "want" than to be coy and ultimately obscure. Johnny and Susie are often forceful arguers out of school, and they can be forceful arguers in school if the moves of the game are not kept from them.

Notes

1. Deborah Meier, *The Power of Their Ideas: Lessons for America from a Small School in Harlem* (Boston: Beacon Press, 1995), 11.

2. Paul Grice, *Studies in the Way of Words* (Cambridge, Mass.: Harvard Univer sity Press, 1989).

3. I acquired Ellen's paper at a workshop for college and high school teachers. As elsewhere here when quoting from student writing, I have changed the student's name.

4. See my earlier discussion of Basil Bernstein's distinction between elaborated and restricted codes in chapter 2.

5. The "So what?" problem has been acutely discussed by University of Chicago compositionist Joseph M. Williams, who writes extensively on "problem formation" as the key enabling step in writing persuasive arguments. (I referred to Williams's work earlier in my discussion of "the problem problem.") Williams observes that when student writers are unaware that they need to pose a problem near the beginning of an essay, they end up either merely summarizing their reading or asserting their opinions in a vacuum. In either case, Williams notes, the writing will lack motivation and prompt readers to ask, "So what, if we don't know that?" (Joseph M. Williams, "Problems into Problems," unpublished essay).

Gerald Graff, "Chapter 8: Why Johnny Can't Argue," *Clueless in Academe: How Schooling Obscures the Life of the Mind*. New Haven: Yale University Press, 2003, pp. 155-172. Reprinted by permission.

What We Eat

Eric Schlosser

Over the last three decades, fast food has infiltrated every nook and cranny of American society. An industry that began with a handful of modest hot dog and hamburger stands in southern California has spread to every corner of the nation, selling a broad range of foods wherever paying customers may be found. Fast food is now served at restaurants and drive-throughs, at stadiums, airports, zoos, high schools, elementary schools, and universities, on cruise ships, trains, and airplanes, at Kmarts, Wal-Marts, gas stations, and even at hospital cafeterias. In 1970, Americans spent about $6 billion on fast food; in 2001, they spent more than $110 billion. Americans now spend more money on fast food than on higher education, personal computers, computer software, or new cars. They spend more on fast food than on movies, books, magazines, newspapers, videos, and recorded music—combined.

Pull open the glass door, feel the rush of cool air, walk in, get on line, study the backlit color photographs above the counter, place your order, hand over a few dollars, watch teenagers in uniforms pushing various buttons, and moments later take hold of a plastic tray full of food wrapped in colored paper and cardboard. The whole experience of buying fast food has become so routine, so thoroughly unexceptional and mundane, that it is now taken for granted, like brushing your teeth or stopping for a red light. It has become a social custom as American as a small, rectangular, hand-held, frozen, and reheated apple pie.

This is . . . about fast food, the values it embodies, and the world it has made. Fast food has proven to be a revolutionary force in American life; I am interested in it both as a commodity and as a metaphor. What people eat (or don't eat) has always been determined by a complex interplay of social, economic, and technological forces. The early Roman Republic was fed by its citizen-farmers; the Roman Empire, by its slaves. A nation's diet can be more revealing than its art or literature. On any given day in the United States about one-quarter of the adult population visits a fast-food restaurant. During a relatively brief period of time, the fast-food industry has helped to transform not only the American diet, but also our landscape, economy, workforce, and popular culture. Fast food and its consequences have become inescapable, regardless of whether you eat it twice a day, try to avoid it, or have never taken a single bite.

The extraordinary growth of the fast-food industry has been driven by fundamental changes in American society. Adjusted for inflation, the hourly wage of the average U.S. worker peaked in 1973 and then steadily declined for the next twenty-five years. During that period, women entered the workforce in record numbers, often motivated less by a feminist perspective than by a need to pay the bills. In 1975, about one-third of American mothers with young children worked outside the home; today almost two-thirds of such mothers are employed. As the sociologists Cameron Lynne Macdonald and Carmen Sirianni have noted, the entry of so many women into the workforce has greatly increased demand for the types of services that housewives traditionally perform: cooking, cleaning, and child care. A generation ago, three-quarters of the money used to buy food in the United States was spent to prepare meals at home. Today about half of the money used to buy food is spent at restaurants—mainly at fast-food restaurants.

The McDonald's Corporation has become a powerful symbol of America's service economy, which is now responsible for 90 percent of the country's new jobs. In 1968, McDonald's operated about one thousand restaurants. Today it has about thirty thousand restaurants worldwide and opens almost two thousand new ones each year. An estimated one out of every eight workers in the United States has at some point been employed by McDonald's. The company annually hires about one million people, more than any other American organization, public or private. McDonald's is the nation's largest purchaser of beef, pork, and potatoes—and the second largest purchaser of chicken. The McDonald's Corporation is the largest owner of retail property in the world. Indeed, the company earns the majority of its profits not from selling food but from collecting rent. McDonald's spends more money on advertising and marketing than any other brand. As a result it has replaced Coca-Cola as the world's most famous brand. McDonald's operates more playgrounds than any other private entity in the United States. It is responsible for the nation's best-selling line of children's clothing (McKids) and is one of the largest distributors of toys. A survey of American schoolchildren found that 96 percent could identify Ronald McDonald. The only fictional character with a higher degree of recognition was Santa Claus. The impact of McDonald's on the way we live today is hard to overstate. The golden arches are now more widely recognized than the Christian cross.

In the early 1970s, the farm activist Jim Hightower warned of "the McDonaldization of America." He viewed the emerging fast food industry as a threat to independent businesses, as a step toward a food economy dominated by giant corporations, and as a homogenizing influence on American life. In *Eat Your Heart Out* (1975), he argued that "bigger is *not* better." Much of what Hightower feared has come to pass. The centralized purchasing decisions of the large restaurant chains and their demand for standardized products have given a handful of corporations an unprecedented degree of power over the nation's food supply. Moreover, the tremendous success of the fast-food industry has encouraged other industries to adopt similar business methods. The basic thinking behind fast food has become the operating system of today's retail economy, wiping out small businesses, obliterating regional differences, and spreading identical stores throughout the country like a self-replicating code.

America's main streets and malls now boast the same Pizza Huts and Taco Bells, Gaps and Banana Republics, Starbucks and Jiffy-Lubes, Foot Lockers, Snip N' Clips, Sunglass Huts, and Hobbytown USAs. Almost every facet of American life has now been franchised or chained. From the maternity ward at a Columbia/HCA hospital to an embalming room owned by Service Corporation International—"the world's largest provider of death-care services," based in Houston, Texas, which since 1968 has grown to include 3,823 funeral homes, 523 cemeteries, and 198 crematoriums, and which today handles the final remains of one out of every nine Americans—a person can now go from the cradle to the grave without spending a nickel at an independently owned business.

The key to a successful franchise, according to many texts on the subject, can be expressed in one word: "uniformity." Franchises and chain stores strive to offer exactly the same product or service at numerous locations. Customers are drawn to familiar brands by an instinct to avoid the unknown. A brand offers a feeling of reassurance when its products are always and everywhere the same. "We have found out . . . that we cannot trust some people who are nonconformists," declared Ray Kroc, one of the founders of McDonald's, angered by some of his franchisees. "We will make conformists out of them in a hurry. . . . The organization cannot trust the individual; the individual must trust the organization."

One of the ironies of America's fast-food industry is that a business so dedicated to conformity was founded by iconoclasts and self-made men, by entrepreneurs willing to defy conventional opinion. Few of the people who built fast-food empires ever attended college, let alone business school. They worked hard, took risks, and followed their own paths. In many respects, the fast-food industry embodies the best and the worst of American capitalism at the start of the twenty-first century—its constant stream of new products and innovations, its widening gulf between rich and poor. The industrialization of the restaurant kitchen has enabled the fast-food chains to rely upon a low-paid and unskilled workforce. While a handful of workers manage to rise up the corporate ladder, the vast majority lack fulltime employment, receive no benefits, learn few skills, exercise little control over their workplace, quit after a few months, and float from job to job. The restaurant industry is now America's largest private employer, and it pays some of the lowest wages. During the economic boom of the 1990s, when many American workers enjoyed their first pay raises in a generation, the real value of wages in the restaurant industry continued to fall. The roughly 3.5 million fast food workers are by far the largest group of minimum-wage earners in the United States.

The only Americans who consistently earn a lower hourly wage are migrant farm workers.

A hamburger and french fries became the quintessential American meal in the 1950s, thanks to the promotional efforts of the fast-food chains. The typical American now consumes approximately three hamburgers and four orders of french fries every week. But the steady barrage of fast-food ads, full of thick juicy burgers and long golden fries, rarely mentions where these foods come from nowadays or what ingredients they contain. The birth of the fast-food industry coincided with Eisenhower-era glorifications of technology, with optimistic slogans like "Better Living through Chemistry" and "Our Friend the Atom." The sort of technological wizardry that Walt Disney promoted on television and at Disneyland eventually reached its fulfillment in the kitchens of fast-food restaurants. Indeed, the corporate culture of McDonald's seems inextricably linked to that of the Disney empire, sharing a reverence for sleek machinery, electronics, and automation. The leading fast food chains still embrace a boundless faith in science—and as a result have changed not just what Americans eat, but also how their food is made.

The current methods for preparing fast food are less likely to be found in cookbooks than in trade journals such as *Food Technologist* and *Food Engineering*. Aside from the salad greens and tomatoes, most fast food is delivered to the restaurant already frozen, canned, dehydrated, or freeze-dried. A fast-food kitchen is merely the final stage in a vast and highly complex system of mass production. Foods that may look familiar have in fact been completely reformulated. What we eat has changed more in the last forty years than in the previous forty thousand. Like Cheyenne Mountain, today's fast food conceals remarkable technological advances behind an ordinary-looking facade. Much of the taste and aroma of American fast food, for example, is now manufactured at a series of large chemical plants off the New Jersey Turnpike.

In the fast-food restaurants of Colorado Springs, behind the counters, amid the plastic seats, in the changing landscape outside the window, you can see all the virtues and destructiveness of our fast-food nation. I chose Colorado Springs as a focal point for this . . . because the changes that have recently swept through the city are emblematic of those that fast food—and the fast-food mentality—have encouraged throughout the United States. Countless other suburban communities, in every part of the country, could have been used to illustrate the same points. The extraordinary growth of Colorado Springs neatly parallels that of the fast-food industry: during the last few decades, the city's population has more than doubled. Subdivisions, shopping malls, and chain restaurants are appearing in the foothills of Cheyenne Mountain and the plains rolling to the east. The Rocky Mountain region as a whole has the fastest-growing economy in the United States, mixing high-tech and service industries in a way that may define America's workforce for years to come. And new restarants are opening there at a faster pace than anywhere else in the nation.

Fast food is now so commonplace that it has acquired an air of inevitability, as though it were somehow unavoidable, a fact of modern life. And yet the dominance of the fast-food giants was no more preordained than the march of Colonial split-levels, golf courses, and man-made lakes across the deserts of the American West. The political philosophy that now prevails in so much of the West—with its demand for lower taxes, smaller government, an unbridled free market—stands in total contradiction to the region's true economic underpinnings. No other region of the United States has been so dependent on government subsidies for so long, from the nineteenth-century construction of its railroads to the twentieth-century financing of its military bases and dams. One historian has described the federal government's 1950s highway-building binge as a case study in "interstate socialism"—a phrase that aptly describes how the West was really won. The fast-food industry took root alongside that interstate highway system, as a new form of restaurant sprang up beside the new off ramps. Moreover, the extraordinary growth of this industry over the past quarter-century did not occur in a political vacuum. It took place during a period when the inflation-adjusted value of the minimum wage declined by about 40 percent, when sophisticated mass-marketing techniques were for the first time directed at small children, and when federal agencies created to protect workers and consumers too often behaved like branch offices of the companies that were supposed to be regulated. Ever since the administration of President Richard Nixon, the fast-food industry has worked closely with its allies in Congress and the White House to oppose new worker safety, food safety, and minimum-wage laws. While publicly espousing support for the free market, the fast-food chains have quietly pursued and greatly benefited from a wide variety of government subsidies. Far from being inevitable, America's fast-food industry in its present form is the logical outcome of certain political and economic choices.

In the potato fields and processing plants of Idaho, in the ranch lands east of Colorado Springs, in the feedlots and slaughterhouses of the High Plains, you can see the effects of fast food on the nation's rural life, its environment, its workers, and its health. The fast-food chains now stand atop a huge food-industrial complex that has gained control of American agriculture. During the 1980s, large multinationals—such as Cargill, ConAgra, and IBP—were allowed to dominate one commodity market after another. Farmers and cattle ranchers are losing their independence, essentially becoming hired hands for the agribusiness giants or being forced off the land. Family farms are now being replaced by gigantic corporate farms with absentee owners. Rural communities are losing their middle class and becoming socially stratified, divided between a small, wealthy elite and large numbers of the working poor. Small towns that seemingly belong in a Norman Rockwell painting are being turned into rural ghettos. The hardy, independent farmers whom Thomas Jefferson considered the bedrock of American democracy are a truly vanishing breed. The United States now has more prison inmates than full-time farmers.

The fast-food chains' vast purchasing power and their demand for a uniform product have encouraged fundamental changes in how cattle are raised, slaughtered, and processed into ground beef. These changes have made meatpacking—once a highly skilled, highly paid occupation—into the most dangerous job in the United States, performed by armies of poor, transient immigrants whose injuries often go unrecorded and uncompensated. And the same meat industry practices that endanger these workers have facilitated the introduction of deadly pathogens, such as *E. coli* 0157:H7,* into America's hamburger meat, a food aggressively marketed to children. Again and again, efforts to prevent the sale of tainted ground beef have been thwarted by meat-industry lobbyists and their allies in Congress. The federal government has the legal authority to recall a defective toaster oven or stuffed animal—but still lacks the power to recall tons of contaminated, potentially lethal meat.

I do not mean to suggest that fast food is solely responsible for every social problem now haunting the United States. In some cases (such as the malling and sprawling of the West) the fast-food industry has been a catalyst and a symptom of larger economic trends. In other cases (such as the rise of franchising and the spread of obesity) fast food has played a more central role. By tracing the diverse influences of fast food I hope to shed light not only on the workings of an important industry, but also on a distinctively American way of viewing the world.

Elitists have always looked down at fast food, criticizing how it tastes and regarding it as another tacky manifestation of American popular culture. The aesthetics of fast food are of much less concern to me than its impact upon the lives of ordinary Americans, both as workers and consumers. Most of all, I am concerned about its impact on the nation's children. Fast food is heavily marketed to children and prepared by people who are barely older than children. This is an industry that both feeds and feeds off the young. During the two years spent researching this book, I ate an enormous amount of fast food. Most of it tasted pretty good. That is one of the main reasons people buy fast food; it has been carefully designed to taste good. It's also inexpensive and convenient. But the value meals, two-for-one deals, and free refills of soda give a distorted sense of how much fast food actually costs. The real price never appears on the menu.

E. coli 0157:H7: One of many strains of the bacterium *Escherichia coli*, which causes severe intestinal problems and has been associated with undercooked hamburger.

The sociologist George Ritzer has attacked the fast-food industry for celebrating a narrow measure of efficiency over every other human value, calling the triumph of McDonald's "the irrationality of rationality." Others consider the fast-food industry proof of the nation's great economic vitality, a beloved American institution that appeals overseas to millions who admire our way of life. Indeed, the values, the culture, and the industrial arrangements of our fast-food nation are now being exported to the rest of the world. Fast food has joined Hollywood movies, blue jeans, and pop music as one of America's most prominent cultural exports. Unlike other commodities, however, fast food isn't viewed, read, played, or worn. It enters the body and becomes part of the consumer. No other industry offers, both literally and figuratively, so much insight into the nature of mass consumption.

Hundreds of millions of people buy fast food every day without giving it much thought, unaware of the subtle and not so subtle ramifications of their purchases. They rarely consider where this food came from, how it was made, what it is doing to the community around them. They just grab their tray off the counter, find a table, take a seat, unwrap the paper, and dig in. The whole experience is transitory and soon forgotten. I've written this…out of a belief that people should know what lies behind the shiny, happy surface of every fast-food transaction. They should know what really lurks between those sesame-seed buns. As the old saying goes: you are what you eat.

Why Look at Fish?

Ginger Strand

What is it about aquariums? Walk into the cool, humming darkness of the zoo's aquatic counterpart and something magical happens. Burbling blue light, darkened corridors, a silvery flash of fin, a ripple of aquatic wings: aquariums quiver with the promise of unearthly visions. In *The Lady from Shanghai*, Orson Welles's passionate clinch with Rita Hayworth unfolds before an aquarial tank: the aquarium's allure, after all, is not unlike the appeal of illicit sex. Aquariums, like adultery, draw us into a shadowy underworld of unspoken sensual pleasures, an engrossing, exotic environment harboring dangers of mythic proportion.

It's partly the mystery of it all. The ocean has long been our repository for ideas of the monstrous and the unknowable. "Canst thou draw out leviathan with a hook?" God demands of Job. We can't control the sea's creatures—we can barely comprehend them. They challenge our most basic ideas of creatureliness. Creatures have recognizable parts—but in the sea they can be diaphanous clouds of membrane, without eyes, face, stomach, spine, or brain. Creatures move, but oysters drift, and corals are rooted like plants. Creatures have physical integrity but a starfish chopped in half will grow into two separate beings. Or consider the Portuguese man-of-war, a creature that acts like an individual but is actually a huge colony of beings moving as one. There are fish that can freeze without dying, and other sea creatures living at temperatures above boiling. Recent research around volcanic vents has found tiny organisms that breathe iron. As for reproduction, even the most ordinary fish can be deliriously perverse. They're hermaphrodites. They switch genders. Males give birth. Some corals and bivalves reproduce by "broadcast spawning," in which males cast off huge nets of sperm that drift capriciously to any available egg, while snails and leeches mate through what scientists call "traumatic insemination," where the male fires a detachable sperm-filled harpoon at the unsuspecting body of a female— Jesse James meets Johnny Wad.

As naturalist Loren Eiseley once wrote, "If there is magic on this planet, it is contained in water."

A visit to an aquarium does little to diminish this sublime terror. Even as it strives to inform, with wall copy and touch screens and neat placards of exhibit-speak, the aquarium mesmerizes visitors, overflowing and short-circuiting its own pedantic intent. No touch screen on earth can match the allure of a live reef shark, rippling your way with a sinister, toothy smile.

We must love this. Aquariums are currently all the rage. Of the forty-one American aquariums accredited by the American Zoo and

Aquarium Association in 2003, more than half opened since 1980, sixteen since 1990 alone. These are not traditional halls of fish tanks but huge, immersive environments with increasingly exotic fish in ever more realistic, habitats: live coral reefs, artificial currents, indoor jungles, and living kelp forests. Massive public/private endeavors, the new breed of aquarium has flourished in an era of ambitious urban renewal aimed at reviving derelict inner-city waterfronts. Their prominent role in such schemes has caused the *Wall Street Journal* to dub the last two decades "the age of aquariums." We are in love with looking at fish. But why?

Poseidon And Athena

There's a standard story about the history of animal display. It begins with the menagerie, a beast-collection used since ancient times as a sign of princely power and dominance. According to zoo historians, Roman praetors introduced the idea in the West, sending tigers, elephants, snakes, and other exotic fauna back to the capitol as symbols of conquest. Other heads of state followed suit. Louis the Fourteenth established a menagerie at Versailles. In England, the tradition of keeping a menagerie at the Tower of London seems to have begun with Henry I, who started his collection of exotic critters at Woodstock. It was common practice for royals to present allies with gift animals.

Sometime in the mid-nineteenth century, the story goes, animal collections evolved a new purpose. As the industrial revolution fostered the rise of an urban working class, animal displays transcended the crass display of dominance, shifting their focus to education. Menageries became "zoological gardens," sites of learning that forwarded human enlightenment and progress not only through scientific knowledge but through edifying contemplation of the Creator's work. Where menageries had been private, aristocratic, and designed to intimidate, zoological gardens were public, democratic, and designed to educate. At the same time, technological advances solved some of the problems of maintaining aquatic environments. The first aquarial exhibit in London opened in 1853 and was quickly followed by others in Europe and America.

Nigel Rothfels, in *Savages and Beasts: The Birth of the Modern Zoo* (2002) outlines how scholars have attacked this idea of a "transformation" from intimidation to education as a sham. In reality, debunkers say, regardless of format, the display animal is always underwritten by social, political and economic imperatives. Modern zoos operate as signs of dominance; but they bear witness to civic pride rather than princely power. The formation of aquariums supports this view. In Paris, for instance, the first public aquarium was built in 1931 for the Colonial Exposition. It brought together a stunning array of sea creatures—the plundered riches of France's far-flung conquests. (The surrealists, grasping the imperialist implications, demonstrated against it.)

America's first public aquarium launched a different struggle. According to Jerry Ryan's *The Forgotten Aquariums of Boston* (Finley Aquatic Books, 2001), the first "pure" aquarium in America was the Boston Aquarial Gardens, begun by James Cutting in 1859. There were already aquarial exhibits in the U.S., most notably at P. T Barnum's American Museum, but these were, according to Ryan, "a collection of curiosities and freaks and, 'pure humbug?'" The Aquarial Gardens, on the other hand, were not crassly commercial, but "dedicated to the apprecia- tion of marine life and the education of the public." No Feejee Mermaids for Cutting.

But not for long. In 1862 Barnum bought the struggling attraction from Cutting, renaming it the Barnum Aquarial Gardens and repurpos- ing it to the kind of hokum and spectacle purveyed by his American Museum. The re-opening, Ryan relates with scorn, involved a "Great National Dog Show." Thereafter, the fish shared the limelight not only with dogs, but babies, midgets, albinos, and "dramatic performances." "The marine life exhibits," Ryan sighs, "were mere background." Thus opens the history of American aquariums: with an agon between study and spectacle, teaching and unabashed trade.

Loaves And Fishes

The current U.S. aquarium boom can be dated from the opening of the New England Aquarium in 1969. Located on an unpromising stretch of Boston's derelict waterfront, the New England Aquarium was the first de- signed by Peter Chermayeff and his groundbreaking exhibit design firm, Cambridge Seven. The Central Wharf, where the aquarium was built, was purchased from the city of Boston for one dollar, and the rest of the proj- ect was financed with $6 million in corporate and individual donations.

Estimates were that somewhere around 600,000 visitors a year would pass through the aquarium's doors. Shortly after the opening, a million had attended. Within walking distance of Faneuil Hall's new com- plex of shops and eateries, the aquarium provided the missing waterfront piece of Boston's urban renaissance. Downtown Boston took off. The site the aquarium occupies is now valued at more than $50 million.

Chermayeff and his associates went on to recreate this magic formula—aquarium + shopping malls = urban renewal—in Baltimore, designing and building the National Aquarium on the dilapidated Inner Harbor. After a 1990 study by the Maryland Department of Economic and Employment Development concluded that the National Aquarium had generated $128.3 million in income for the local economy, blighted city centers began lining up for their fish. New Orleans already had its project in place; it opened in 1990. In the decade following, Corpus Christi, Columbus, Dallas, Tampa, Charlotte, Pittsburgh, and Charleston,

all became proud owners of new aquariums. Soon, even smaller struggling cities began to see aquariums as economic development catalysts:
one of the first was Camden, New Jersey, already federally designated
an "Empowerment zone." Others followed: Long Beach, California;
Chattanooga, Tennessee; even Newport, Kentucky, a riverfront adult-
entertainment strip known to its Cincinnati neighbors as "sin city."

"A lot of cities have looked at aquariums as an economic pana-
cea," Debra Kerr Fassnacht, executive vice president of Chicago's Shedd
Aquarium told the *Christian Science Monitor*. So many cities added
an aquarium to their development wish list that recent articles in the
Monitor and the *Wall Street Journal* raise the specter of a market oversatu-
rated with fish. Even so, a number of new aquariums are in the works:
Atlanta, Georgia; New Bedford, Massachusetts; Los Angeles, California.
One project currently in proposal stage is the Great Waters Aquarium for
Cleveland, Ohio. It's planned for the riverfront of the Cuyahoga—a body
of water so polluted that it holds the dubious distinction of being the
only moving river ever to have caught fire.

Biophilia

What is the link between aquariums and urban renewal? True, an aquarium is more likely to generate popular interest than, say, an art museum.
But there are deeper connections, too. Since the nineteenth century, animal displays have been argued to provide moral uplift for the working
classes. In an attempt to secure funds for Hamburg's zoological gardens in
1911, Dr. J. Vosseler summarized the view:

> Intimacy with the living world makes people indigenous, and awakens and
> sustains the sense of home and the love of Nature and her creatures as the
> best counterbalance to the social disadvantages of modern life.

The "social disadvantages of modern life" assuaged by the zoo are represented more explicitly for us by a 1904 visitor to the New York Zoological
Park:

> It matters little whether Michael Flynn knows the difference between the
> caribou and the red deer. It does matter a lot, however, that he has not sat
> around the flat disconsolate, or in the back room of the saloon, but has
> taken the little Flynns and Madam Flynn out into the fresh air and sunshine
> for one mighty good day in which they have forgotten themselves and their
> perhaps stuffy city rooms.

In this way, zoological gardens and parks were more critical to the "lower orders" than they were for the upper classes, providing not only relief from "stuffy city rooms," but an alternative to the inevitably degraded amusements they would seek otherwise. In 1869, as concerned citizens raised money to establish a zoological garden in Central Park, the *New York Times* published an editorial titled "The Necessity of Amusements for the Poor." The editors argued that "the class of amusements supplied now to the poor is nasty and odious... If there be no amusements of even a pretence of decency, the young man and young girl seek their enjoyment in such places as the Water-street dance-cellars, or the innumerable liquor saloons" (July 4, 1869).

But zoos were more than just distractions; they were, sites of instruction, offering "moral improvement" for the working classes not only by diverting their natural tendencies towards drinking, gambling and fighting, but by illustrating the higher principles on which society depended. Zoos provided the working class with training in middle-class behavior standards, banning alcohol, polka music, littering, the shooting of songbirds, and even, in some cases, restaurants, for fear of creating a "low" atmosphere. Furthermore, the zoological garden's focus on taxonomies upholds a view of the world—including the human part of it—as hierarchical. The *New York Times* editorialized:

> The true destination of Zoological Gardens would be to serve as a stage for facts and experiments in natural history An investigation into the laws, by virtue of which animals pass from the savage into the domestic state, attempts at acclimatization, the improvement of the conquered races and re-education of those that remain to conquer—such, in our view, is the field of practical studies in which Zoological Gardens ought to limit their instructions. (July 18, 1868)

Assimilation is in the best interest, then, of cows as well as people. In a nation doubling in population, as the U.S. did between 1860 and 1900 in part due to immigration, that message could hardly fall on deaf ears.

Today's "Michael Flynns" continue to be offered moral betterment through education in the normative—defined now as conservation. But it's a particularly personal form of conservation that aquariums propound. Visitors are urged to take individual action: stop littering, use public transportation, avoid banned products like corals, snakeskin, and sea horses. And they are exhorted to care. The local, urban population, particularly urban youth, is the primary focus of this message. As the Monterey Bay Aquarium says on its web site:

Children today need to grow up to be better stewards of nature because of all of the threats to this world. But if they don't know about the sea and its creatures, how can they care about them?

The implication is that individual action is what counts—and that city kids, with less exposure to nature, are a bigger threat to conservation than, say, the executive board at ExxonMobil, or the sycophants at George Bush's new, pollution-friendly EPA.

In a more general sense, aquariums are argued to support moral improvement by inspiring a broad appreciation for life itself. Again, Chermayeff has led the charge, moving away from the educational, information-heavy designs of earlier aquariums like Boston's, and towards a more spectacular, emotion-based approach meant to create a sense of wonder in the viewer. An aquarium should be "an emotional thing, not a science lesson," he told *Harvard Magazine*. Chermayeff frequently borrows biologist E. O. Wilson's term "biophilia" to describe the response he is aiming for: the innate human attraction to other forms of life. According to Wilson, biophilia is one of the things that defines our humanity. We are human in part because we long to look.

Rich And Strange

Looking at fish is not like looking at zoo animals. Most zoo creatures are at least partly familiar. Even the creepy denizens of the reptile house or the bat exhibit are critters we might come across in our daily lives. But fish don't come from our habitat. The aquarium is a terrestrial embassy from a nonterrestrial world. If fish went about on land, making themselves visible out the kitchen window or from the car as we sped past them on the highway, they wouldn't be half as fascinating. We'd look— we're lookers after all—but we wouldn't look with the same feeling of excitement, that thrill of transgression we get from gazing through that foot or so of acrylic that makes the formerly unseeable seen.

John Berger's classic essay, "Why Look at Animals?" printed in the collection *About Looking* (Pantheon, 1980), asks why we are so doomed to disappointment at animal parks. The inevitable feeling at a zoo, he claims, is baffled unfulfillment: "Why are these animals less than I believed?"

Berger proposes an answer: while we long to see animals as connected to us, in fact the very conditions of their visibility highlight how separate they are. Placed in faked habitats, lit by artificial means and footnoted with informational copy, they become merely "objects of our ever-extending knowledge." We see them, but the gaze is one-way. They don't see us. The technologies that make them visible and interpretable only serve to differentiate and distance them further: "What we know about them is an index of our power, and thus an index of what separates us from them."

Berger blames this on modernity: the very historical conditions that gave rise to zoos also ensured the disappearance of animals from everyday life. With urbanization and the industrial revolution, machines replaced animal labor, while factories took over breeding them. Along with cuddly animal toys, anthropomorphized animal imagery, and urban pets, zoos became monuments to the disappearance of true beasts from our lives, "an epitaph to a relationship which was as old as man."

Following Berger's construct, one might read the aquarium boom of the eighties and nineties as a monument to the disappearance of sea creatures not only from our lives, but from the planet. In *The Empty Ocean* (Shearwater Books, 2003) biologist Richard Ellis outlines the various ecological disasters now making the oceans what he calls "the next environmental battleground." Among them is the disappearance of fish. A seemingly inexhaustible resource has been depleted, in many cases beyond recovery. Among the missing: miles-long swarms of cod off the Grand Banks, gray whales that once roamed the Atlantic, the giant Patagonian toothfish of South America, nearly extinguished in the two short decades since its 1982 L.A. debut under the stage name Chilean sea bass. The world's leading sardine canneries, on Cannery Row in Monterey, closed in the seventies when sardine stocks became too skimpy to support an industry. As if to illustrate Berger's point, the old cannery has become the site of the highly acclaimed Monterey Bay Aquarium, built by Lucile and David Packard of Hewlett-Packard.

But Berger's formula falters when we consider aquarium technology. For Berger, the zoo's technology distances the animals from us. But fish are invisible without those technologies. Hence, in aquariums, technology is not disguised. Habitats may aim for realism, but the pumps and plate glass aren't embarrassing necessities, like the camouflaged fence limning the captive tiger's fake jungle. In aquariums, the technology that makes the creatures available to us is part of what we come to admire, what creates our sensation of awe and wonder. Aquariums know this and are immensely fond of citing their stats: the number of tank gallons, the thickness of the acrylic walls, the sophisticated filtration and aeration systems that make it all possible. In flaunting this technological prowess, aquariums reach for the sublime.

The ocean has always been sublime, which is to say it has always been capable of instilling wonder and awe, appreciation tinged with terror. The age of reason borrowed the notion of the sublime from the ancients as a counterpoint to mere beauty. In the late eighteenth and early nineteenth centuries, poets and painters valorized the sublime, and turned to nature to evoke it. Then, only the natural world had the scale and complexity to be sublime. Today, that's no longer true: sublimity resides best in the manmade world. David Nye, in *American Technological Sublime* (MIT Press, 1994), argues that this is an American phenomenon:

where once we looked at nature and gleaned a sense of the divine, now we look at technology and glean a feeling of national pride. Leviathan is superseded by levees.

We have come a long way from the question of why aquariums might be good devices for slum clearance. Or have we?

An Art That Nature Makes

Writing in *Communique*, the magazine of the American Zoo and Aquarium Association, John Bierlein, exhibit manager at Seattle's Woodland Park Zoo, states a truism in contemporary exhibit design: animal displays must create awareness and appreciation not only of animals, but of the habitats that sustain them. "One of our goals:," he writes, "is to accentuate the inseparable connection between the survival of animal species and the survival of their wild habitats," (March, 2003).

But the zoo or aquarium's very existence suggests the opposite. Increasingly, endangered animal populations are kept alive only by conservation parks—the best husbandry might be done not by nature but by man. Without zoo and aquarium captive-breeding programs, many recovering animal species, including the California condor and the Arabian oryx, might still be languishing on the endangered list, or worse, might be entirely extinct. No longer viewed as unfortunate captives or pale imitations of their wild counterparts, zoo and aquarium animals are now considered a fortunate, treasured few.

The aquarium not only improves on nature; in substituting the technological sublime for the natural sublime, it improves on our relationship to it. Ecologically adept and technologically brilliant, the aquarium is a twenty-first-century utopia, a place where culture and nature unite to induce wonder. Publicity photos offered by aquariums make this clear. They have evolved a standard vocabulary of awe and absorption to indicate the new heights of sensation achieved in this artificial world.

Publicity photos are mostly of two types. First is the animal close-up. These tend to feature either anthropomorphized creatures—otters, toads, turtles—or wildly strange or scary ones—sharks, jellies, lionfish, seahorses. Regardless of subject, they follow an unwritten set of rules. Framed according to the conventions of traditional portraiture and engaging the camera eye directly, the fish—or otter or shark or turtle—is a direct refutation of Berger's claim that the animal has no gaze with which to return ours. (There are exceptions: the leafy sea dragon, a creature straight out of a cartoon, is almost always shown in profile: to grant it a gaze would undermine its adaptive resemblance to its kelp habitat.) They look right at us, and their expressions mirror the intelligence and thoughtful interest that these encounters promise to inspire in us. Sometimes they appear in pairs or groups, and their relationships are always idyllic—devoted couples, attentive parents, cooperative social units. Signs of strife, dominance or struggle are absent—as they largely are in the aquarium itself, where the copper sulfate used to treat water for algae and parasites also reduces the natural aggressiveness of fish and sharks.

The second kind of photo shows humans interacting with the aquarium environment. Here, too, a standard vocabulary prevails, its predominant gestures connoting both the aquarium's magnitude and the human response to it. Pointing or reaching hands are common. Faces are shown angled upward, lips parted in wonder. The sensation of sublimity is often indicated by composition as well. One of the most popular shots, for instance, is a panorama of a large, backlit tank with one or more people silhouetted in front of it. The aquarium environment, the shot tells you, is completely absorbing: you lose yourself in it.

The Tennessee Aquarium media library includes one particularly interesting photo. It shows a young African-American boy in a pop-up tank—a large tank with a bubble-shaped window on its floor, giving viewers a vantage point from inside the tank habitat.

The boy is looking at a seahorse, and the angle of the shot makes it look as if the seahorse is gazing back at him. His expression—eyes wide, mouth a circle of delighted astonishment—is striking. Next to him, you can just make out the pink coat and hair braids of a slightly taller girl— his classmate? His sister? It doesn't matter. The boy's expression of joy is the shot's focal point. He is Tennessee's twenty-first-century answer to "Michael Flynn," a (presumably) urban youth having his eyes—literally— opened, his perspective changed through contact with another living thing. The highly mediated nature of that contact is elided—the tank walls separating seahorse and boy vanish—and yet that very mediation is in some sense the subject of the photo. The photo is not depicting the boy, nor the aquarium's nifty acrylic sphere, but the experience made possible by their encounter. That experience is coded as an exchange of sympathies between two beings— our Michael Flynn and a sea horse— and by extension, between gritty urban reality and the magical world of nature.

Those Are The Pearls

The new aquariums propose a reconciliation of nature and technology. In doing so, they offer to reconcile environmentalism and corporate culture. Sometimes this can be quite explicit: in Baltimore, for example, each exhibit has a corporate sponsor. Placards over each tank inform you that, for instance, the electric eels are brought to you by Tristate Electricity Suppliers. That connection may inspire a chuckle, but for the most part, the signs are subtle. It takes some looking to realize that every inch of the so-called National Aquarium is underwritten by American business. The picture is clearer on the web site. The section on corporate sponsors lists 216 corporations and businesses that have supported the aquarium to the tune of anywhere from $850 to more than $25,000. It includes General Motors, IBM, Proctor and Gamble, Castrol HDL, Lockheed Martin Naval Electronics, Aegon, and, alone in the "Corporate Circle," defense contractor Northrop Grumman.

Baltimore isn't alone. Clearly, corporate P.R. departments have seen the relatively worry-free advantage of associating themselves with something as crowd-pleasing and uncontroversial as an aquarium—no *Piss Christs* or Mapplethorpes here. Coca-Cola and SunTrust Banks are presenting sponsors of the Tennessee Aquarium. Coca-Cola reappears as an institutional sponsor of the New England Aquarium, along with Comcast and Sovereign Bank. PepsiCo underwrites the Oregon Coast Aquarium in Newport, Oregon, and the South Carolina Aquarium in Charleston, South Carolina where it is joined by Philip Morris, Alcoa, BMW and Chevron.

Somehow, it seems appropriate for the new breed of mega-aquariums to thrive on corporate sponsorship. With their expensive, advanced technology, they seem like they must be brought to us by the companies that build printers or cars. But it's more than that. We expect public museums to be like the outdated National Aquarium in Washington, D.C.—rows of medium-sized fish tanks in the basement of the Department of Commerce. It's interesting—they're still fish—but bland, staid, educational. Instead, the highly planned, affective environments of the splashy new aquariums have a corporate feel: the glitzy crowd appeal, the slick presentation of easy-to-digest facts, the obsession with their own stats. It's the real thing.

Furthermore, aquariums are telling a pro-corporate story They posit a world in which the chief danger to nature is individual apathy. Baltimore's National Aquarium, for instance, offers cautious tips, for how individuals can promote conservation: recycle! Install water-saving showerheads! Conserve electricity! As for cars, they suggest Americans drive a fuel-efficient vehicle—which they define as thirty-two miles to the gallon, knocking about ten miles off what environmentalists typically advocate. When it comes to driving less, they are more guarded. "Sharing a ride just once or twice a month," they point out, "can have a tremendous impact."

Corporate behavior, on the other hand, is never questioned. In fact, it is nature's friend. Example: the star exhibit at the Audubon Aquarium of the Americas in New Orleans, a 400,000 gallon Gulf of Mexico tank boasting a replica of an abandoned oil rig. Behind thirteen inches of acrylic, sharks, rays, groupers, gars, and turtles meander around shellfish-encrusted pilings. Abandoned oil rigs, the wall copy explains, should be considered valuable ecosystems, improvements on nature, not eyesores.

Another placard, likely to be passed over by schoolchildren, displays the logos of companies that sponsor the Gulf of Mexico tank: Amoco. Shell. ExxonMobil. Chevron. Kerr-McGee. Auto parts maker Tenneco. Oil-field couplings manufacturer Wheeling Machine Products.

The one aquarium that has tried to avoid leaping into the sponsor-ship fray is the pioneering New England Aquarium in Boston. Its freedom from corporate donors is evident when you read its display copy: global warming, overfishing, overuse of fossil fuels—no punches are pulled in its conservation message. Sadly, this freedom can't last. The New England Aquarium's dire financial situation caused the AZA to revoke its ac-creditation in March of 2003. According to President and CEO Edmund Toomey, "the Aquarium is engaged in an ambitious strategic planning process and has launched several initiatives to strengthen its financial position." Undoubtedly these initiatives will include increasing the num-ber of corporate underwriters—and whatever content adjustments are required to keep them happy.

Roll On, Thou Deep And Dark Blue Ocean

Built as part of a plan to redevelop Chattanooga's riverfront, the Tennessee Aquarium focuses on the Tennessee River ecosystem. But the Tennessee River can really no longer be considered a river at all. Rather, it's a system of reservoirs, linked by some thirty-five dams. In recreating the "original" Tennessee River environment, the aquarium is creating a monument to a body of water that no longer exists. This is not odd: more and more, it's part of what aquariums do. In fact, it wouldn't be unrea-sonable, every time you saw a fancy new aquarium, to ask *What body of water has been destroyed here?* You might then want to look at the corpo-rate donors and ask a further question: *How might they be implicated?*

Witness the Florida Aquarium in Tampa. One of the nation's top ten busiest ports, Tampa Bay is Florida's largest open-water estuary. Its natu-rally shallow harbor requires continual dredging and channel-digging to support the port's heavy traffic in phosphates, petroleum, and seafood. By the late 1970s, this constant dredging and filling, combined with nitrogen-polluted water, had led to algae-bloom, fish kills, and the death of more than half the sea grasses that provided natural nurseries for the area's fish.

The Florida Aquarium opened on Tampa Bay in 1995. One of its corporate sponsors is Cargill, developers of the phosphate industries that necessitate the harbor's regular dredging, and one of the world's larg-est producers of the nitrogen fertilizers that choke the Bay. Today, these fertilizers pour down the Mississippi from the Corn Belt and into the Gulf of Mexico, where, according to a National Oceanic and Atmospheric Administration report, they are the primary drivers of a seasonal "Dead

Zone": an area the size of New Jersey—and growing—in which nothing can live from May to September.

Or consider the Great Lakes Aquarium, a freshwater aquarium located in Duluth, Minnesota. Duluth Harbor was created in 1871, when mayor J. B. Culver and fifty men with picks and shovels, racing against a federal injunction, dug a channel in the sandbar that separated the St. Louis River from Lake Superior. By the time the "cease and desist" order arrived, it was all, as they say, water under the bridge. Since then, Duluth Harbor has become one of the busiest Great Lakes ports, and the St. Louis River has become one of Lake Superior's most polluted tributaries. Local industries, most notably U.S. Steel, released PCBs, mercury, cyanide, and other volatile organic compounds into it for over fifty years. In the eighties, the area was designated a Superfund site and the closed U.S. Steel plant put on the National Priorities List. U.S. Steel is a business partner at the Great Lakes Aquarium.

There are many more examples. Paper and packaging giant Sonoco, having dumped thousands of pounds of PCBs into Lake Michigan via the Fox River, sponsors the South Carolina Aquarium. Cinergy, the coal-heavy utility singularly responsible for 1 percent of the earth's greenhouse gas emissions, bought naming rights to the Cinergy Theater at Kentucky's Newport Aquarium. Aquariums have become a sort of consolation prize for communities whose drinking water has been despoiled, whose fish have been poisoned, whose runoff has turned toxic, and whose waterfronts have been left to die.

"In a world full of simulations and clever illusions, zoos and aquariums increasingly become the authenticators of what is real and still alive," John Bierlein writes. But it isn't just fish we want to imagine alive; it's the sea itself. Baltimore's Inner Harbor. Charleston Harbor. Monterey Bay, the Tennessee River, Lake Superior, even the noxious Cuyahoga. Few big aquarium projects are landlocked, because the aquarium feeds nostalgia not only for vanishing sea creatures, but for a lost connection to the waterfront itself. Inland water travel is a distant memory; sea travel is a hobby for retirees; even our fishing and canning industries are dying as our fisheries, one by one, are depleted. The vibrant maritime metropolis celebrated in Alfred Stieglitz's early-twentieth-century photos of docks, ships, disembarking crowds, and commercial water traffic has vanished.

In his brilliant photo essay *Fish Story* (Richter Verlag, 1995), Allan Sekula recounts how the rise of container shipping in the 1960s led to the removal of commercial ports to the urban margins. New York's port, for instance, is now in Elizabeth, New Jersey. As the increasingly automated working harbor moved out of sight, city dwellers lost track of the huge amounts of labor—grubby, back breaking, and poorly remunerated—that underwrites a global economy predicated on the transfer of goods and workers. The container, according to Sekula, is "the very coffin of remote labor-power," a banknote-shaped sarcophagus enabling "the transnational bourgeoisie's fantasy of a world of wealth without workers, a world of uninhibited flows."

Thus bereft of purpose and meaning, urban waterfronts became derelict and dangerous, ripe for commercial redevelopment. They're reborn as retail-driven fantasy ports like Baltimore's Inner Harbor, now trumpeted as "one of America's oldest seaports—and one of the world's newest travel destinations." Tampa Bay's Channelside is similar, as is Chattanooga's riverfront, rechristened Ross's Landing, where the Tennessee Aquarium paved the way for one hundred new stores and restaurants, property value increases of 124 percent, and an economic impact estimated to be around a billion dollars. All these waterfront complexes, in addition to aquariums, feature Disney-like recreations of waterfront life: scenic boat tours, shopping malls with seaside themes, maritime museums and plenty of chain-operated seafood restaurants to serve up the last of the vanishing cod, once so thick off the Grand Banks that fishermen drew them up by the basketful.

We want to see the ocean as rich and teeming with life when all over the world it is dying, fisheries collapsed, tidal basins clogged by development, coral reefs bleached to lifelessness. We want to see the waterfront as a vital source for economic growth, but magically free of the ugly trappings of hazardous cargos, grimy industry, and unions. Even as it becomes more obviously the barometer of our ability to kill, we cling to the notion of the sea as the cradle of life. And we are nostalgically reconstructing the seaside—an improved, sanitized version—before we have even finished eradicating it.

The zoo, as Berger contends, may be an epitaph for our lost connection to animals, but the aquarium is a headstone—a great big, titanium-clad one—for our lost connection to water.

A Shadow Of Man's Ravage

On Good Friday, 1989, the Exxon Valdez, a 987-foot, single-hulled tanker, ran aground on Bligh Reef in Alaska's Prince William Sound. At least eleven million gallons of heavy crude oil—125 Olympic-pools-full—gushed into the sound's pristine waters and began to spread, eventually oiling 1,300 miles of coastline. The immediate, countable damage was dramatic: at least a quarter-million dead seabirds, 2,800 dead sea otters, 300 dead harbor seals, 250 dead bald eagles. The uncountable effects on the ecosystem were even more disastrous, including what scientists estimate to be billions of destroyed salmon and herring eggs and juveniles, along with genetic malformations affecting generations to come.

The Exxon Valdez disaster put Prince William Sound on the map. News footage and photos of seabirds, otters, and eagles slicked with oil were a P.R. disaster for one of the world's wealthiest corporations. Exxon went to work immediately to repair its image. More than a decade after the spill, it seemed to have succeeded. Exxon stock had tripled, and it merged with Mobil to become the world's largest oil corporation, with more than $12 billion in profits annually. The *Economist* recently declared it "the world's best-run energy company." But even before the merger, as it appealed the 1994 U.S. District Court decision slapping it with $5 billion in punitive damages, Exxon had repaired its public image enough to turn its massive resources to the job of helping to sink U.S. participation in the Kyoto Protocol on global warming, a goal met in March 2001 with President Bush's scrapping of the accord.

The environmental clean up has been less successful than the publicity one. While Exxon describes the sound's environment as "healthy, robust and thriving," the Oil Spill Trustee Council, an organization created by the government to disburse the millions of dollars in reparations Exxon paid in settlements, disagrees. Of the thirty "injured resources" being tracked, the OSTC lists only seven as recovered fifteen years later. Among the species posted as "not recovering" are the common loon, three species of cormorants, harbor seals, the harlequin duck, the pigeon guillemot, and one of the sound's foundation species, the Pacific herring.

Around thirty-nine million dollars of the Exxon Valdez Oil Spill Settlement Fund went towards building an aquarium. The Alaska SeaLife Center in Seward opened in May 1998, with the declared purpose of "understanding and maintaining the integrity of the marine ecosystem of Alaska through research, rehabilitation and public education." Designed by the Cambridge Seven, the Center was designed to combine a marine research and rehabilitation center with a tourist attraction.

Many of the species still suffering from the effects of the spill—and facing further threats from climate change and overfishing—can now be seen in the Center. Harbor seals, the pigeon guillemot, and the Pacific herring are thriving at the Center, even as they falter in the wild. One can find Steller's sea lions there, a marine mammal whose 93 percent decline in population over the last thirty years has landed them on the endangered list. "We probably have the best habitat in the world for these animals," then-executive director Kim Sundberg told the *Seattle Post-Intelligencer* in 1998. "Everything's been designed to accommodate full-sized adult Steller sea lions." It's a far cry from their natural habitat, particularly Prince William Sound, where the continued post-spill lack of nutrient-rich herring has driven sea lions to eat pollack, a fish that marine biologists call "the junk food of the sea." At the SeaLife Center, the sea lions enjoy their herring iced: it's Canyon Ranch for marine mammals.

The SeaLife Center is officially owned by the city of Seward, population 2,500, and operated by the Seward Association for the Advancement of Marine Science, a non-profit affiliated with the University of Alaska.

Exxon, however, has done little to disguise its role. Most of the press around the opening of the Center mentioned Exxon's restitution settlement as its main finding source. But Exxon's fingerprints remain on more than the money. The corporation's very language has structured discussion of the disaster from the beginning, and now shapes debate on the status of the clean-up.

According to Exxon's press release on the state of Prince William Sound, the Oil Spill Trustee Council's declarations of incomplete recovery can't be trusted. This is because some populations might have been in decline before the Valdez' spill. Addressing the issue of the common murre, a seabird failing to thrive, Exxon's release states that "there was little information about the size of the murre population prior to the spill. Yet for the Trustees, murre population recovery is dependent on a return to pre-spill conditions—when it is obvious that no one knows what those conditions were, or what the population would have been had no oil been spilled."

The SeaLife Center s executive director, Tylan Schrock, uses very similar language to describe the Center's function. "When the Exxon Valdez went aground and had that terrible natural disaster," he told KNLS, a World Christian Broadcasting radio station, "one of the things that came out of that was a recognition that we didn't even know what the baseline information from that ecosystem was. That was one of the real strong messages that came out of the oil spill. We can construct a world-class research institution that will provide that baseline data. And we never want to see that type of a natural disaster up here again, but we're not gonna kick ourselves for not having the information the second time around if it does happen to us."

Schrock, intentionally or not, is telling an authorized story—as does the SeaLife Center itself. The Cambridge Seven design, borrowing features from other successful projects, is calculated to tell an uplifting story of cooperation between corporate culture and the public trust. Like the firm's other designs, the Center leads visitors through a predetermined tour route, starting with an escalator trip to the second level. When the Center opened, after an initial exhibit introducing Alaska's marine life, visitors were led into a room entirely devoted to the Valdez disaster. Text, photos, maps, and day-by-day accounts described the damage and the clean-up effort.

Emerging from this area, visitors would see the Center's research facility, overlooking the research deck and wet lab, as they moved towards the realistic Resurrection Bay habitat in which many of the area's struggling species—sea lions, seals, puffins, and murres—could be seen enjoying themselves. They then descended to the first level, where they got an underwater view of the habitat.

The progression of the tour could best be described as triumphal. The viewer began, after some preliminary facts, with disaster. The negative feelings spurred by this display were immediately qualified by the Center's scientific capabilities. The final impression was one of a better-than-real-life habitat in which endangered species were hearty, thriving, and accessible. As the *Atlanta Journal-Constitution* reported in a 1998 article on the Center, "Here, children could spend hours communing with the noses and faces of chocolate-brown seals and sea lions." Through its rehabilitation programs and its ability to make animals visible, the Center posed itself as an example of how technology can improve on nature.

Today the Center is arranged on a slightly different plan. The Valdez disaster display has been relocated from the beginning of the tour to the end. After viewing the underwater tanks, visitors can listen to an audio exhibit called "Exxon Valdez Oil Spill: The Continuing Legacy." The text gives an update on species affected by the disaster. The final display, however, is a video of Stellar's sea lions. The visitor ends, again, with the image of thriving, magnificent animals.

The SeaLife Center suggests a story that is in keeping with the one Exxon tells through its press releases—the story of a tragic accident that, through corporate accountability and the use of advanced technology, was prevented from causing serious, long-term harm. It's tempting to see this narrative as a brazen and prejudicial imposition on an unwilling public. But what's happening is more complicated. If Exxon's story appeals, it isn't just because Exxon wants it to. Exxon is telling the story people long to believe, the story at the heart of our use of aquariums as agents of urban renewal. People want to believe that technology and nature can be united, that corporate culture tends to forward the public good. That's the story aquariums tell, all by themselves. In yoking technology and nature as if there were no conflicts between them, aquariums sit astride what Leo Marx called "the contradiction at the heart of culture that would deify the Nature it is engaged in plundering."

Refining The Future

Senegalese conservationist Baba Dioum once said, "In the end, we will conserve only what we love." The quote is often cited as a rationale for spending large sums on animal display. Aquariums, their promoters claim, help us to love fish. They help us love the wonders of the sea, in all their richness and all their strangeness too. Only by looking a harbor seal or a leafy sea dragon in the eye will we really see that there is something there to be valued.

Do aquariums achieve this end? And if they do, does it matter? A recent book of photographs is the best current document of the worldwide aquarium boom. *Aquarium* by Diane Cook and Len Jenshel (Aperture,

2003) juxtaposes two photographers whose pictures pose very different answers to such questions. Cook's black and white photos are texturally rich and often abstract, focusing mostly on what mesmerizes aquarium visitors themselves: the delicate tendrils of a jellyfish, the comic cartwheel of a crab, the rippling rows of suckers on an octopus's underneath. When there are human subjects in them, they commune with the animals. In one, a walrus turns its head as it swims past a child's hand pressed to the tank window. The window seems to disappear, so the walrus appears to be pressing its muzzle against the child's stubby fingers. It's a false sense of intimacy—exactly what aquariums, at their best, create.

Len Jenshel's color pictures, in contrast, draw out the separation between human and animal, between observers and observed. His people are blurred and indistinct; his viewing subjects always seem to be missing the view. A single woman in a red skirt stands in an underwater tunnel at the Bahamas' Atlantis resort, a large gold handbag under her arm. A school of silvery fish arc over the tunnel above her, their luminescent curves echoing her shiny bag. She gazes, not up at them, but at something unseen off to the left, so the school's spectacular swoop goes unnoticed, except to us. In another tunnel shot in the same aquarium, a woman in shorts and a bikini top is seen leaving as a mournful looking fish floats in the foreground, disconsolate. A joke on a break up scene, the photo dramatizes the separation that, as John Berger would have it, is the only relationship possible between displayed animals and their observers.

Looking at Cook's photos, one is struck with the awe and wonder that sea creatures have the ability to inspire. Looking at Jenshel's, one takes a step back from that awe and asks *Is it enough*? Will our oceans be saved by a sea turtle's wise face, or the luminous, ethereal beauty of a tank full of jellies? A more fundamental question underlies that one: what does education have to do with love? Is instilling a sense of wonder truly a higher educational goal, the root of real understanding? Or is it simply the easiest effect to induce in the overstimulated, MTV generation? David Powell, former director of live-exhibit development at the esteemed Monterey Bay Aquarium, would argue for wonder. "My original goal," he writes in his memoir, *A Fascination for Fish* (2001), "was to bring as much factual understanding as possible to the visitor... Now I see things quite differently. I've come to realize that perhaps our true goal in the aquarium world is to inspire awe, to create a sense of wonder and appreciation that will grow into caring. Communicating facts is all well and good, but without awakening a sense of caring we have accomplished little."

It's a convincing argument, but it fails to account for the ways in which aquariums are making an argument, even as they seem to offer simply the visual spectacle of nature in all its glory. *Here is where you can find this*, they say, presenting their acres of sparkling acrylic. *Here is what we have done for nature.*

When you visit an aquarium, there are usually boxes or cute parking meters where you can drop in a quarter for wetlands preservation, or a "save the Amazon rainforest" charity. But you're more likely to be overwhelmed by the technological sophistication of a facility that could clearly be funded only by corporate America. ExxonMobil, and its cronies, continue to support the aquarium boom. And they continue to bankroll the ever-dwindling number of scientists who will question the reality of global warming and the still plentiful politicians who will ignore it.

Meanwhile, the ocean fisheries dwindle, the waterfront retreats from view, and historical memory founders on the reefs of complacency. After the Valdez disaster, Congress legislated that all oil tankers in Prince William Sound must be double-hulled by the year 2015. Most tanker-owners are beginning to comply. The only major oil company that has not yet built a double-hulled tanker is ExxonMobil. As for the Valdez, Exxon refloated it, towed it to San Diego (after Portland refused to harbor it), and repaired it. It changed the ship's name to the Mediterranean, and its subsidiary's name from Exxon Shipping to Sea River Maritime. Exxon then petitioned to have a 1990 law barring the ship from Alaskan waters declared unconstitutional. When that failed, it filed a "takings" claim against the federal government, demanding $125 million in reparations. Currently, the Sea River Mediterranean carries oil between Europe, Africa, and the South Pacific. At last sight, it was continuing ExxonMobil's commitment to education: as part of a project called "Refining the Future," the children of Hallett Cove South Primary school in Adelaide, Australia, are in regular email contact with the ship and its crew.

PROGRAM
AWARDS

Student Writing Awards

We invite students to submit work for the English 100 Program Student Writing Awards. Submitted writing must have been completed for an English 100 course during the 2008-2009 academic year.

The three award categories are:

Narrative: This may include descriptive or reflective writing, memoir, or other forms of essays that engage a topic from a personal point of view.

Explanatory/Exploratory: This may include essays that explain or explore the ideas of others, processes, or events.

Critical: This may include essays that perform critical analysis of a text (including cultural or popular texts like film or web-based texts) or make a critical argument about an issue or idea.

Guidelines for Submission

- Remove your instructor's grades and comments. Papers should be typed, free of mechanical errors, and clearly legible for photocopying. You may consult your instructor about final revision and editing of your work.

- Please include only the essay's title and award category (if applicable) on the first page of a written essay. Include a completed and signed "permission to publish" form with the essay.

- Please make certain that your name, your title, and your instructor's name appear clearly and only on the "permission to publish" form.

- Please sign, to verify that your essays are your own work and that any research is properly documented.

- Turn in the paper essay, along with an electronic file of the paper (MS Word doc), and completed "permission to publish" form to Morris Young, Director of English 100, 6187C H.C. White or to your instructor. Use a separate "permission to publish" form for each submission.

Deadline for Submission

- For Fall 2008:   February 1, 2008

- For Spring 2009:   June 1, 2009

   (Writing submitted from a Spring 2009 English 100 course will be considered for the awards given in 2010.)

Permission to Publish

I hereby grant permission to the Department of English at the University of Wisconsin-Madison to use, print, or publish, in any place, in any form, all or any part of the following composition:

Title:

If my composition is in digital form, I give permission for all files to be hosted on the Department of English's server and for the English 100 Web Site to display those compositions.

Further, I hereby swear that the above work is my own. Or, if the work is dependent on a source other than me, I have explicitly and clearly stated the source(s) and its usage in my composition.

I also understand that if my work is selected by the English Department, I am required to submit an electronic version of the text. If I fail to submit texts in the appropriate format, I understand that my work may not be published.

Name (*please print*): _____

Signed: _____

Instructor's Name: _____ Course: _____

Award Category/ies (if applicable; you may circle more than one):

_____

☐ Narrative

☐ Explanatory/Exploratory

☐ Critical

Contact Information (Please provide the best contact information—some correspondence may occur before or after the academic term.)

Phone Number: _____

E-Mail Address: _____

Address: _____

To submit, please bring a clean copy, along with this form (signed and completed), to Morris Young, Director of English 100, 6187C H.C. White,—or submit it electronically to English100@english.wisc.edu. An electronic submission from a student's email address constitutes acknowledgment of the rules and verification that the work submitted is your own.

Outstanding Teacher Award

We invite students to nominate instructors for the English 100 Program's "Outstanding Teacher" Award.

To be eligible for the award the instructor will have taught in the English 100 Program during the 2008-2009 academic year.

To nominate an instructor

Please submit a brief paragraph (200-250 words) describing why you find this instructor outstanding in the teaching of English 100.

You may want to consider some of the following in making your nomination:

- Attention to students
- Quality of feedback and advice
- Impact on your learning and development as a writer
- Quality of writing activities and assignments
- Overall course experience

Deadline for Nominations

- **For Fall 2008:**   December 15, 2008
- **For Spring 2009:**   April 15, 2009

   Please send nominations to Morris Young, Director of English 100 (*msyoung4@wisc.edu*).